D1220851

Allan Ramsay
and the Search for Horace's Villa

Allan Ramsay and the Search for Horace's Villa

Edited by Bernard D. Frischer
and Iain Gordon Brown

with contributions by
Patricia R. Andrew,
John Dixon Hunt and
Martin Goalen

ASHGATE

Published with the assistance of the Getty Grant Program.

Published by
Ashgate Publishing Limited
Gower House
Croft Road
Aldershot
Hants GU11 3HR
England

Ashgate Publishing Company
131 Main Street
Burlington, VT 05036–9704 USA

British Library Cataloguing-in-Publication Data
Allan Ramsay and the search for Horace's villa. –
   (Reinterpreting classicism)
   1. Horace – Homes and haunts 2. Excavations (Archaeology) –
   Italy – Licenza Valley 3. Civilization, Western – Roman
   influences 4. Licenza Valley (Italy) – Antiquities
   I. Frischer, Bernard D.
   874'.01

Library of Congress Cataloging-in-Publication Data
Allan Ramsay and the search for Horace's villa / edited by Bernard D. Frischer and
Iain Gordon Brown with contributions by Patricia R. Andrew, John Dixon Hunt,
Martin Goalen.
      p. cm. – (Reinterpreting classicism)
   Includes bibliographical references and index.
   1. Horace – Homes and haunts – Italy – Licenza. 2. Ramsay, Allan, 1713–1784. Enquiry
   into the situation and circumstances of Horace's Sabine villa. 3. Ramsay, Allan,
   1713–1784 – Journeys – Italy – Licenza. 4. Farm life – Licenza – Historiography.
   5. Villa of Horace (Licenza, Italy) 6. Licenza (Italy) – Antiquities. 7. Poets, Latin –
   Biography. I. Frischer, Bernard. II. Brown, Iain Gordon. III. Ramsay, Allan,
   1713–1784. Enquiry into the situation and circumstances of Horace's Sabine villa. IV.
   Series.

PA6411 .A45 2001
874'.01–dc21   00-054326

ISBN 07546 0004 1

Printed on acid-free paper
Typeset in Palatino by Bournemouth Colour Press, Parkstone, Poole, Dorset, and printed
in Belgium

FRONTISPIECE
Allan Ramsay, self-portrait in red chalk, drawn on Ischia, 1776

Contents

List of Text Illustrations

An Enquiry into the Situation and Circumstances of Horace's Sabine Villa

List of Colour Plates

List of Abbreviations

BL	British Library
BM	British Museum
CIL	*Corpus Inscriptionum Latinarum*
EUL	Edinburgh University Library
NAS	National Archives of Scotland (formerly Scottish Record Office)
NGS	National Gallery of Scotland
NLS	National Library of Scotland
OED	*Oxford English Dictionary*
PIR I	*Prosopographia imperii romanii, saec.* I.II.III., pars I, Berlin 1897
PIR II	*Prosopographia imperii romanii, saec.* I.II.III., pars II, Leipzig, 1936
RSA	Royal Scottish Academy
SNPG	Scottish National Portrait Gallery
UCLA	University of California, Los Angeles

Notes on Contributors

Bernard D. Frischer is a graduate of Wesleyan University and received his Ph.D. in Classical philology from the Universität Heidelberg. He is presently Professor of Classics at the University of California, Los Angeles, where he also directs the UCLA Cultural Virtual Reality Lab. Since 1997 he has been Director of excavations at Horace's Villa, under the auspices of the American Academy in Rome and the Archaeological Superintendency of Lazio. His special research interests include Augustan Rome, Roman topography, the reception of ancient culture since the Renaissance, and the use of virtual reality technology for the study and presentation of cultural heritage.

Iain Gordon Brown is a graduate of the universities of Edinburgh and Cambridge and is now Principal Curator of Manuscripts in the National Library of Scotland. He has published widely in the field of eighteenth-century cultural history, where his research has concentrated on the literature, architecture, antiquarian thought and taste of the age. His books, articles and essays cover such topics as the careers of Allan Ramsay and Robert Adam, and he has a particular interest in the history of the Grand Tour. He is a Fellow of the Society of Antiquaries of London and the Royal Society of Edinburgh.

Patricia R. Andrew studied at the University of Nottingham and received her Ph.D. in art history from the University of Edinburgh, specializing in the work of Jacob More and his circle in Edinburgh and Rome. She has worked in museums in England and Scotland and is currently Assistant Director (Professional Services) for the Scottish Museums Council. Special research interests include the colony of British artists active in late eighteenth-century Italy, and research for exhibitions covering a wide variety of subject areas, both historical and contemporary.

John Dixon Hunt is a garden historian and editor of the international quarterly *Studies in the History of Gardens and Designed Landscapes*. He also edits the University of Pennsylvania Press monograph series *Penn Studies in Landscape Architecture*, in which his own work, *Greater Perfections: The Practice of Garden Theory* (published jointly with Thames & Hudson), has recently appeared. He has written widely on Italian, Dutch, English and American garden design, including *Garden and Grove: The Italian Renaissance Garden in the English Imagination 1600–1750*.

Martin Goalen, a practising architect, has taught at the universities of London and Cambridge and is currently Visiting Professor at University College London. He worked as architect to British School of Archaeology at Athens excavations at Perachora, Mycenae and Aghios Stephanos, and is currently collaborating in investigations at the Villa del Discobolo at Castelporziano, Lazio. His architectural work includes widely published new buildings as well as work at historical sites such as the Palace of Westminster. He publishes on the reception and interpretation of ancient architecture in the modern world, and has been a Sargent Fellow in Fine Art at the British School at Rome and Visiting Fellow at the British School of Archaeology in Athens.

Preface by the Series Editor

When the Scottish painter Allan Ramsay set out for Italy in the 1770s to investigate the remains of what for some time had been thought to be Horace's villa, he was, considered superficially, simply engaging in an exercise of archaeological reconstruction. But the search for the poet's house was also an attempt to obtain first-hand knowledge of Horace and everything he stood for by scrutinizing the remains of his estate and the landscape around it. The result of that search, Ramsay's 'Enquiry into the Situation and Circumstances of Horace's Sabine Villa, Written during Travels through Italy in the Years 1775, 76 and 77', is not only a summary of and considerable contribution to what was known at that time about Horace's farm. Ramsay's text also reveals in what manner the poet who embodied the ideals of British neo-classicism was reinterpreted at the end of the eighteenth-century. As so often in late eighteenth-century archaeology, investigating the classical past was not only an exercise in the acquisition of historical knowlege, but also a reconsideration of the meaning of that past for the present, and a way of constructing the identity of the investigator. Through his search for Horace's villa and its written account, Ramsay, the portrait painter whose career was in decline and whose health was failing, redefined himself as an archaeologist, a man of letters and an authority on one of the key figures in British neo-classicism. And knowing as we now know from the new excavations undertaken by Bernard Frischer, that the remains Ramsay investigated belonged primarily not to the structure of Horace's day but to a later complex on the site owned by a member of the imperial court, only adds to the appreciation of the importance of the 'Enquiry' as a central document of neo-classicist self-fashioning in late eighteenth-century Great Britain.

Ramsay's 'Enquiry' is published here for the first time. The accompanying essays not only offer an analysis of the 'Enquiry' and its place in Ramsay's life and career; they also place Ramsay's work within the wider context of the European classical tradition. Thus Iain Gordon Brown reconstructs Ramsay's life and his pre-occupation with Horace; Bernard Frischer analyses the work of his predecessors and the genesis of the 'Enquiry'; and Patricia Andrew examines the work of the artists commissioned by Ramsay to prepare illustrations intended to accompany his text. John Dixon Hunt shows how eighteenth-century imitations of the Horatian country estate fitted within the tradition of imitations of classical literature and art. Finally, Martin Goalen looks at the ideal of the villa rather than its actual remains, and shows how this ideal formed a continuous thread in Western architecture from Alberti to Le Corbusier, including Ramsay's reconstruction of Horace's villa. Together these essays show how Ramsay's exercise in imaginative reconstruction can be read as a testimony to the artistic and aesthetic attitudes of British neo-classicism.

The co-editors, Bernard Frischer and Iain Gordon Brown, collaborated closely on all aspects of the production of this book and made equal contributions to it. As Series Editor, I therefore found the listing of their names a difficult task. In the end, this was resolved by giving more weight to the central role in the book played by Ramsay's 'Enquiry', which was Bernard Frischer's primary responsibility.

Caroline van Eck

Allan Ramsay and the Search for Horace's Villa is published in the series
REINTERPRETING CLASSICISM: CULTURE,
REACTION AND APPROPRIATION
edited by Caroline van Eck, Vrije Universiteit, Amsterdam

This new series provides a forum for the interdisciplinary study of classicism in the arts and architecture in the Western World from the Renaissance to the present day, investigating its complex nature and development, the selection and use of ancient sources, its cultural, political or ideological role, and its relation to other existing traditions and styles. The series is inspired by recent re-examinations of the discourses of interpretation used in art history.

IN THE SAME SERIES

Producing the Past
Aspects of Antiquarian Culture and Practice 1700–1850
Edited by Martin Myrone and Lucy Peltz
Preface by Stephen Bann

Sir John Soane and the Country Estate
Ptolemy Dean

The Built Surface Volume 1
Edited by Christy Anderson

Building on Ruins
The Rediscovery of Rome and English Architecture
Frank Salmon

Preface and Acknowledgements

It had long been my hope to transcribe, edit, comment upon and prepare for publication the surviving manuscripts of Allan Ramsay's 'Enquiry into the Situation and Circumstances of Horace's Sabine Villa'. In 1984 I had taken more than passing account of this then little-known work both in my *Poet and Painter* and in the exhibition on Ramsay held in the National Library of Scotland to mark the bicentenary of his death. Four years later I was able only to list the manuscripts in an Appendix to a long article on the entire literary output of the author. An unpublished treatise by such a distinguished figure in British and European culture of the eighteenth century on a subject close to the hearts and minds of his contemporaries has its own intrinsic interest; and as one of the two known unprinted works from Ramsay's versatile pen it surely merited wider circulation rather before now. The growth of interest in all aspects of Ramsay's life and work, due in large part to the scholarship of the late Professor Alastair Smart, has convinced us that such a publication will now be welcomed.

When, some years ago, Professor Bernard Frischer first wrote to me expressing interest in working on the manuscripts of the 'Enquiry' preserved in two of Edinburgh's great libraries, I saw this as a chance to make a reality of the project.* Bernard Frischer could apply not only his classical and textual scholarship, but also his wide-ranging familiarity with the Italian cultural scene, and a valuable range of contacts in the academic and archaeological community. We divided the work between us, with Bernard Frischer undertaking the transcription and editing of the manuscripts themselves. I have checked all the transcription and have collated the two authorial manuscripts known before the autumn of 2000, but by far the greatest share of this aspect of the project has been Bernard Frischer's alone, and to him must be given full credit for completing a task that proved rather more difficult than had first appeared.

We had hoped that James Holloway, who (in an article published in *Master Drawings* in 1976 and a small but important exhibition at the National Gallery of Scotland in 1977) was one of the first to take a serious interest in Ramsay's work at Horace's villa and to attempt to reconstruct Ramsay's efforts towards a programme of illustration of his 'Enquiry', would join us to discuss these various contemporary projects to illustrate the treatise. But owing to other commitments he was unable to do so, and we turned instead to Patricia Andrew. She has brought to the task her special knowledge of the artistic

*At the time, and indeed until October 2000, neither Bernard Frischer nor I knew of the existence of a *third* manuscript of Ramsay's 'Enquiry', which had been lurking unrecognized at Professor Frischer's own university in Los Angeles. We are grateful to Dr Paul Naiditch, Rare Books Librarian at UCLA, for bringing this to our attention, however late in the day. The existence of this third manuscript, which appears to be a fair copy doubtless made to Ramsay's order in the last months or perhaps even weeks of his life, was unknown both to all Ramsay scholars and to those interested in the history of the exploration of Horace's villa. Even the UCLA Library itself had no idea of the real significance of the manuscript, which, lacking an author's name on the title page, was catalogued under 'Anonymous … England ca 1785', until Professor Frischer first saw it on 19 October 2000 and immediately recognized it for what it was.

background against which Ramsay selected his landscape draughtsmen, and she has applied to it, moreover, a determination and enthusiasm that have been vital to the success of the enterprise.

A chance meeting with Alec McAulay, then of Scolar Press, brought me into fruitful contact with Ashgate Publishing and with Pamela Edwardes, our patient and imperturbable commissioning editor. Professor John Wilton-Ely and Professor John Dixon Hunt spoke warmly in favour of the initial proposal for the book, and the latter was persuaded to contribute an essay on those aspects of the wider subject on which he is an authority.

All the authors who have joined in this exercise of comment and analysis have published extensively on the topics on which they have chosen to write here. Bernard Frischer is currently engaged on a larger work on Horace's Villa in all its aspects and is directing new excavations at the site. John Dixon Hunt has written at length on the history of the English appreciation of Italian landscape, and of the creation of English landscape that evoked classical and Italian Renaissance and Baroque patterns, in relation to the poetry and painting of the age. Patricia Andrew is the leading authority on Jacob More, the Scottish landscape painter known as 'More of Rome', whom Ramsay commissioned to illustrate his treatise. Martin Goalen, a practising architect, has published a number of articles and papers on classical architecture and its impact on later architectural thought. I myself have written on aspects of the careers and achievement of both Allan Ramsay the painter and of his father, the poet of the same name; on their Scottish cultural world; and on the antiquarian and architectural background against which the younger Ramsay's Horace's Villa enterprise must be viewed. An overview of the story of Allan Ramsay and his search for and identification of Horace's Villa is the subject of my contribution to the volume *Archives and Excavations*, shortly to be published by the British School at Rome.

The present book is intended to supplement existing standard works on the life and art of Allan Ramsay and to offer scholars an edition, with commentary, of one of Ramsay's most important literary undertakings. It provides, we hope, through his own words and those of modern commentators, a discussion of one eighteenth-century scholar's approach to literary and topographical investigation, and to the elucidation of classical textual problems by archaeological research in all its forms. Above all, this is a study in sensibility to place and association.

As co-ordinator of the project I have certain general acknowledgements to make. Museums, galleries and libraries that have granted permission for reproduction of material in their collections are individually acknowledged in the appropriate places. We are indebted to Dr Murray Simpson, now Director of Special Collections in the National Library of Scotland and previously Keeper of Special Collections in Edinburgh University Library, for making available (in his former capacity) the more finished of the two earlier versions of the 'Enquiry' and for permitting its use as the base text – though this has now been set aside in favour of the third version, published here. Ian McGowan, Librarian of the National Library of Scotland, has kindly awarded a grant from the Ruth Ratcliff Fund to help with publication costs. Steve

McAvoy of the National Library has gone to a vast amount of trouble to make photographs for this work. Professor Brian Allen of the Paul Mellon Centre for Studies in British Art gave useful support and advice.

Bernard Frischer is indebted to various institutions for financial support of the ongoing work at Horace's Villa: the Steinmetz Family of Los Angeles; the Vincenzo Romagnoli Group; the American Academy in Rome; the American Council of Learned Societies; the Kress Foundation; the Creative Kids Education Foundation; the Center for Advanced Study in the Visual Arts, National Gallery, Washington, DC; the University Research Expedition Program of the University of California; and the Academic Senate of the University of California, Los Angeles. For various kinds of help while working on this book he would also like to thank Alitalia; the Archivio Capitolino, Rome; the Biblioteca Angelica, Rome; the British Library, London; the Department of Prints and Drawings, British Museum, London; the Center for Hellenic Studies, Washington, DC; the Comune di Licenza; the Deutsches Archäologisches Institut, Rome; the Edinburgh University Library; the Free Public Library, Philadelphia; the Library of Congress, Washington, DC; the National Gallery of Scotland; the National Library of Scotland; the Soprintendenza Archeologica per il Lazio; Dean Abernathy; Caroline Bruzelius; Adele Chatfield-Taylor; Jane Crawford; Maria Grazia Fiore; John and Mary Fort; Elizabeth Fentress; Deborah Hall; Charles Henderson; Christine Huemer; Valerie Hunter; Jama Laurent; Lester Little; Paolo Liverani; Franco and Ester Macconi; Claudio Marra; Gabriele Marriotti; Archer Martin; Antonio von Marx; Kirk Mathews; Mary Pedley; John Rae; Anna Maria Reggiani; Giovanna Romagnoli; Luciano Romanzi; Ann and Russell Scott; Richard Thomas; David and Yvonne Tweedie; and Guido Vitali.

Patricia Andrew is grateful to Lesley Castell, Elizabeth Garland, Keith Hartley, Dr Sarah Hyde, Dr Kim Sloan, the late Professor Alastair Smart, the National Galleries of Scotland and the National Library of Scotland. The research for Martin Goalen's contribution was begun as Sargent Senior Fellow in Fine Art at the British School at Rome; he would like to thank all those at the British School and in particular Amanda Claridge, then Assistant Director.

In respect of my own contribution I am indebted to Dr Ilaria Bignamini, Professor Martin Kemp, John Ingamells and Jonathan Scott, as well as to Deborah Hunter and Katrina Thomson of the National Galleries of Scotland. On a more personal level, I remember warmly the friendship and shared enthusiasm of Professor Alastair Smart. I am more grateful than they know to Irene Young and Alison Morrison-Low for all kinds of help and support during the months when the oft-repeated excuses 'Horace' or 'Ramsay' – neither character seemingly as companionable nor as easy-going as their contemporaries had allegedly found them – meant that other activities had to be abandoned or postponed.

Iain Gordon Brown

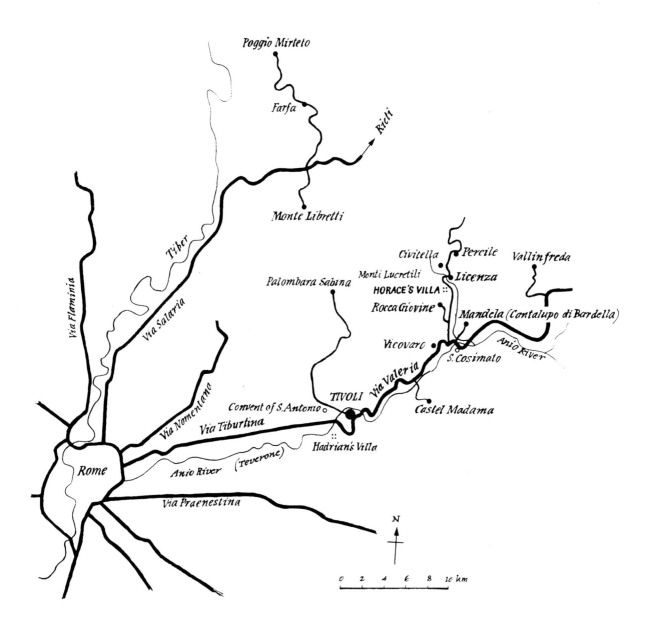

i. Modern map of Rome and
the Sabine Hill country,
showing the location of
Horace's Villa in relation to
other sites around Tivoli

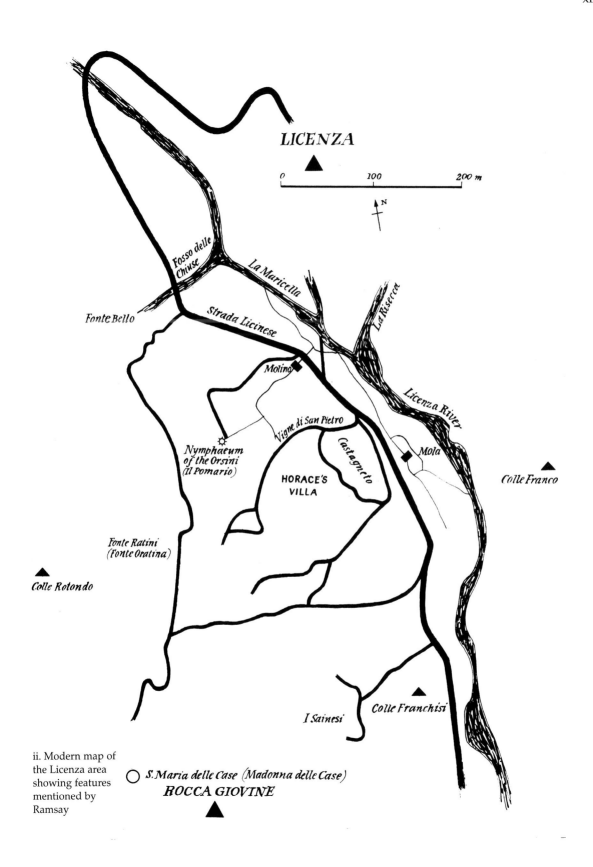

LICENZA ▲

0   100   200 m

N

Fosso delle Chiuse

La Maricella

La Riserca

Fonte Bello

Strada Licinese

Molino ◆

Vigne di San Pietro

Licenza River

Castagneto

Mola ◆

Colle Franco ▲

Nymphaeum of the Orsini (Il Pomario) ☼

HORACE'S VILLA

Fonte Ratini (Fonte Oratina)

Colle Rotondo ▲

Colle Franchisi ▲

I Sainesi

ii. Modern map of the Licenza area showing features mentioned by Ramsay

○ S. Maria delle Case (Madonna delle Case)
ROCCA GIOVINE
▲

iii. Autograph page from Ramsay's 'Enquiry', in which he criticizes the topographical work of De Chaupy; from the version in the National Library of Scotland

and in other Maps of that Country. But in that of the Valley of Licenza, drawn by Abbé de Chaupy for the illustration of his book upon Horace's Country house, the good Abbé has suffered his pencil to be guided rather by his prepossessions than his eyesight, and has moved heaven and earth in order to make the actual situation of things correspond with what he believed to be Horace's description of them. For in his Maps the Village of Licenza is placed almost west of San Cosimato, instead of being, as it is in reality, exactly North of it. He judged, indeed, very right in supposing that Horace could not be mistaken with regard to the four points of the compass in a place where he had spent all the hours of the day and all the months of the Year; but after seeing that the situation of the ground did not agree with the description, he ought to have suspected that he had mistaken Horace's meaning. Upon a reconsideration of the Passage, I find it will admit of another construction much less exceptionable than that which is generally given to it, by making Sed ut relate not to dissocientur but to opaca, and interpret it thus! A cluster of hills, except in this place where they are seperated by a deep Valley; yet not so deep as to be deprived of the rays of the Sun when rising, or when he is going to set. Here however some small allowance must be given to the exaggerating Poet, and the fond proprietor, for the description cannot be strictly true of any small valley surroun

Introduction

Iain Gordon Brown

'I love Ramsay,' pronounced Dr Samuel Johnson of his host at dinner the previous day, when the talk among the guests – James Boswell, Sir Joshua Reynolds, Lord Binning, the historian William Robertson and Mrs Boscawen, the bluestocking – had turned to the posthumous fame of authors ancient and modern, and to 'antiquarian researches'. 'You will not find a man in whose conversation there is more instruction, more information, and more elegance than in Ramsay's.'[1] Boswell thus recorded Johnson's encomium of the man who, though now chiefly celebrated as one of the finest and most sensitive portrait painters of the eighteenth century, was also known to his contemporaries as an essayist, classical scholar and archaeologist.

Earlier in that month of April 1778 Johnson and Boswell had been entertained by Reynolds. Also at dinner that afternoon were Ramsay, Edward Gibbon, Richard Owen Cambridge, Bennet Langton and Jonathan Shipley, Bishop of St Asaph's. On that occasion the conversation had centred upon one ancient author in particular, whose fame was evergreen and whose celebrated dwelling had been the subject of Ramsay's own intense antiquarian research. The *Life of Johnson* records that 'Mr Ramsay had lately returned from Italy, and entertained us with his observations upon Horace's villa, which he had examined with great care. I relished this much, as it brought fresh into my mind what I had viewed with great pleasure thirteen years before. The Bishop, Dr Johnson and Mr Cambridge joined with Mr Ramsay in recollecting the various lines in Horace relating to the subject.'[2] Boswell's private journal contains more particulars of the occasion: 'Allan Ramsay talked much of Horace's villa … He said he had put his observations in writing. BOSWELL: "Pray put them in the press and let them come out again. Let us have them."'[3]

Allan Ramsay (1713–84) published much on a wide variety of subjects. His 'Enquiry into the Situation and Circumstances of Horace's Sabine Villa, Written during Travels in Italy in the Years 1775, 76 and 77' was, however, not destined to appear in print during the author's lifetime. Substantially the product of his third visit to Italy, the work was revised and expanded in the course of his fourth and final visit in the early 1780s. Ramsay died at Dover on 10 August 1784, immediately upon his return from the Continent, leaving (as we now know) three versions of his essay on the site and remains that were thought in the eighteenth century to be those of the Roman poet's country retreat. Of these manuscripts, one (largely autograph, but with passages in the hand of his wife as amanuensis) survives in the National Library of Scotland (MS730; Fig.iii). A fuller, more finished manuscript, largely in the hand of his wife, is in Edinburgh University Library (MS La.III.492; Fig.iv). A third version, a contemporary manuscript in a fine copyist's hand, in which the illustrations of inscriptions and of architectural

46

a part of the Rocca Giovine territory; but from the nature of the ground, which is there flat, might have anciently belonged to either. Within the boundary I have described, and at the south east corner of it near the river is a hill, part of the foot of Mount Lucretilis, called Colle Franchisi. Near the high way from Vico Varo where in turning the east corner of this hill, we first get sight of the open Valley and Horace's Villa, Bernardo Pomfili, the proprietor told me he had some years ago dug up the stone sides of a Portone or Gate, which pointed from that part of the highway, slanting towards Horace's house, and that there was a neat pavement went from the gate, part of which he had likewise dug up. I had not an opportunity of digging when I was last at Licenza in June 1777, but was shown upon the spot some dozens of these stones said to have composed this pavement, and which were scattered about in the land. They are a sort of Wedges of about 7 inches deep, the heads of them which formed the outside of the pavement being a square of about 3 inches and a half of the common white rock of these hills which is a coarse marble. The fact, as related by Bernardo would have been of consequence for shewing that Horace's ground extended at least so far south, and the more conclusive that at the remains of the Villa itself, which is about three quarters of a mile off there are thousands of stones to be gathered exactly formed like this pretended pavement. But as these stones being proper for causewaying, are formed precisely like those made use of in the Opus reticulatum to be found in the mausoleum of Augustus and almost all the buildings of the first Emperors as far down as Caracalla, Thus.

a. Opus reticulatum in Walls

b. head or surface of the stones about 3 inches and 1/2

c. depth of them about 7

Taken from Licenza looking towards Mons Lucretilis
Horace's villa a little above the house that is in this drawing

iv. Page of Ramsay's
'Enquiry' in the hand of
Margaret Ramsay, with
corrections, sketches and
added descriptions by Allan
Ramsay, from the version in
Edinburgh University
Library

v. The Licenza valley, Mons
Lucretilis and the site of
Horace's Villa; a landscape
sketch by Ramsay appended
to the National Library of
Scotland manuscript of the
'Enquiry'

and decorative features are drawn in a neat and elegant form even as the text itself is carefully set out, was discovered in the Charles E. Young Research Library, UCLA, in October 2000 (Bound Manuscripts Collection 170/376). Although not authorial in the sense that it is neither in Ramsay's holograph nor in the hands of his wife or son as his regular amanuenses, this version nevertheless must carry considerable textual authority. For further information see pp.105–107 below. Associated watercolours and drawings, prepared with the illustration of Ramsay's treatise in mind, are appended to the version in the National Library (Fig.v), in the Print Room of the National Gallery of Scotland, and in public and private collections elsewhere.

This corpus of material forms the core of the present book. Herein will be found the first publication of Ramsay's original work, edited from the UCLA manuscript and collated with the EUL and NLS versions. The aim has been to present a text corresponding as nearly as possible to that which Ramsay, had he lived, is likely to have offered the scholarly world soon after his return from Italy, perhaps in the winter of 1784–5. To this end, the drawings, watercolours and gouaches commissioned from two of the foremost landscape draughtsmen of the day, Jacob More and Jakob Philipp Hackert, have been assembled here to indicate the range of pictures produced by artists with whom Ramsay was associated in the course of the project. From these works he would have been able to select the illustrations that (as engraved plates) might have formed the visual part of his treatise or might have accompanied it as a supplementary album of prints. It is known that maps were to be included in the projected book, and a selection of these has been included here in an attempt to make as complete as possible the study that Ramsay had in prospect, so adding to the body of his published writings this final work on a subject clearly close to his heart.

Allan Ramsay and the Search for Horace's Villa is more than mere exhumation of a long-forgotten manuscript treatise and its now scattered illustrations. Ramsay was a very early visitor to the villa, and his 'Enquiry' is one of the first works specifically devoted to the site; it is, moreover, the first such account in English. Ramsay knew that his project would tap a vein of contemporary enthusiasm. His initial expedition to the villa site in the summer of 1755, in pursuit of 'the curiositys of Nature and Antiquity', had been, as he told Sir Alexander Dick, 'one which you or any man of elegant taste would have been glad to have partaken of.'[4] Ramsay was convinced of the essentials necessary for any archaeological and historical study of an ancient site in its landscape. He had written to Dick, in the letter cited above, of his first 'jaunt' to the villa: 'But the particulars … and my observations upon the ground compared with the passages that relate to it in the Poet I will defer till I can communicate to you at the same time the plan of the situations and some of the principal Views without which any description by words must remain obscure & defective.' Ramsay's wish to present all the materials of his study – his comparison of Horace's verse with the topography of the site, the presentation of the results of field survey and excavation, the evaluation and interpretation of the ancient literary and epigraphic sources, together with maps, plans and landscape views – is now fulfilled. The pleasure and instruction that was denied to Boswell, and which Johnson thought could not be known because it was not in the ancient texts themselves (which he viewed as the only necessary or valid evidence)[5] is at long last granted to today's readers.

For the classicist and literary scholar, Ramsay's 'Enquiry' offers accurate verbal descriptions and visual depictions of a site believed to be that of the Sabine farm, which Horace (65–8 BC) made a principal theme of many of his most celebrated lyric verses. The villa remains, in fact, the only house of an ancient writer that was thought to have been identified with certainty. According to ancient tradition, the villa had been the gift of Horace's patron, Maecenas. Lying in the Licenza valley, in the hills beyond Tivoli (ancient Tibur) to the north-east of Rome (Fig.i), it was relatively remote in antiquity, being located in the less fashionable Sabine country rather than in the Tiburtine villa-belt of 'gentlemanly retreat'.[6] The site (Fig.ii) was still remote in Ramsay's time and for long afterwards, and was not on what might be called any regular tourist itinerary of the day. The villa was in a relatively untouched condition when Ramsay explored it, whereas by the time the Italian government sponsored official excavations between 1911 and 1914, some of what the Scottish painter reported had been irretrievably lost through agriculture, erosion, stone-robbing and neglect. Ramsay's treatise therefore provides valuable primary materials for the archaeological study of this important late-Republican villa site (now forming part of a regional conservation park) on which a final excavation report has not yet been published.

The 'Enquiry' is an important document in the history of antiquarian scholarship, and it remains one of the key sources for the discovery and interpretation of this particular site, with its literary resonance, sentimental significance and historical importance.

Notes

1.　J. Boswell, *Life of Johnson*, 1934, vol.3, p.336. For the subjects of conversation see ibid., pp.332–3. The dinner took place on 29 April 1778 at Ramsay's house in Harley Street, London. For another version of Johnson's remarks ('Ramsay is a fine fellow …') see J. Boswell, *Boswell in Extremes*, 1971, p.327.

2.　Boswell, *Life of Johnson*, vol.3, p.250. The date of the dinner was 9 April 1778.

3.　Boswell, *Boswell in Extremes*, p. 253.

4.　Ramsay to Dick, 12 November 1755, NAS, Dick Cunyngham of Prestonfield Muniments, GD331/5/18; see I.G. Brown, *Poet and Painter*, 1985, no.232.

5.　J. Boswell, *Life of Johnson*, 1934, vol.3, p.333. Johnson, unmoved by the possibilities of what we would call archaeological research in the widest sense, declared, 'We *can* know no more than the old writers have told us.'

6.　See R.O.A.M. Lyne, *Horace*, p.7; D. Armstrong, *Horace*, p.48.

1

Allan Ramsay: Artist, Author, Antiquary

Iain Gordon Brown

'Horace, the Prince of the Roman lyric poets, was possessed of a Villa or farm in the Sabina…': thus does Allan Ramsay open his 'Enquiry into the Situation and Circumstances of Horace's Sabine Villa'. Behind his enterprise lies the long tradition of adulation of the poet, which forms a continuous thread through Western literature since the Renaissance. Admiration of Horace was at its peak in the eighteenth century. Perhaps the most significant of the presiding *genii* of 'Augustan' Britain, Horace was, as has been well said, 'a kind of cultural hero of the age' (Fig.1.1).[1] He was the most frequently quoted and deferred to of any classical author, not excepting Virgil and Cicero.[2] There were substantially more translations of Horace into English in the period 1660–1800 than of any other Latin or Greek author.[3] In the *Satires* especially, Horace was thought by John Dryden to be 'teaching us in every line'. Dryden, in his translation of André Dacier's Preface to his great and influential edition of 1683–97, defined Horace's contribution thus: 'In a Word, he labours to render us happy in relation to our selves, agreeable and faithful to our Friends, and discreet, serviceable, and well bred in relation to those with whom we are oblig'd to live, and to converse.'[4] Alexander Pope may speak for his age when he maintains that 'An Answer from Horace was both more full, and of more Dignity, than any I cou'd have made in my own person.'[5] As he had put it in 'An Essay on Criticism' (1711)

> Horace still charms with graceful negligence
> And without method talks us into sense,
> Will, like a friend, familiarly convey
> The truest notions in the easiest way.[6]

Reuben Brower has observed that the 'Augustans saw in Horace's poetry a concentrated image of a life and a civilization to which they more or less consciously aspired'.[7] This all-pervasive admiration of Horace and his works and way of life was shared by Ramsay and his poet father, Allan Ramsay the elder (1684–1758). Both the Ramsays read Horace with pleasure and imitated his sentiments; and their desire to emulate his life-style, either in actuality or in the realm of wishful thinking, was constantly stressed in their various writings in verse and prose (Fig.1.2). Poems and letters of the elder Ramsay praise the philosophical calm of a life of tranquil retirement at some agreeable villa. The Horatian creed of *'beatus ille'* famously expressed in *Epodes* 2 ('happy the man' who enjoys such an ideal of peaceful, rural existence) found in him a fervent votary. Pleasure in the rewards of patronage, and the fame and immortality conveyed by artistic or literary achievement, are other Horatian notions that feature prominently in the Ramsay mind.

When Allan Ramsay the painter wrote in a brief memoir[8] of his father's

1.1. Tribute to Horace; an
emblematic engraving from
R. Bentley, ed., *Q. Horatius
Flaccus*, 1711

1.2. Idealized portrait of Horace, engraving from J. Pine's edition of the works of Horace, 1733–7

'catching the spirit of the Odes of Horace' he was in fact giving a good definition of the contemporary literary form known as an 'imitation'. By this men in the circle of Pope (or the elder Ramsay) would have understood the desire to adapt the Horatian original – its mood, words and sense – to produce something not only original in itself but also a re-interpretation or a re-creation of Horatian themes.[9] It has been said that men of letters of the period wrote with the Latin poet 'over their shoulder' (Fig.1.3).[10] The elder Ramsay composed several of these Horatian variations, and adapted Odes and Epistles with varying degrees of success: at worst mere 'dilutions', banal and unsubtle, of the Horatian originals; at best successful and powerful examples of naturalization of the Roman's thoughts by domesticating them to the Scottish psyche and landscape.[11]

The elder Ramsay appears as a Scottish equivalent of the Horace of the conventional view, 'a genial but rather superficial character whose most typical activity was drinking wine and uttering proverbial wisdom under a tree' (Fig.1.4).[12] There is much of the spirit of smug moralizing; professed contempt for vulgar vanity, filthy lucre, town life, wordly hurry; slightly pompous views from 'the sumit [*sic*] of Philosophy'; and a deal of gratuitous advice on contentment in repose at someone else's country house. For Allan Ramsay the elder, as for Alexander Pope – the two admired each other in varying degrees – time wrought 'a life and a literary career that became progressively an Imitatio Horati'.[13] The elder Ramsay shared with Pope a deep interest in the visual arts. His artistic inclinations and contacts had a profound influence on his son, who would allude to the unity of the arts in his *Dialogue on Taste*: 'The polite arts, and all the several branches of true learning, have so immediate a connection that they always march together … and indeed there is so great a likeness betwixt two of them, poetry and painting, that their sisterhood will be readily allowed.'[14]

Remarkably, whereas Ramsay the elder had wanted originally to be a painter, and maintained a particular interest in the world of art, his son, who attained such genuine distinction (and riches) as a painter, displayed an intense and persistent desire for literary reputation. The younger Ramsay was a considerable Latinist, and as a classical scholar concerned himself long and deeply with Horace. In his erudite 'Enquiry into the Principles of English Versification'[15] he was to defend the study of ancient languages and literature: 'It is the source of every thing that is correct and elegant, and it will be difficult to produce an instance of any man in modern times who has distinguished himself by his excellence in any of the higher kinds of poetry and oratory, without having drunk at this source.' In later life it was as a man of letters that he appeared to seek the greater recognition; indeed, he developed what might be regarded as a secondary career as a pamphleteer. From the late 1750s Horace Walpole began to think of Ramsay as both artist and writer;[16] and so the younger Ramsay entered the mythology of Scottish cultural history as 'one born with a genius both for poetry and painting', for he had 'inherited his father's genius, and rose to eminence both as a painter and a schollar'.[17]

Ramsay's artistic career was one of brilliance and paradox (Fig.1.5). His achievement as a painter, obviously his greatest claim to fame, has recently been re-assessed and accorded the recognition it deserves. His output as a writer (which, arguably, distracted him from attaining even greater triumph as an artist) has also been investigated.[18] Ramsay early displayed a precocious talent. He studied art in Edinburgh, London, Rome and Naples, whence he returned to take London by storm in 1738. There he was initially 'much cried up by the Scotch Gentry';[19] but English patrons soon flocked to his painting room. His success was enormous, and material and social reward came quickly. He enjoyed aristocratic patronage and Royal favour, being appointed Principal Painter in Ordinary to King George III: his coronation portraits of the monarch and his consort are the definitive images of British Hanoverian kingship, even if many were replicas executed on a production-line basis by studio assistants.

Until about 1760 Ramsay was the outstanding British portrait painter, his style moving from Baroque convention to a new, informal manner blending intimate characterization with 'naturalness' and so granting charming individuality to his sitters, especially women. This remarkable directness, in which there is, nevertheless, elegance, extreme sophistication, subtlety of design (based on extensive preparatory drawing), delicacy in colouring and psychological insight, was much influenced by contemporary French masters. It seems also to reflect the empiricism of the thinkers of the Scottish Enlightenment, notably his friend David Hume. Hume's sceptical philosophy profoundly influenced Ramsay, not only in the art of his greatest period but also in the method of his various investigations into aesthetics, literary problems (such as the 'Enquiry' into the situation and circumstances of Horace's Villa) and political controversy, which were published as a series of essays and pamphlets. Ramsay's choice of 'The Investigator' as his pseudonym indicates his belief in empirical method.

1.3. A Roman writer and the
books inspired by his
example, engraving from
J. Pine's edition of the works
of Horace, 1733–7

Ramsay's serious interest in classical archaeology began during the first of his four Italian visits, in 1736–38 (Fig.1.6). Then he encountered the monuments at first hand, and had the opportunity of studying in Roman and Neapolitan collections. It was Ramsay who purchased for the great physician, collector and connoisseur Dr Richard Mead a volume of watercolour copies by Pietro Santi Bartoli of ancient wall-paintings in the sepulchre of the Nasonii on the Via Flaminia just north of Rome.[20] The acquisition of this magnificient album, now in Glasgow University Library, represented a considerable antiquarian coup, which, quite apart from its intrinsic importance in the history of the study of ancient painting, served also to bring Ramsay to the notice of Mead's influential antiquarian circle in London. The tomb from which the paintings came was thought to be that of Ovid's family, and it was believed that Ovid himself and his muse Erato were depicted in one mural – a portrait of an ancient poet by an ancient painter.

Ramsay's friend Camillo Paderni also made drawings after these same ancient originals, together with other fragments of antique wall-decorations, and Ramsay was instrumental in engaging Paderni's services in the production of the plates for George Turnbull's *A Treatise on Ancient Painting* (1740).[21] Here Turnbull argued that the painting of antiquity had hitherto been neglected, and that increased knowledge of the subject might serve both to enhance taste and to illuminate the study of classical authors. This suggestion that archaeological evidence might have a bearing on the literary record may well have set Ramsay on the path that led him ultimately to Horace's Villa.

On his second trip to Italy, in the 1750s, Ramsay not only applied himself to academic drawing as a student once more, but also kept company with a remarkable circle of brilliant men in mutual pursuit of Antiquity and the neo-classical ideal: his fellow Scot Robert Adam, Charles-Louis Clérisseau and Giovanni Battista Piranesi. Ramsay's contemporaries recognized the fact that he was always more than a mere face-painter, and his breadth of learning was clear to his Roman friends of the 1750s. Piranesi best epitomized Ramsay's intellectual range, although his tribute is to be found in the most unlikely of contexts.[22] In Piranesi's febrile fantasy vision of the junction of the tomb-lined Appian Way and the Via Ardeatina at Porta Capena, which plate forms the frontispiece to the second volume of *Le Antichità Romane* (1756), appears a monument to the then very-much-alive Allan Ramsay: the Latin inscription on the would-be mausoleum lauds this 'eminent painter renowned for his abilities in all the noble arts'.

A severe injury to his arm in 1773 caused Ramsay to abandon the art of which he had in any case, perhaps, grown weary; and he devoted ever greater time to literature in its widest sense, and to political and economic observation, analysis and comment. Two further visits to Italy followed in the 1770s and 1780s, the last being anodyne against his grief at the death of his beloved second wife Margaret Lindsay, subject of the loveliest and most exquisite of all his portraits. His son John's schoolboy diary records the last artistic contacts in Italy of the enfeebled scholar-painter.

His second visit to Italy had seen Ramsay exploring Rome and the Campagna with a new passion for antiquity. Horace's Villa entered his consciousness, even as he sketched the monuments of Rome and drew at Hadrian's Villa and the numinous falls of Tivoli. Yet controversy now became inextricably linked to his vision of the past, and in a most unexpected way this was to result in Ramsay's provoking indirectly some of the most significant contributions to eighteenth-century archaeology.

In *A Dialogue on Taste*, published in 1755 while Ramsay was in Rome, the discussion between Colonel Freeman, who is Ramsay, and Lord Modish, who represents the conventional views of the day, turns upon architectural taste. In arguing his alter ego's position Ramsay wrote: 'In history we shall find that every nation received its mode of architecture from that nation which, in all other respects, was the highest in credit, riches and general estimation.' The Greeks acknowledged the primacy of the Egyptians, the Romans that of the Greeks; Ramsay paints a picture of nasty and brutish Romans who, 'destitute of money, and profoundly ignorant of all the arts of peace', and having

> never raised any buildings of which they could boast ... decreed the Greeks to be the only architects in the world, and submitted willingly to receive laws in the Arts from those whom their Arms has subdued ... An admiration, to a degree of bigotry, seized the Roman artists and connoisseurs, and put a stop to any farther change or improvement in architecture.

The Romans were, in short, 'a gang of mere plunderers, sprung from those who had been, but a little while before their conquest of Greece, naked thieves and runaway slaves'.[23] These views were hardly likely to appeal to Piranesi, the publication of whose own monumental four-volume *Le Antichità Romane*, a glorification of the grandeur of ancient Rome and a tribute to the genius of her architects and engineers, was announced in the year of the first appearance of Ramsay's pamphlet. It is Piranesi's reaction to *A Dialogue on*

1.4. Lyric poetry inspired by Falernian wine in a garden, engraving from J. Pine's edition of the works of Horace, 1733–7

Taste that lends to the little book its peculiar interest. Seldom can one small octavo have given rise to so many massive folios.

Ramsay's *Dialogue* had been published originally with the whimsical title of *The Investigator. Number* CCCXXII. When re-issued in 1762 it formed part of a volume containing four of his early pamphlets with the omnium gatherum title of *The Investigator*. It was under this pseudonymous disguise that Ramsay was attacked by Piranesi: 'l'Investigatore (e questo il nome assunto da un certo critico) … l'autore di alcuni dialoghi intitolati L'INVESTIGATORE'. In his polemical *Della magnificenza ed architettura de' Romani* Piranesi systematically refuted all the assertions made by Ramsay that, as Piranesi saw it, minimized the Roman achievement: point by point Ramsay's arguments were cited by the Italian and buried under a vast weight of verbal and visual evidence in response, the purpose of which was to make the original contentions appear trifling or flippant. The *Investigator*'s publication was to be followed by the much more profound and heavyweight arguments of Winckelmann and Le Roy, but it appears that Piranesi's volcanic reaction was provoked by Ramsay's work alone. The crusading text of *Della magnificenza*, with its superb plates, was the first of many subsequent blows struck for Rome: other polemical works with erudite texts and powerful illustrations praise the ancient Roman contribution to architecture and engineering and are convincing refutations of *The Investigator*'s position. Nevertheless, to have been, in part at least, the instigator of books that have influenced the tastes of Western culture ever since, and which are a monument to the eighteenth-century vision of Antiquity, is no mean achievement.[24] No doubt Piranesi would have expected some equally sparky work from Ramsay's pen when he learned that 'The Investigator' was turning his attention to the Sabine villa of Horace.

In the eighteenth century, before the discoveries of Roman houses in the buried cities of Vesuvius had become familiar to Europeans, the five most

celebrated domestic (as opposed to monumental public or religious) buildings of the Roman world were Hadrian's imperial villa at Tivoli; Diocletian's palace at Split in Dalmatia; Pliny the Younger's Laurentine and Tuscan villas; and Horace's Sabine farm.

The first had long been known from its extensive ruins which, surviving in an idyllic rural setting, had been studied since the Renaissance by architects and scholars: the site had become a prime source of classical statuary and works of art for the decoration of the palaces of modern Rome and for the enhancement of princely collections.[25] At Split, Diocletian's fortress-palace had been transformed over 1400 years into a unique example of organic urban growth: like an extraordinary palimpsest, a bustling town had developed, age by age, through, over and around a structure that was part reclusive dwelling and part military camp. In the eighteenth century the palace became the proving-ground for Robert Adam's reputation as an interpreter of classicism.[26] Pliny's opulent villas, known only from descriptions in his letters and not from physical remains, were lost buildings that nevertheless inspired learned and laborious exercises in literary reconstruction by gentlemen architects of the neo-Palladian generation, to which elegant pursuit the handsome folio of Robert Castell's *Villas of the Ancients* (1728) is the best testimony (see Fig.2.4).[27]

Horace's farm or villa – the terms were used interchangeably – had both a literary, or cerebral, and a physical existence: a site at once real and of the imagination, an ideal and an actual place embedded in the Western mind and soul and known to the Augustan generation from schooldays. Since the seventeenth-century scholar Lucas Holstenius had drawn the connection between the Sabine farm and the valley of the Licenza, Ramsay's contemporaries were at last able to 'give to airy nothing/ a local habitation and a name'. The conception was that his villa was modest: his house 'plain' and his estate 'small'. 'In this neighbourhood and at his villa Horace seems to have passed the greatest part of his time, much in the same manner as we less significant people do in the country. He read, slept and sauntered, lived pleasingly and forgot the bustle of the town. He composed much and thought and talked much of moral subjects. (Fig.1.7)'[28]

For the eighteenth-century mind, then, the discovery or positive identification of the site of the immortal Horace's celebrated Sabine farm – a favourite spot, praised by the poet himself in verses familiar to every educated person – would have had special significance. As Boswell's accounts indicate, the quest for the poet's villa, and the whole topic of the interrelationship of actual topography and idealized poetic description of landscape, was the stuff of dinner-party conversation among that circle of intellectuals and men and women of learning and taste for whom a diet of classical literature was as familiar as their own pabulum of Addison and Pope, *The Spectator* or *The Annual Register*. Where Horace had lived and loved, written, read and wandered, mused on town and country life, entertained friends, drunk his cool wine or watched the sun go down, and in what circumstances, was a matter of interest to a whole society. It is

1.5. *Allan Ramsay*, self-portrait in black chalk, possibly drawn in Rome around 1756

1.6. *Roma sotterranea*: archaeological treasure-hunting in the Renaissance, as illustrated in the title-page decoration of G. R. Volpi, *Vetus Latium Profanum*, vols iii–x, 1726–45

interesting to note that when David Hume was defending his decision to accept a diplomatic appointment in Paris and thus to allow himself to be 'dragged from [his] retreat', his thoughts turned to Horace. He would take with him only four books: a Virgil, a Horace, a Tasso and a Tacitus. 'I own', he wrote, 'that in common decency, I ought to have left my *Horace* behind me, and that I ought to be ashamed to look him in the face. For I am sensible that at my years no temptation would have seduced *him* from his retreat; nor would he ever have been induced to enter so late into the path of ambition.'[29]

James Boswell was especially interested in Ramsay's talk of the villa, and greatly hoped to see those observations in print (see Introduction), because he himself had visited the site in 1765, half-way between Ramsay's first informal expedition to the Licenza valley in 1755 and his specific investigations of the Sabine hill country twenty years later. Boswell had made his trip under the guidance of the Scottish antiquary and Roman *cicerone* Andrew Lumisden, and both men wrote accounts of their visit in the form of rough memoranda and more polished letters. Boswell labelled his notes 'Horace jaunt', and prepared his mind in customary fashion with the exhortation: 'At Villa be in enthusiasm'. 'Saw ruins; fell on knees and uttered some enthusiastic words'. Unable to contain himself, Boswell wrote to a friend from the villa site, telling of this magic spot where the very odes that 'charmed my youthful soul' had been written.[30] To judge by this, Ramsay, himself always emotionally controlled, may have been wary of reviving in Bozzy an excessive display of enthusiasm at the dinner table. Lumisden, for his part, wrote a report of this 'classical excursion' in epistolary form to the Edinburgh connoisseur John MacGouan, and this was published only in 1797. Here archaeological discovery took second place to more general 'classical curiosity': in the end buildings are destroyed and ruins themselves

1.7. Map, more decorative than topographically or archaeologically accurate, showing the villa country around Tivoli, ancient Tibur; the villa of Horace shown here is not the Sabine farm but rather the putative site of a house Horace was then believed to have owned at Tibur itself; engraving from J. Pine's edition of the works of Horace, 1733–7

disappear, but the poems of Horace constitute his 'monumentum aere perennius'.[31]

Some years later, Sir Walter Scott, himself soon to set foot on classic ground for the first (and only) time, observed that 'fame depends on literature not on architecture'. In apparent contradiction, however, he went on to state that we are 'eager to see a broken column from Cicero's villa',[32] as if admitting that an encounter with the physical remains somehow enhanced the perception of the writings. Andrew Lumisden was, in the last analysis, concerned more with the poetry of Horace, and with the spirit of place, than with the stones themselves; with literary remains rather than the physical remains upon which Ramsay placed equal weight in his investigation of the villa. Allan Ramsay was a lover of literature and a classical scholar of some distinction, and he was certainly a man of sensibility, moved by association. But he was also an antiquary concerned for the progress of the science of archaeology, and one who valued the evidence that excavation or museology could afford.

For Ramsay's contemporaries the story of the search for the villa, and any published work which might result from that assiduous quest, had a relevance and appeal intimately bound up with the appreciation and enjoyment of the poetry of the uniquely sympathetic, companionable and enduringly popular Horace who had almost come to do duty 'as an English landowner and country-gentleman'.[33] The place of composition of the immortal verses was deemed important. As a modern scholar has written: 'Amidst the acreage of pasture-land, olive groves, gardens and grazing herds Horace found inspiration for his second book of *Satires*, the *Epodes*, and the first three books of *Odes*, no mean return from the benefice of his patron Maecenas.'[34] In a short work now unjustly forgotten, T.R. Glover observes of Horace's life at the Sabine villa that 'in rest and peace and sunshine the man develops and his genius is seen'. Glover makes the telling comparison with Robert Burns: 'Did any farm, at Mossgiel or anywhere else, yield such a crop as that which "gave Horace to himself" and to us?'[35] Maecenas's generosity was, in short, 'one of the most fortunate gifts in literature. (Fig.1.8)'[36]

To a generation devoted to the villa ideal – in architectural terms that of actual houses built for rural (often suburban) retreat, and in ideological terms that of the pursuit on *villeggiatura* of a life of cultivated leisure, refined ease and intellectually profitable repose in the manner (as it was supposed) of the ancients – the discovery of the bricks and mortar of real Roman villas was important. There was a profound interest in what archaeology was beginning to reveal of the domestic architecture of the Romans. Neo-classical architects, who had themselves studied the actual buildings of antiquity, partly as a result of the new discoveries at Pompeii and Herculaneum, were able to offer their patrons a more accurate vision of the past adapted to the life of the present.[37]

Just as the Ramsays, father and son, imitated the Odes and Epistles of Horace, so they had attempted to imitate the villa setting in which the poetry had been composed and the ideal life pursued.[38] In 1733, even before the painter made his first visit to Italy, he had begun a project to establish himself and his father in a remarkable house in the shadow of Edinburgh Castle. This he saw as some kind of temple of the arts; and indeed it was invested with the grandiloquent title of the 'House of the Muses'. The villa on the Castle Bank was at once a fastness for a poet in Horatian retirement and a studio for a painter with a reputation in the making. Here Ramsay was later to produce some of the key images of the society that engendered the Scottish Enlightenment, and from his headquarters here played his part in the intellectual life of Edinburgh as founder of the influential Select Society and as the friend and correspondent of many of the leading literati.

The muses' seat on the Castlehill was rapidly nicknamed the Guse-Pie (that is, Goose-Pie, from its octagonal shape). Clearly, Edinburgh wits appreciated less than the founders of the house this attempt to create an Horatian retreat – an architectural equivalent of an 'imitation' of the Roman poet, a place in which his imagined manner of living might be translated. More sympathetic minds, however, endorsed the Ramsays' project. Notable among them was the greatest exponent in Scotland of the neo-Roman life, Sir John Clerk of Penicuik. He it was who furnished the Latin inscription for the 'House of the Muses', and who acted as architectural adviser. Clerk appended to his Latin text the famous lines from Horace's *Ars Poetica* 9: 'pictoribus atque poetis/Quidlibet audiendi semper fuit aequa potestas' ('painters and poets, you say, have always had an equal licence in daring invention').[39]

Sir John himself lived by the precepts of Horace, Cicero and Pliny and imitated a Roman life of virtuous ease ('otium'), not only at his principal seat of Penicuik but also (and perhaps chiefly) at his exquisite suburban villa of Mavisbank.[40] It was Clerk, indeed, who first used the term 'villa' in a British context to describe the kind of house that was to be defined more in terms of its use than by its strict adherence to any particular architectural type, as that may be distinguished by factors ranging from location, through dimensions, to plan and even rhythm of bays and modulation of facade.[41] By 'villa' Clerk meant a secondary seat to which a man of affairs might withdraw from the cares of court or city to pursue a more simple, rural, honourable and scholarly existence. The Roman precedents were clear. As an architectural type – small though often elaborate, and situated near the town where lay its owner's duty or business ('negotium', in Roman terms: the negation of leisure) – the villa became established as the prevalent building type of the mid and later eighteenth century and one intimately connected with the idea of the cultivation of leisure and friendship in rural peace and quiet.[42] To this was linked the exercise of patronage by the villa owner, and the creation of literary and cultural circles.

By the time he came to study seriously the subject of Horace's Villa, Ramsay himself had already contributed to the debate on architectural propriety and which ancient building types should rightly form models for emulation or adaptation. He touches upon these matters in *A Dialogue on Taste*:

The present taste in architecture was formed, not upon the palaces and dwelling-houses of the ancient Greeks and Romans, of which there were no vestiges at the revival of the arts, but upon their temples and other public buildings, from which the ornamental part has been borrowed and applied to domestic use, in a manner abundantly absurd, for the most part; and which, nevertheless, custom has rendered agreeable to the sight.[43]

Robert Adam followed Ramsay in explaining why the modern architect should select with care those ancient buildings most capable of offering instruction in, and inspiration for, the design of town and country houses; and in so doing he appears to acknowledge the value of ancient literary references to sites such as Horace's Villa. Adam and Ramsay must surely have discussed this topic when in Rome together in the mid-1750s. The following quotations are taken from the introduction to Adam's *Ruins of the Palace of the Emperor Diocletian at Spalatro in Dalmatia*, to which Ramsay subscribed:

Scarce any monuments now remain of Grecian or of Roman magnificence but public buildings … the private but splendid edifices in which the citizens of Athens and Rome resided, have all perished; few vestiges remain of those innumerable villas with which Italy was crowded … Some accidental allusions in the ancient poets, some occasional descriptions in their historians, convey such ideas of the magnificence, both of their houses in town and of their villas, as astonish an artist of the present age ... There is not any misfortune which an Architect is more apt to regret than the destruction of these buildings, nor could any thing more sensibly gratify his curiosity, or improve his taste, than to have an opportunity of viewing the private edifices of the Ancients, and of collecting, from his own observation, such ideas concerning the disposition, the form, the ornaments, and uses of the several apartments, as no description can supply.

This thought often occured to me during my residence in Italy; nor could I help considering my knowledge of Architecture as imperfect, unless I should be able to add the observation of a private edifice of the Ancients to my study of their public works.

Adam's publication was the result of a thoroughgoing attempt to study Roman domestic architecture, albeit building on a monumental, almost public scale. Ramsay's decision to explore the much more modest site of the Sabine villa, from which would have come but a small publication in his old age, contrasts with Adam's more grandiose and less altruistic plans to exploit the palace at Split as part of a carefully orchestrated exercise in image-making, in which Antiquity itself was laid under tribute as the servant of Adam's reputation.

As we have noted, Ramsay's was an age in which the ideal of the unity of the arts was propounded by aesthetic theorists. Poetry and painting were the 'sister arts': their interrelationship was close, and both were linked in the arts of landscape. In gardens throughout Britain, landscapes of allusion or association were created to evoke the spirit of classical antiquity. The poetical world of Virgil and Horace was made palpable in English woods and waters, grottoes, temples, statues and evocative inscriptions. 'Poetry, Painting and Gardening, or the science of landscape', wrote Horace Walpole, 'will forever by men of taste be deemed Three Sisters or The Three New Graces, who dress and adorn nature.'[44] In his search for Horace's Villa, Allan Ramsay added to his accomplishments as painter and man of letters the study of ancient buildings in their landscape.

In investigating the locality of Horace's country estate, Ramsay realized that the arbitrary preservation or destruction of the villa buildings and gardens was in part the result of accidents of nature and in part the product of human intervention by the *contadini* of the Licenza valley. Throughout the 'Enquiry' he took pains to study the culture of the country people and made perceptive observations. Such passages are at variance with many of the more arid or coolly analytical sections of the 'Enquiry', and it may be that part of the attraction for Ramsay in his search for Horace's Villa was the pursuit of an ideal of rustic simplicity and virtue. His disenchantment with the state of British politics and society in the 1760s and 1770s may have heightened the appeal of what must to him have seemed a lost idyll. Britain had lost the American colonies, and much of Ramsay's pamphleteering was directed to questions such as her Imperial rôle. The villa site itself presented, even in its physical decay, a symbol of peace and contemplation, and the discovery of the rural villa-world of Horace represented a retreat to a golden age free of corruption and decline. For all the rigour of his scholarship and

1.8. Horace at work with Pegasus to inspire him; engraving from J. Pine's edition of the works of Horace, 1733–7

his empirical methodology, Ramsay succumbed as much as anyone to the dream of a better world seen through Horace's eyes.

Ramsay was followed by later commentators on the putative site of the Sabine farm. Because for so long Horace had been regarded as a sort of honorary Englishman, villa-hunting had come to be an especially British pastime, pursued in the face of the opprobrium of Piranesi, among others (see pp.85–6 below). Urbanity, gentlemanliness, worldly-wisdom, love of country life and the rest of the ancient Roman's endearing qualities led the British, as modern Romans, to seek out the house of their soul-mate from Antiquity. It has been suggested that in the nineteenth century the local villagers of the Sabine Hills believed that Horace had been an *Inglese* because so many British visitors came on pilgrimage to his house.[45] The source of this pleasing conceit is a letter of George Dennis, who in 1842, taking time out from his discovery of the Etruscans, wrote from Licenza giving a narrative of his visit to the villa, which he described as his 'pilgrimage to this spot, more holy to us both than Mecca, Loreto or Compostella'. Few travellers came from Rome to Horace's villa, Dennis noted; and of these few the greater number were English. 'In fact, it is commonly believed by the peasantry, that Horace was our countryman, for they cannot conceive of any other source of interest in one so long dead, and unsainted, than that of co-patriotism or consanguinity.'[46]

In a work that was to become a standard companion-guide for travellers in Italy, John Moore cited as among the principal attractions of the area the Horatian associations of Tivoli and the proximity of what he agreed to be in all probability the authentic site of the Sabine farm (Fig.1.9). Reading Horace on the spot was certain to intensify the pleasure of a literary and topographical experience: the man of feeling would surely 'see the philosophic poet wandering among the groves'.[47] It would be left for Robert Bradstreet, musing in the early nineteenth century, to describe in verse how

1.9. Romanticized view of Horace in his landscape at Tivoli; engraving from G. R. Volpi, *Vetus Latium Profanum*, vol. x, 1745

antiquarian proofs, gathered over the preceding fifty years or so of fieldwork and documentary research, had come to supplement the evidence of nature and the verse descriptions of Horace himself:

> Lo! The sweet knoll, whose trees of various green,
> Half hide, and half admit the circling scene;
> While, at the foot of its o'erhanging groves,
> With dove-like murmur cool Digentia roves;
> Whose broad, and winding bed of pebbles white,
> Seems a wide river to the stranger's sight,
> Which parts him from the wooded mountain round,
> And yon fair conic hills with hamlets crown'd –
> Did not a thousand proofs around appear.
> Imagination's self would fix it here.
>
> Here then, O shade of Horace! let me kneel,
> And kiss those fragments with a pilgrim-zeal![48]

Over the past hundred and fifty years the theme of the Sabine farm, and the quest for its actual setting, has attracted a steady procession of devotees. Giving full credit to the Abbé Bertrand Capmartin De Chaupy for his contribution, but wholly ignorant of Ramsay, Henry Hart Milman described how the site of Horace's villa had, since the eighteenth century, been visited by 'other antiquarians and scholars, who have found almost every name mentioned by the poet still clinging to the mountains and valleys, the towns and villages of the neighbourhood'.[49] The anonymous writer of an article in *The Builder* (1883) described the site as 'the most sincerely sacred' of all the 'hallowed shrines' on Addison's 'classic ground'. Like Ramsay, Gaston Boissier linked his study of Horace and Virgil with the various landscapes of their lives and poetry.[50]

G. H. Hallam, his studies warmed by his own long-term residence in that very place, wrote lovingly (but almost certainly incorrectly) of Horace at Tivoli (ancient Tibur), where he was long alleged to have had a villa, shown to visitors since antiquity with a local pride that claimed the house of San Antonio as in origin the poet's dwelling. Hallam's essay also deals with the Sabine Hill country beyond Tibur, that region in which Horace's actual residence is more accurately to be placed, and which Hallam, in fact, knew intimately from frequent visits to the villa site.[51]

L. P. Wilkinson, in a fine study published in 1945 and revised in 1951, recommended – like Ramsay – personal inspection of the topography as a way of understanding the essential veracity of Horace's description of an actual rather than an imagined landscape (although Wilkinson did liken it to the Yorkshire Dales). Nevertheless, this scholar wrote with a feeling for the landscape and for its present-day inhabitants in a way uncannily reminiscent of Ramsay's own sentiments.[52] In this manner Gilbert Highet's wise, delightful and evocative study *Poets in a Landscape* follows, and accords to Horace's Villa, and to the theme of the relationship of place to poems, one of the most perceptive of treatments.

Most remarkable of all is Alfred Noyes's evocation of life at the Sabine farm across the divide of two thousand years. This fulsome, yet somehow completely credible picture is based on literature, archaeology, topographical familiarity (book-learned or otherwise) and keen sensitivity to and appreciation of place. Noyes reconstructs Horace's villa in its landscape of the Licenza valley with its encircling hills; his fields, woods and streams; his immortal fountain; his herds and flocks; his garden; his house with its different rooms and their decoration; his possessions; his library; his table and his food and wine; even his manner of living and the pattern of his day. The portrait is completed by an evocation of the process of literary creation itself:

But the Sabine farm was the real home of Horace, and we may surely picture him, by his water-spring on many a golden morning, or by that ruined temple on the hill, concentrating his whole mind on the attempt to give the last touches of perfection to lines that he had written earlier in the din and smoke of Rome; lines that only needed time and patience, the labour of the file, and Horace, to make them unforgettable. He had brought many of these unfinished poems with him. He liked to hold them back from publication until he felt sure of them; and in that stillness, with only the peaceful sound of the stream below – 'thy stream, Digentia' – or the rustling of a light breeze through the stone pine that shadowed his roof, he had his opportunity. Hour after hour would slip by while, forgetful even of food and wine, hardly lifting his eyes, he endured the happy torment of all true artists.[53]

Notes

1. R. A. Brower, *Alexander Pope*, 1959, p.165. On Horace in the eighteenth century see G. Showerman, *Horace*, 1922, pp.121–5; L. G. Burgevin, 'A Little Farm' in *Horace*, 1936, pp.57, 65–72; and, generally, C. Martindale and D. Hopkins, *Horace Made New*, 1993.

2. C. Goad, *Horace in English Literature*, 1918, p.7.

3. P. Ayres, *Classical Culture*, 1997, pp.31–2.

4. Quoted in F. Stack, *Pope and Horace*, 1985, pp.4–5.

5. Advertisement to 'Imitations of Horace', in Pope, *The Poems*, 1968, p.613.

6. On Pope and Horace see the essay by R. Sowerby in C. Martindale and D. Hopkins, *Horace Made New*, 1993, pp.159–83.

7. Brower, *Alexander Pope*, 1959, p.176.

8. For the life and work of Ramsay's father see A. Ramsay [the elder], *The Works of Allan Ramsay*, vol.4, 1970, Biographical and Critical Introduction by A. M. Kinghorn, Appendix A, pp.71–6, which includes a memoir of the father by the son, surviving in Edinburgh University Library (MS.La.II.212/41, 42); see also I. G. Brown, *Poet and Painter*, 1984.

9. See J. Butt, *Pope: Imitations*, 1966, pp.10–12.

10. R. A. Brower, *Alexander Pope*, 1959, p.163.

11. See A. M. Kinghorn, 'Biographical and Critical Introduction', in A. Ramsay [the elder], *The Works of Allan Ramsay*, vol. 4, 1970, pp.110, 112.

12. L. P. Wilkinson, *Horace and his Lyric Poetry*, 1968, p.2.

13. R. A. Brower, *Alexander Pope*, 1959, p.165.

14. A. Ramsay [the younger], *The Investigator*, 1762, pp.45, 52.

15. Begun around 1775, this survives in manuscript in the British Library, Add. MS. 39999: see I.G. Brown, 'The Pamphlets of Allan Ramsay', 1988, pp.84–5.

16. H. Walpole, *Correspondence*, 1937–83, vol. 31, p.416.

17. A. Ramsay [the elder], *The Poems of Allan Ramsay*, 1800, vol. 1, pp.lii, ix.

18. For the fullest modern assessment of Ramsay and his art see the works by A. Smart in the Bibliography; see also I.G. Brown, 'Ramsay's Rise and Reputation', and *Poet and Painter*, both 1984. On Ramsay's literary productions see also Brown, 'The Pamphlets of Allan Ramsay', 1988.

19. G. Vertue, *Notebooks*, 1934, p.96.

20. I.G. Brown, 'Ramsay's Rise and Reputation', 1984, Appendix II, 'Allan Ramsay's Purchases for Dr Richard Mead', and note 101; see also C. Pace, 'Pietro Santi Bartoli', 1979.

21. See Brown, 'Ramsay's Rise and Reputation', Appendix II.

22. See I.G. Brown, *The Hobby-Horsical Antiquary*, 1980, pp.25–6; Brown, 'Ramsay's Rise and Reputation', 1984, pp. 214–5.

23. A. Ramsay [the younger], *The Investigator*, 1762, pp.37, 38, 40.

24. For a summary and assessment of the dispute with Piranesi see I.G. Brown, *Poet and Painter*, 1984, pp.40–41.

25. See W.J. MacDonald and J.A. Pinto, *Hadrian's Villa*, 1995.

26. See I.G. Brown, *Monumental Reputation*, 1992.

27. See P. du Prey, *The Villas of Pliny*, 1994.

28. Remarks attributed to the mysterious 'Mr T—' and preserved by J. Spence, *Observations*, vol. 2, 1966, pp.672, 674, 677–8.

29. D. Hume, *Letters*, vol. 1, 1932, p.401.

30. F.A. Pottle, *James Boswell*, 1966, pp.216–17, 511; M.S. Pottle, C.C. Abbott and F.A. Pottle, *Catalogue*, vol. 1, 1993, p.274 (letter 754, to John Johnston, May 1765).

31. A. Lumisden, *Remarks on the Antiquities of Rome*, 1797, pp.400, 425.

32. W. Scott, *Journal*, 1972, p.523.

33. C. Martindale and D. Hopkins, *Horace Made New*, 1993, p.1.

34. A.G. McKay, *Houses, Villas and Palaces*, 1975, p.112.

35. T.R. Glover, *Horace*, 1932, p.44. The reference is to Horace, *Epistles*, I.14.1: 'the little farm which makes me myself again'.

36. A. Noyes, *Portrait of Horace*, 1947, p.110.

37. For a valuable treatment of this topic see G. Worsley, *Classical Architecture*, 1995, chap. VII, passim.

38. On Horace's idea of rural life see D. Armstrong, *Horace*, 1989, pp. 48–9, 58–9.

39. For the inscription see I.G. Brown, 'Ramsay's Rise and Reputation', 1984, p.229 and note 87.

40. On Clerk see I.G. Brown, 'Sir John Clerk', 1980, especially chaps 7 and 8; see also Brown, *The Clerks of Penicuik*, 1987.

41. On Clerk's use of 'villa' see I. Gow, 'The Edinburgh Villa', 1991, p.38, quoting Brown, 'Sir John Clerk', 1980.

42. Cf. J. Summerson, 'The Classical Country House in Eighteenth-Century England', originally published in *Journal of the Royal Society of Arts*, 1959, reprinted in Summerson, *The Unromantic Castle*, 1990, pp.86, 92–3, 106; see also J. Ackerman, *The Villa*, 1990, pp.9, 39.

43. A. Ramsay [the younger], *The Investigator*, 1762, p.52.

44. The quotation is from Walpole's *The History of the Modern Taste in Gardening*, quoted in J. Ackerman, *The Villa*, 1990, p.182.

45. On this point see most recently P. Levi, *Horace*, 1997, p.85.

46. For Dennis's letter see H.H. Milman, *The Works of Quintus Horatius Flaccus*, 1849, pp.97, 108–9.

47. J. Moore, *A View of Society*, vol. 2, 1787, pp.330–31.

48. From the poem 'Poetical Pilgrimage', in R. Bradstreet, *The Sabine Farm*, 1810, Preface and p.85.

49. H.H. Milman, *The Works of Quintus Horatius Flaccus*, 1849, p.53

50. G. Boissier, *The Country of Horace and Virgil*, 1896.

51. G.H. Hallam, *Horace at Tibur*, 1927. That Hallam visited the villa very regularly is clear from the visitors' book of the period, which B. Frischer has found in the archive of the Archaeological Superintendency for Lazio.

52. L.P. Wilkinson, *Horace and His Lyric Poetry*, 1968, pp.55–6.

53. A. Noyes, *Portrait of Horace*, 1947, pp.1–5, 11, 13, 111–14, 140.

2

Some Reflections on the Idea of Horace's Farm

John Dixon Hunt

The American landscape architect Laurie Olin, in a book of essays on English country houses and their relationship to the land, writes that 'behind these country gardens and parks as well as the more recent garden city movement and modern flight to the suburbs lies the ghost of Virgil and the image of Horace's farm.'[1] It is unusual these days to hear a professional landscape architect invoke, even as ghostly presences, the authority and model of classical villa life; but it was a commonplace of earlier periods. One has only to look at the manuscripts of John Aubrey, which document the history of seventeenth-century English garden art, to notice his frequent glossing of local English examples with literary references, mainly Latin.[2]

A different question is addressed here: namely, what was special about the Horatian example for British villa-making and villa-living in the eighteenth century? There are essentially two answers. One depends upon the classical facts themselves, the other derives from the fashion in which those 'facts' were made available to English readers. The latter was effected above all through the life and writings of Alexander Pope, whose triple authority as poet, translator and gardenist contributed greatly to eighteenth-century ideas of Horace's villa. It is the mode of translation that Pope developed through his 'imitations' of Horace[3] that is especially relevant to the 'translation' into English of classical gardens and villas.

Although Pope's versions of Homer from the late 1710s and 1720s abided by notions of translation that we would generally recognize and share today – rendering the Greek in a servicable, unjarringly modern but literary form – his work with Horace in the 1730s was much more committed to (re-)shaping the Latin to make the *sermones proprii* sound and feel wholly local and contemporary. Part of Pope's strategy was to direct his reader's attention to the ways in which Horace's world was by no means readily analogous to Hanoverian England's nor particularly apt for sustaining straightforward parallels; Horace had, in fact, to undergo revision – alteration, addition and subtraction – before he was consumable in the 1730s. Not that parallels between modern Britain and classical Rome could not be identified; but a careful comparison of here and now with there and then would significantly highlight contrasts in crucial matters. The simplest way to appreciate these comparisons and contrasts is to remind ourselves of the original *mise en page* of Pope's *Horatian Imitations*, where the Latin faced the English (Fig.2.1). Not only did this enable a reader with good Latin to appreciate the English equivalents that had been found for it in English, but actual *lacunae* also signalled the slippages between the two cultures.[4] On a personal level, for instance, Pope's own indisposition ('this long disease, my life') must have paralleled Horace's 'very weak health', upon which Allan Ramsay dilates. More important, however, are the instances in which Pope contrasts Horace's

8   E P I S T L E S

²¹ Si latus, aut renes morbo tententur acuto,

Quere fugam morbi —

— ²² Vis recte vivere ? quis non ?

Si Virtus hoc una potest dare, fortis omissis

Hoc age deliciis ——

— ²³ Virtutem verba putas, ut

Lucum ligna ? ²⁴ cave ne portus occupet alter,

Ne Cybiratica, ne Bithyna negotia perdas.

²⁵ Mille talenta rotundentur, totidem altera : porro

Tertia succedant, & quæ pars quadret acervum.

OF H O R A C E.   9

²¹ Rack'd with Sciatics, martyr'd with the Stone,
Will any mortal let himself alone ?   55
Rather than so, see Ward invited over,
And desp'rate Misery lays hold on Dover.
The case is easier in the Mind's disease ;
There, all Men may be cur'd, whene'er they please.
Would ye be ²² blest ? despise low Joys, low Gains ;
Disdain whatever CORNBURY disdains ;   61
Be Virtuous, and be happy for your pains.
²³ But art thou one, whom new opinions sway,
One, who believes as Tindal leads the way,
Who Virtue and a Church alike disowns,   65
Thinks that but words, and this but brick and stones?
Fly ²⁴ then, on all the wings of wild desire!
Admire whate'er the maddest can admire.
Is Wealth thy passion ? Hence ! from Pole to Pole,
Where winds can carry, or where waves can roll,
For Indian spices, for Peruvian gold,   71
Prevent the greedy, and out-bid the bold :
²⁵ Advance thy golden Mountain to the skies;
On the broad base of fifty thousand rise,

D

2.1. Opening page from Alexander Pope's 'Imitations of Horace', 1733

ownership of his Sabine estate with his own rented accommodation of the Twickenham villa (for Catholics in Hanoverian England were legally forbidden to own property).

Pope's recognition of the differences in habitation between Horace and himself is part of his larger concern with the difficulties that would attend any attempt to reproduce the Italian legacy of landscape architecture (ancient and modern) in the British Isles. He plays with making his villa and garden at Twickenham the equivalent of Horace's Sabine farm: Horace's famous 'Secretum iter, et fallentis semita vitae' ('the secluded journey and the pathway of a life unnoticed', *Epistles* 1.18.103) was inscribed over the garden entrance to Pope's grotto.[6] But despite such gestures – or rather, because of such similarities – Pope's garden was quite deliberate in its self-conscious divergence from Horace's; in practice, the two places clearly were not comparable for reasons at once cultural, political and aesthetic. If gardens declared their gardener – and the Roman Cato had long ago insisted on what was by Pope's time a commonplace that 'Scito idem agrum quod hominem' ('remember that a farm is like a man')[7] – then Pope no more walked around

EPISTOLARVM LIBER I.   121

EPISTOLA X.
AD FVSCVM ARISTIVM.

RBIS amatorem Fuscum salvere jube-
mus

Ruris amatores; hac in re scilicet una

Multum diffimiles, ad caetera pene
gemelli,

Fraternis animis : quidquid negat alter, et alter :

Annuimus pariter, vetuli notique columbi.   5

Tu nidum servas : ego laudo ruris amoeni

Rivos, et musco circumlita saxa, nemusque.

Quid quaeris? vivo, et regno, simul ista reliqui,

Quae vos ad coelum fertis rumore secundo.

Vtque sacerdotis fugitivus, liba recufo,   10

Pane egeo, jam mellitis potiore placentis.

Vivere naturae si convenienter oportet,

Ponendaeque domo quaerenda est area primum;

Novistine locum potiorem rure beato?.

2.2. Opening page of
Horace's *Epistles*, from J.
Pine's edition of the works of
Horace, vol.i, 1733

in a toga and had a wealthy patron like Maecenas than the design of the Twickenham garden would have resembled any image that could be imagined for a Roman *villa suburbana*. (Indeed, as a Roman Catholic Pope would see his garden-making in terms of a cathedral of trees, and the climax of his site was an obelisk commemorating his revered mother).[8]

There was, nevertheless, a strong desire to secure a place for modern English gardening in the tradition or 'progress' of gardening that stretched from classical times, to modern Italy, and then northwards through the countries of England's neighbours and finally across the Channel.[9] The Palladian movement in British architecture offered a plausible model: Palladio had himself studied classical buildings, from which he had drawn inspiration for modern and largely Veneto architecture; this in its turn had been imitated further and further north, especially in England among the circle around Lord Burlington.[10] An equivalent activity in landscape architecture, what has been called 'Palladian gardening',[11] was made difficult by the scarcity of antique remains upon which to model modern gardens and estate layouts. Even if traces of Roman landscape architecture had been frequent and full enough to direct modern design, the materials of garden and estate design – above all, the plantings – could not be transposed into a northern climate and culture. To make the Horace who was villa-owner and agrarian 'speak good English'[12] required somewhat more tricky negotiation than was needed to render his poetry. For Pope, as for many landscapers in early and mid eighteenth-century Britain (some of whom he advised), it was necessary both to show off classical obligations and simultanously to declare indigenous skills and achievements.[13] How was that possible in the matter of villa-making?

Pope was in some paradoxical way lucky that he never had the chance to visit Italy. Despite some second-hand knowledge of its riches undoubtedly contributed by such friends as William Kent, who had spent years there, the renegotiation of classical villa design would have to remain largely within Pope's imagination. This was surely a freer zone than one based on archaeological enquiry, as some contemporary documents show. Purchasers of John Pine's 1733 edition of *Quinti Horatii Flacci Opera*, published in London exactly at the period when Pope was in the midst of his imitations of the Latin poet, were not readers who needed Horace to 'speak good English', since presumably they themselves had good Latin. And as part of this experience of communing directly with the Roman past, Pine's handsome edition was decorated with images that purported to be accurate representations of classical gardens (Fig.2.2). They were, however, no more than reproductions of imaginary reconstructions from earlier guidebooks published in Rome, visual representations that depended as much upon contemporary Renaissance architectural forms as upon archaeological remains.[14]

In the absence of sufficient and reliable remains of classical gardens, the issue became how the modern reader translated Latin verbal descriptions of gardens and villas into visual, let alone actual and material forms that

Notes

1.   L. Olin, *Across the Open Field: Essays Drawn from English Landscapes*, 1999, p.220.

2.   See, for instance, Bodleian Library MS. Aubrey 2, an analysis of Wilton House gardens and Sir John Danvers's property at Chelsea, among other sites; Aubrey glosses his account of English examples with references to the elder Pliny and Juvenal. That he does not cite Horace perhaps indicates the greater relevance of that Roman poet to the eighteenth-century English situation.

3.   On Pope and Horace, see F. Stack, *Pope and Horace*, 1985, and J. Fuchs, *Pope's Imitations of Horace*, 1989; see also D. Chambers, 'The Translation of Antiquity', 1991.

4.   It is a familiar experience in books of this period to find Latin passages rendered into lengthier English ones, a result of the conciseness of Latin yet an effect that draws attention to the fashion in which the two languages were not equitable; for another example beside Pope's, see B. Kennett, *Romae Antiquitiae Notitia*, 1699, pp.178 (Lucan), 181–2 (Juvenal) and 203–4 (Virgil).

5.   See A. Ramsay, 'Enquiry', p.58 (Ramsay's pagination, here and following).

6.   See the anonymous 'An Epistolary Description of the late Mr. Pope's House and Garden at Twickenham', 1747, reprinted in J. D. Hunt and P. Willis, *The Genius of the Place*, 1988.

7.   Cato, *De re rustica* 4.45. Cf. T. Fuller's remark that 'As is the Gardener, so is the Garden', *Gnomologia*, 1732, adage no.701.

8.   It has not, I believe, been remarked how even this famous item in Pope's garden may have its origin in Horace; see Ramsay, 'Enquiry', p.60. Yet here again, the Catholic Alexander Pope's

celebration of maternal virtues would have been culturally determined in ways that distanced his allusion from its classical 'source'.

9. This was, of course, part of a much larger focus upon Roman culture: see P. Ayres, *Classical Culture*, 1997. M. Mack has explored this theme for Pope in *The Garden and the City*, 1969; see also J.D. Hunt, 'Pope's Twickenham Revisited', 1983.

10. See J. Lees-Milne, *Earls of Creation*, 1962; J. Carré and J. Harris, *Palladian Revival*, 1994.

11. See J.D. Hunt, 'Pope, Kent and "Palladian" Gardening', 1988.

12. The phrase is Sir William Trumbull's, urging Pope to continue with his translations of Homer: see A. Pope, *Correspondence*, vol.1, 1956, pp.45–6. In this connection see J.D. Hunt, 'Gard'ning can Speak Proper English', 1992, and 'Making Virgil Look English', 1993.

13. See J.D. Hunt, op. cit., notes 10 and 11 above; see also Hunt, *Garden and Grove*, 1996, passim.

14. For other images in Pine's Horace, see Figs 1.2–4 and 1.8. Both Pope and his landscape gardener friend, William Kent, subscribed to Pine's edition.

15. I reproduce this engraving again in this book because when originally published in my *Garden and Grove*, 1986, its usefulness was somewhat defeated by the removal of the original seventeenth-century caption, here restored, upon which this argument depends.

16. In this connection see P. du Prey, *The Villas of Pliny*, 1994.

17. See A. Ramsay, 'Enquiry', pp.30 and 49, respectively.

18. 'Enquiry', pp.43–6 and 21–2, respectively.

19. In 'An Epistle to Lord Burlington', 1731; see A. Pope, *Poems*, vol.3/ii, 1951. For earlier and more generous notions of *genius loci* as applied to place-making see J.D. Hunt, 'Evelyn's Idea of the Garden: A Theory for All Seasons', in T. O'Malley and J. Wolschke-Bulmahn, *John Evelyn*, 1988, pp.269–88.

20. S. Switzer, *Ichnographia Rustica*, vol.1, 1718, pp.xxxvii–xxxviii.

21. Ramsay, 'Enquiry', p.56.

22. See N. Everett, *The Tory View of Landscape*,1994, especially pp.116–22.

23. Ramsay, 'Enquiry', pp.56–7.

24. ibid., p.10. Cf. B. Frischer, 'Fu la villa Ercolanese', 1995.

25. See A.G. McKay, *Houses, Villas and Palaces*, 1975, pp.116 and 247, note 191.

26. See J.D. Hunt and P. Willis, *The Genius of the Place*, 1988, pp.197–203. On Clerk, see I.G. Brown, 'Sir John Clerk of Penicuik', 1980.

3

Describing the Villa: *un rêve virgilien*

Martin Goalen

Plato … gives some useful advice: a grand name will lend a place great dignity and authority. That the emperor Hadrian approved of this is demonstrated in the famous names such as Licus, Canopeius, Achademia, and Tempe that he gave the rooms of his [Tivoli] villa.[1]
L.B. Alberti, *De re aedificatoria*, 1485

Nothing renders [Tivoli] so interesting as the frequent mention Horace makes of it in his writings … If you ever come to Tivoli … be sure to put Horace in your pocket. You will read him with more enthusiasm than elsewhere; you will imagine you see the philosophic poet wandering among the groves …[2]
John Moore, *A View of Society and Manners in Italy*, 1781

Returning to France in 1929 on the steamer *Lutetia*, the architect Le Corbusier prepared for publication ten lectures on architecture and urbanism that he had given in Buenos Aires. The twelve-day sea journey and the memory of flying over the landscape of South America – reminding him 'on a bigger scale of Renaissance engravings in books on the art of gardens' – provoked a lyrical response as he set out to recompose his 'Buenos Aires song'.[3] The fifth lecture, 'The Plan of the Modern House', describes the design of the villa that he was then building for the Savoye family at Poissy outside Paris, offered as a model for transplantation to 'a corner of the beautiful Argentine countryside'.[4] The Poissy villa is described in terms of its site: 'une vaste pelouse, bombée en dôme aplati', with orientation, views, the compass of the surrounding forest and the sweep of the chauffeur-driven motor car arriving from Paris all giving rise to an image of the house as a hanging garden, raised above the ground, offering an abstracted, framed spectacle of nature to its urbanite owners. 'It is in its right place in the rural landscape of Poissy', claimed Le Corbusier, although in Biarritz, 'it would be magnificent … the hanging garden would simply be turned around', and in Argentina:

We shall have twenty houses rising from the high grass of an orchard where cows continue to graze … nothing will be disturbed, neither trees nor herds. The inhabitants, drawn because the countryside is beautiful with its *vie de campagne*, will contemplate it, maintained intact, from their hanging gardens …Their home life will be set in a Virgilian dream.[5]

These words hold a justifiable place in Le Corbusier criticism. It is now some fifty years since Colin Rowe drew attention to the parallels between this description of the Villa Savoye and the account that Andrea Palladio gives us in *I quattro libri dell'architettura* of the villa built for Monsignor Paolo Almerico on the outskirts of Vicenza, the so-called Villa Rotonda of *c.*1550. The Villa Rotonda, Palladio wrote, is built on a site

as pleasant and delightful as can be found, because it is on a small hill … and is watered on one side by … a navigable river; and on the other it is encompassed about with most pleasant risings which look like a very great theatre and are all cultivated about with most excellent fruits and most exquisite vines; and therefore as it enjoys from every part most beautiful views … there are loggias made in all four fronts.[6]

The parallel responses of the two architects to site and views are clear, but to make the comparison more telling, Rowe seized on what for him was Le Corbusier's key phrase: 'un rêve virgilien'. The two architects are united, Rowe argued, in sharing the pastoral mood of the Augustan poet. Rowe asked that we picture the visitor to the Villa Savoye 'pausing while ascending the ramp' leading to the roof garden where 'the memory of the *Georgics* … interposes itself'. 'The historical reference may even add a stimulus as the car pulls out for Paris', he concluded.[7]

Literary association is not, though, the main thrust of Rowe's argument. The essay proceeds to a discussion of other buildings by the two architects, and comparisons follow more from analysis of geometry and proportion than literary association.[8] What are we to make of Rowe's point of departure? Is it Virgil's *Georgics* (or the *Eclogues*, perhaps) that is recalled at Poissy, and does Palladio's account of ancient *villeggiatura* really stem from Virgil?[9] The answer to these questions will offer a much clearer account of the reciprocal relationship between the literature, the 'ideological myth' of rural life,[10] and the architectural and landscape settings made for the enjoyment of that life: a relationship as intriguing for Allan Ramsay in the eighteenth century as it is for the visitor to the Licenza valley today.

A relationship with an abstracted and distanced nature is a constant theme in Le Corbusier's work, but the specifically Virgilian metaphor of his Buenos Aires lecture is an isolated one. More characteristic is the comment 'a little like the paintings of Carpaccio', used to describe the view over the trees of the Parc St-James from the house he was designing for Mme Meyer in 1925 (Fig.3.1).[11]

The world of painting is central to Le Corbusier. He and his colleague Amadée Ozenfant championed, through the pages of the magazine *L'Esprit Nouveau*, which they edited together between 1920 and 1925, 'la grande lignée des peintres français – Fouquet, Poussin, Ingres, Corot, Cézanne, Seurat – whose strengths they perceived as 'clarté de conception, de la langue, économie des moyens.'[12] Poussin had a special appeal: it is no coincidence that the issue of *L'Esprit Nouveau* (no.7, April 1921) that included a study of the editors' own paintings also contained a detailed study of the Poussin canvases in the Louvre signed 'de Fayet' – a pseudonym mainly used by Ozenfant, but also by Le Corbusier.[13] Three plates (the whole canvas and two details) showed Poussin's *Eleazer and Rebecca at the Well* of 1648 (Fig.3.2). Here the interplay of elemental geometry set against an Arcadian landscape is surely the visual image of Le Corbusier's 'rêve virgilien', although the two details of Poussin's canvas are cropped to stress forms characteristic of Ozenfant's and Le Corbusier's own painting. It is to painting that one should turn to follow Le Corbusier's thought, not the pages of the *Georgics*.[14]

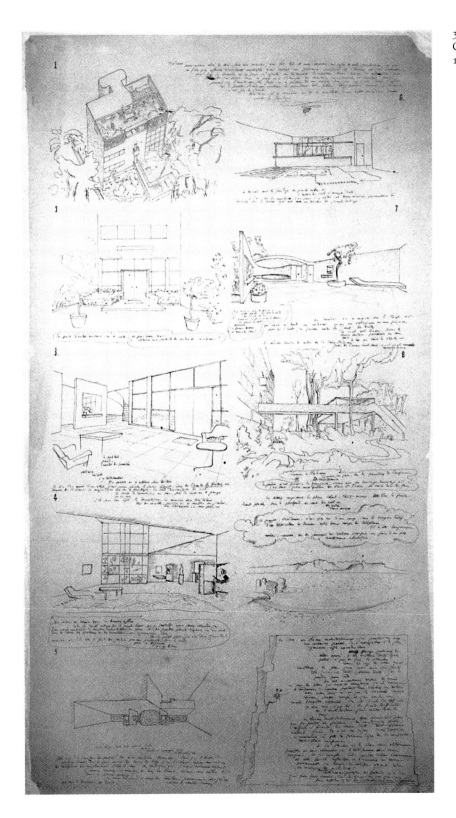

3.1. Detail of a letter from Le Corbusier to Mme Meyer, 1925

For Palladio, on the other hand, the connection to ancient literature was a close one. The classical learning of Palladio's circle of patrons is well known,[15] and the aim of his *I quattro libri* of 1570 was, in part, literary: 'I proposed to myself Vitruvius for my master and guide', he noted in his preface. When Palladio, as the scheme of his book required,[16] came to describe Roman dwellings, he wrote that 'as we have but very few examples from the ancients … I shall insert the plans and elevations of many fabrics I have erected.'[17] In setting the scene for sixteenth-century villa building he recalled the world of the ancient villa: 'the ancient sages commonly used to retire to such places; where being oftentimes visited by their virtuous friends and relations, having houses, gardens, fountains and such like pleasant places, and above all their virtue, they could easily attain as much happiness as can be attained here below'.[18]

'Perhaps these were the dreams of Virgil', Colin Rowe rhetorically questioned this passage,[19] but Palladio's urbane setting of 'brilliant friends … lodgings, gardens, fountains' is not the world of Virgil, not the world of shepherd's songs sung 'under the canopy of a spreading beech'[20], of 'the home fields and the ploughlands that I love' or the 'turf piled high on my poor cottage roof',[21] all made more evanescent by the threatened imminence of their loss. Virgil's 'ignobilis oti', 'inglorious ease' (as he characterized the *Eclogues* in the conclusion of the *Georgics*),[22] is set in the fields and by the streams of a rustic idyll, not in the sophisticated rural retreat of a city-dweller. The *Georgics* too, addressed to those who have the care 'of the fields, of the cattle and the trees',[23] is concerned not with rural ease but with rural virtue and rural husbandry. When Virgil recommended 'a bubbling spring nearby, a pool moss bordered, and a rill ghosting through the grass' at the beginning of *Georgics*, 4, it is not the siting of a villa but that of a beehive that he was recommending, ' for thus, when the new queens lead out the earliest swarms … the bank may be handy to welcome them in out of the heat'.[24]

If Virgil (70–19 BC) was not then the source of Palladio's account of ancient villa life, one might ask whether it was Virgil's younger friend Horace (65–8 BC) from whom Palladio took his view. The poetry of Horace's Sabine farm, though, is not a poetry of urbane *villeggiatura* – the 'brilliant friends' … gardens, fountains' of Palladio's description. Horace, too, affected rustic simplicity. When he wrote of a 'nap on the grass by a stream' ('prope rivum somnus in herba'[25]) his rest was in a meadow rather than in a villa garden, a meadow that was, moreover, a cause of labour and anxiety: 'when you are dead tired, the brook brings fresh work, for if rain has fallen, it must be taught by many a mounded dam to spare the sunny meadow'.[26] Horace emphasized the natural aspects of his valley – its hillsides, its streams, its meadows – but described the dwelling on his farm only negatively: 'not ivory or gilded panel gleams in my home, nor do beams of Hymettian marble rest on pillars quarried in farthest Africa.'[27] To find a parallel to Palladio's urbane view of a rural retreat one must look further, forward almost a century to the letters of the younger Pliny (*c.*AD 61–112).

Two of Pliny's villas (there were others) – one on the coast of Latium, the

3.2. *Eleazer and Rebecca at the Well* by Poussin, 1648; as it appeared in *L'Esprit Nouveau*, no.7, April 1921

other in Tuscany – are each the subject of two long, detailed and famous letters.[28] Pliny described the landscape, climate and products of the region as did Horace, but he did not stop there. The two letters describe the villas in detail: the sequences of rooms, the play of sunlight and breeze, the sea spray, the views: 'the dining-room … lightly washed by the spray of the spent breakers … at the back has a view through the inner-hall, the courtyard with the two colonnades, and the entrance hall to the woods and mountains in the distance.'[29] Pliny described all the pleasures of the two villas, the architecture as well as the landscape. The Tuscan villa, for example, had 'a suite of rooms slightly set back and round a small court shaded by four plane trees. In the centre a fountain plays in a marble basin, watering the plane trees round it and the ground beneath them with a light spray', with nearby 'an informal dining-room where I can entertain my personal friends' and 'a small fountain with a bowl surrounded by jets which together make a lovely murmuring sound ('iucundissimum murmur')'.[30] In the garden,

'roses grow … and cool shadow alternates with the pleasant warmth of the sun … Between the grass lawns here and there are box shrubs clipped into innumerable shapes … small obelisques of box alternate with fruit trees, and then suddenly in the midst of this ornamental ('urbannissimo') scene is what looks like a piece of rural countryside planted there ('ruris imitatio')'.[31]

This is not the rural idyll of the Augustan poets, but a wordly *villeggiatura*: the 'good life' referred to by Palladio. Even in excusing himself from a discussion of Pliny's villas, Palladio acknowledged his awareness of the descriptions: 'I

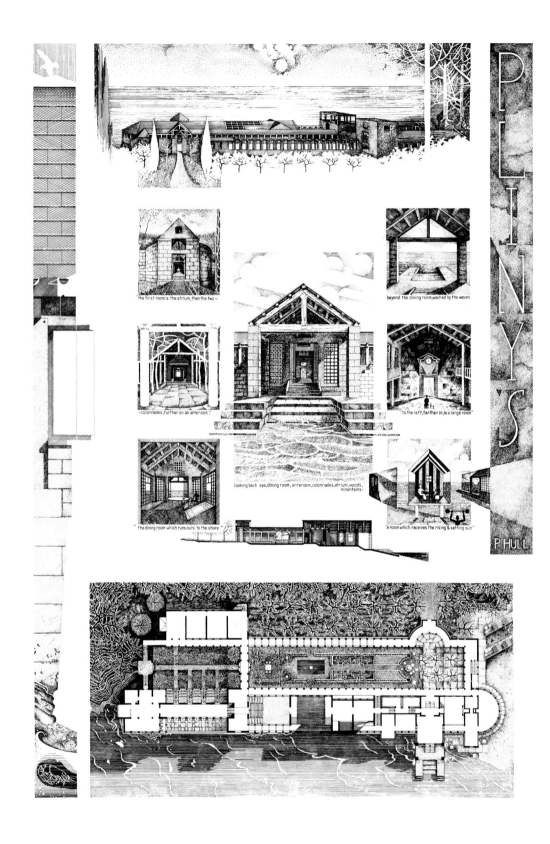

the first room is the atrium, then the two—

beyond the dining room, washed by the waves

—colonnades, further on an anteroom.

to the left, farther in, is a large room

looking back sea, dining room, anteroom, colonnades, atrium, woods, mountains

the dining room which runs out to the shore

'a room which receives the rising & setting sun'

P. HULL

will not include an account of what Pliny says … because now my main aim is solely to demonstrate how one should understand Vitruvius on the subject'.[32]

Pliny's two descriptions follow a common pattern of exposition: first, an introduction, suggesting rhetorically that the description is an answer to his correspondent's question or concern:

You may wonder why my Laurentine place … is such a joy to me (2.17.1)	I am touched by your kind concern when you try to dissuade me from my intention to stay in Tuscany this summer. You think the place is unhealthy, but … (5.6.1)

second, a description of climate and situation:

its extensive seafront … seventeen miles from Rome, so that it is possible to spend the time there after the necessary business is done … it can be approached by more than one route. Whichever way you go … the view on either side is full of variety (2.17.2–3)	The countryside is very beautiful. Picture to yourself a vast amphitheatre … the ancient plain is ringed round by mountains, their summits crowned by ancient woods of tall trees … below them the vineyards … then come the meadows … bright with flowers … the river Tiber flowing through the fields … It is a great pleasure to look down on the countryside from the mountain, for the scene seems to be a painted scene of unusual beauty rather than a real landscape (5.6.7–13)

third, an approach to the main sequence of courts and rooms, and of their views back to the scene just described:

The house is large enough for my needs but not expensive to keep up. It opens into a hall … then two colonnades, rounded like a letter 'D' … opposite the middle is a cheerful inner hall, then a dining-room which really is rather fine … it seems to look out onto three seas, and at the back has a view through the inner hall, the courtyard with the two colonnades, then the entrance hall to the woods and mountains in the distance (2.17.4–6)	My house is on the lower slope of the hill but commands as good a view as if it were higher up … It faces mainly south, and so from midday onwards in summer (a little earlier in winter) it seems to invite the sun into the colonnade. This is broad and long in proportion … from the end of the colonnade projects a dining-room: through its folding doors it looks on to the end of the terrace, the adjacent meadow, and the stretch of open country beyond (5.6.14–19)

then, the internal delights of the villas:

The bright light of the sun reflected from the sea … the sound of the breakers … as a dying murmur … a terrace scented with violets (2.17.17)	… an ornamental pool, a pleasure both see and to hear, with its water falling from a height and foaming white when it strikes the marble (5.6.23–4)

and finally, a conclusion referring back to the rhetorical question of the opening of the letters:

And now do you think I have a good case for making this retreat my haunt and home … You are too polite a townsman if you don't covet it. But I hope you will, for then the many attractions of my treasured house will have another strong recommendation in your company (2.17.29)	But to return to my starting point (5.6.45)

It is clear that the letters are self-conscious literary creations, and as such they take their place in an evolving rhetorical and literary tradition. In an aside towards the end of the Tuscan letter, Pliny compared his own descriptions of the villas with the *ekphraseis* of Homer and Virgil describing the arms of Achilles and Aeneas,[33] and even in that comparison making another: 'comparing small things with great' (following Virgil's comparison of the domestic economy of the bees with that of the Cyclops in the *Georgics*).[34]

The pattern of Horace's *Epistles* 1.16, with which Allan Ramsay prefaced his literary-topographical search for the site of the Sabine farm, is easily recognizable in Pliny's descriptions. Horace's 'letter' begins with just the sort of mock question as do Pliny's: 'Lest you, my good Quinctius, should have to ask me about my farm, whether it supports its master with plough-land or makes him rich with olives … I will describe for you in rambling style the nature and lie of the land'.[35]

Similarly, Horace discussed the situation and climate: 'There are hills, quite unbroken were they not cleft by one shady valley, yet such that the rising sun looks on its right side, and when departing in his flying car warms the left. The climate would win your praise',[36] and the site blessed with water: 'A spring too, fit to give its name to a river'.[37]

But if the tradition in which Pliny wrote was inaugurated by Horace, it nevertheless goes beyond the world of the Augustan poets. To find descriptions of villas themselves we must move forward from Horace some three generations to Statius (*c.*AD 40–79). His collection, the *Silvae*, includes highly coloured encomia of two villas: that of Manilius Vopiscus at Tivoli and that of Pollius Felix at Sorrento.[38] 'Shall I marvel at the gilded beams … the patterned veins of glittering marbles', Statius asked rhetorically of the villa of Manilius Vopiscus, almost directly recalling Horace's *Odes* 2.18 cited above, although inverting its sense.[39] In Pollius' villa 'here the sound of the sea in the chambers, here they know of the roaring of the waters … each chamber has its own delight, its own particular sea … each window commands a different landscape'.[40] Echos of these lines recur throughout Pliny's two descriptions.[41]

There is another form of literary production that provides a model for Pliny's villa descriptions. Pliny had heard Quintilian's lectures in rhetoric as a young man,[42] and as an advocate was a daily practioner of forensic rhetoric. One of the skills that a speaker must have is a trained memory, and the art of memory is one of the themes of the rhetorical handbooks such as that of Quintilian. The following much quoted passage sets out such a procedure:

Some space is chosen … such as a spacious house divided into a number of rooms. Everything of note there is carefully committed to the memory, in order that thought may be able to run through all the details without let or hindrance … Particular symbols that serve to jog the memory … are then arranged as follows. The first thought is placed, as it were, in the vestibulium; the second, let us say, in the atrium; the remainder are placed in due order all around the impluvium and entrusted not merely to the cubicula and exedrae but even to the care of statues and the like. This done … all those places are visited in turn … [and] the sight of each recalls the respective details.[43]

Pliny's letters guide us through his two villas exactly thus: from vestibulium, to atrium, to cubicula, to exedrae. Surely his reader was intended to recall the mnemonic procedure of the textbooks of rhetoric, or of his daily forensic practice.

By placing his descriptions so clearly within a literary/rhetorical tradition, Pliny drew attention to the letters as literary constructions. Indeed, one editor and translator of the letters, Ann-Marie Guillemin, has suggested that the villa descriptions are so much a product of art that the two villas might not have existed at all, but were invented for the sake of a virtuoso literary performance.[44] There exist, however, a number of villa sites along the Laurentine coast to the south of Ostia that, in spite of generations of remodelling after Pliny's time and their ruined state in the undergrowth of the Presidential estate at Castelporziano, may provide the basis for the Laurentine description. Current work on the Castelporziano littoral is revealing an ancient seafront that, in Pliny's words, 'gains much from the pleasing variety of the villas built either in groups or far apart; from the sea or shore these look like a number of cities.'[45] The search for the physical remains of the Laurentine villa is one that has been pursued since at least the seventeenth century, precisely paralleling the story of the search for Horace's Villa.[46]

Even if the physical remains of Pliny's villa cannot be precisely identified, his description is so vivid that it has encouraged generations of architects to make paper reconstructions. Palladio refrained from this task, he tells us, to focus on Vitruvius' much more technical descriptions. Palladio's professional successor, Vincenzo Scamozzi, repaired the omission, in his *Idea dell'architettura universale* of 1615, and inaugurated a sequence of such exercises through to the present day.[47] These exercises in architectural composition parallel Pliny's exercises in literary composition.

Although the physical remains of Pliny's two villas may be elusive, the same cannot be said of Hadrian's Villa – the sprawling complex of house, palace, park, administrative centre, gardens, pavilions, baths and gymnasia that the emperor built at Tibur (modern Tivoli) in the years following his accession in AD 117.

Allan Ramsay visited the site in 1755. His friend Piranesi had been working there on and off from his arrival in Rome as a young man of twenty-one until his death thirty-seven years later in 1778. Piranesi spent ten of these years working on a huge plan of the villa at a scale of 1:1000; its six folio sheets measure over ten metres long when hung together.[48] Piranesi codified in the plan an aspect of the villa that had fascinated visitors since its rediscovery in the fifteenth century – the fact that Hadrian, according to his biographer in the *Scriptores Historiae Augustae*, named parts of the villa after places in the empire: the vale of Tempe in Thessaly, Plato's Academy at Athens, the Canopus near Alexandria, 'and, in order to omit nothing, he even made a Hell.'[49]

'A grand name', noted Alberti in the epigraph set at the head of this essay, 'will lend a place great dignity and authority. That the emperor Hadrian approved of this is demonstrated in the famous names ... that he gave the rooms of his Tiburtine villa.' From its rediscovery (or recognition) in the fifteenth century, the experience of Hadrian's Villa was mediated by a literary conceit: by naming. The first extended modern description that we have of the site, that of Cardinal Hippolite D'Este's architect Pirro Ligorio, takes this 'naming' as an underpinning for the account. Subsequent writers too give the conceit a fundamental importance, neatly characterized by Pierre Grimal: 'la vallée qui s'étend à l'Est de la Villa Hadriana était délicieuse; elle devint encore plus séduisante le jour où l'Empereur la baptisa Tempé. ... Ce nom, à lui seul, conférait une sorte d'authenticité supplémentaire au plaisir que l'on prenait au bocage romain.'[50]

At the Villa Adriana, then, we have the situation at the villas of Horace and Pliny precisely reversed. For Ramsay, as for us, the remains in the Licenza valley and the Laurentine littoral acquire a particular resonance from the fact that Horace and Pliny dwelt, wrote in and described them. At Tivoli, on the other hand, the vast and extensive ruins become illuminated by a single sentence. The naming of the parts – the Canopus, the Academy, the Poikile, and so on – amplifies the physical experience of the site into a more complicated experience, in which associations are bound together with the sight, sound and smell of the place. We must assume that it was thus for Hadrian in his vast villa. These imaginative links with the wider world of literature, history and myth are also made in the wall-paintings, well known from Pompeii and Herculaneum, that covered every wall of even quite small houses. Vitruvius recommended that these paintings take as their subjects 'harbours, headlands, shores, rivers, springs, straits, temples, groves, hills, cattle, shepherds', but also Homeric scenes: 'the battles of Troy and the wanderings of Ulysses' (Pl.IV).[51]

'I am now writing a book', remarked James Joyce to his friend Frank Bugden as they strolled by the Zürich lake in 1918, 'based on the wanderings of Ulysses. The *Odyssey*, that is to say, serves me as my ground plan. Only my time is recent time and my hero's wanderings take no more than eighteen hours.'[52] The two literary modes of Aristotle's *Poetics* are combined in *Ulysses*: the tragic with the epic.

T. S. Eliot spoke appreciatively of the 'significance of the method employed'

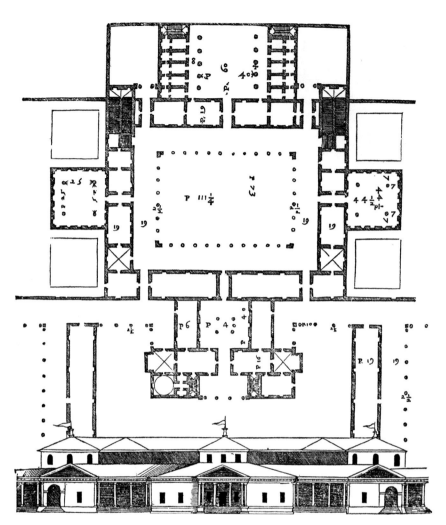

3.4 Reconstruction drawing of the Roman villa after Vitruvius, from A. Palladio, *I quattro libri dell' architettura*, 1570

by Joyce: 'the parallel to the *Odyssey* and the use of appropriate styles and symbols to each division [of the narrative] … manipulating a continuous parallel between contempraneity and antiquity.'[53] The 'divisions' referred to by Eliot are the naming of the eighteen chapters as Telemache, Nestor, Hades, Lestrygonians, Penelope and so on, to fashion a scaffolding for the epic narrative reduced to a single Dublin day: 16 June 1904. Joyce follows the peregrinations of Leopold Bloom from bed to butcher's shop, to chemist, funeral, lunch, through the streets of Dublin, to bar, pub and bawdy house, with final return to Molly's bed. The formal structure given by the parallel to the wanderings of Odysseus/Ulysses gives a significance and resonance to the otherwise quotidian events and is further paralleled by Joyce's virtuosity in working through different literary modes, conventions and rhetorics in each of the eighteen episodes. In the 'Penelope' episode, for instance, not only is a particular literary mode employed appropriate to the point in the narrative – the soliloquy is in vastly long unpunctuated sentences following the semi-conscious somnambulant state of Molly – but the naming of the section as 'Penelope' expands and parallels the immediate narrative by association, allowing simultaneous readings of Molly both as Molly and as the archetypal figure of Penelope. The naming of the chapters serves as a release for the reader's imagination and a spur for invention and bravura in the writer.

Towards the end of his life Joyce was said to have regretted making public that this scaffolding had existed. 'A whim … a terrible mistake', he is reported to have said to Vladimir Nabokov.[54] In the light of the history of the writing of *Ulysses*, this denial seems hardly convincing. Not only did Joyce's many discussions with Frank Bugden make the parallels central to the project, but Joyce had prepared elaborate schemas gradually released with exhortation to secrecy to his friends but eventually published separately under their Homeric titles – from the 'Telemachus' in 1918, to the 'Oxen of the Sun' in 1920.[56] When the complete work was eventually published, the chapter headings were omitted; 'I may have oversystematized *Ulysses*,' Joyce later confided to Samuel Beckett.[57] Joyce's ambiguities in relation to the schema, which had sustained what he estimated as 20,000 hours of writing over a period of seven years, have not been followed in the book's critical reception; Eliot set the pattern. To the reader now, the schema is as suggestive as it was to Joyce when describing the book to Bugden in 1918. Perhaps Joyce's denials are an attempt to redress the balance, to prevent either of the two worlds – the epic/Homeric and the tragic/quotidian – from driving out the other in the reader's mind, and to hold them in the tension from which so much of the novel's power resides.

There is something of the same tension in the naming of the elements of Hadrian's Villa. The names provide a continuous cycle from the present and physical to the remembered and imagined. For John Moore, in the epigraph placed at the head of this essay, Horace's verse is set in an analogous relationship to the landscape of Tivoli. Allan Ramsay, in turn, inscribes the verses of Horace in the Licenza valley, not in the topographical order that one might expect but in the verbal order of the edition that he was using, placing his *verba* in a series of *loci* like Quintilian's orator. Originally, perhaps, adding merely that 'supplementary authenticity' of which Pierre Grimal spoke in the 'vale of Tempe' at Tivoli, the *name* – that is, the text, with all the mental associations that it brings with it – and the *named* – that is, the landscape – coalesce into a new whole.

Notes

1. L.B. Alberti, *De re aedificatoria*, 1988, p.162. The reference to Plato is to *Laws* 4.704a: the naming of a city.

2. Moore, vol.2, 1781, pp.324, 326. Moore went on to say that he knew of the opinion that Horace's Sabine farm was in the Licenza valley and added, 'those who hold this opinion say, that when Horace talks of Tibur [modern Tivoli], he alludes to the villa of Maecenas; but when he mentions Digentia, or Lucretilis, his own house and farm are to be understood'; ibid., p.326. I am indebted to Patricia Andrew for the quotation.

3. Le Corbusier, *Précisions*, [1930], pp.4, 7 and 21.

4. For a recent summary of the voluminous literature on the Villa Savoye, see W.J.R. Curtis, *Modern Architecture since 1900*, 1996, pp.275–85.

5. 'Il est à sa juste place dans l'agreste paysage de Poissy … Cette même maison, je vais l'implanter dans un coin de belle campagne argentine: nous aurons vingt maisons surgissant des hautes herbes d'un verger ou continueront de pâitre les vaches … L'herbe sera au bord des chemins, rien ne sera troublé, ni arbres, ni fleurs, ni troupeaux. Les habitants, venus ici parce que cette campagne agreste était belle avec *sa vie de campagne*, ils la contempleront, maintenue intacte, du haut de leur jardin–suspendu ou les quatres faces de leurs fenêtres en longeur. Leur vie domestique sera insérée dans un rêve virgilien'; Le Corbuser, *Précisions*, p.138. Perhaps there is an echo, in the phrase 'agreste paysage', of Horace's 'Graecia capta ferum victorem cepit et artis / intulit agresti Latio' (*Epistles* 2.1.156–7).

6. C. Rowe, 'The Mathematics of the Ideal Villa', 1947, pp.101–104. Reprinted in Rowe, *The Mathematics of the Ideal Villa and Other Essays*, 1976.

7. Rowe, loc. cit. William Curtis called Rowe's tone one of 'puckish cynicism'; see W. Curtis, 'Principle v Pastiche', 1984, p.18. For a more sympathetic account of Rowe's criticism see A. Forty, *Words and Buildings*, 2000, pp.23–7.

8. Rowe was a student of Rudolf Wittkower; cf. Wittkower's *Architectural Principles*, 1949.

9. cf. R. Williams, *The Country and the City*, 1973, p.9, where Williams pursues backwards in time the point at which 'a way of life that has come down to us from Virgil has suddenly ended'.

10. J. Ackerman, *The Villa*, 1990, p.10.

11. Le Corbusier and P. Jeanneret, *The Complete Architectural Works*, 1964, vol.1, p.89. It is not clear what painting of Vittore Carpaccio Le Corbusier had in mind. The Louvre has only the *Sermon of St Stephen*, the Musée Jacquemart-André *Theseus Receiving the Embassy of Hippolyta;* neither of these works seems to offer the particular mixture of building and landscape implied in Le Corbusier's text. Perhaps he was thinking of a work like the *Saint Reading* of c.1504 (Washington, DC, National Gallery), in which the saint sits by a parapet wall overlooking a sunny rural landscape.

12. *L'Esprit Nouveau*, no.7 (April 1921), p.751.

13. Le Corbusier was only one of the pseudonyms of Charles Edouard Jeanneret adopted in the pages of *L'Esprit Nouveau*. See the entry 'Pseudonymes' in J. Lucan, *Le Corbusier: une encyclopédie*, 1987.

14. cf. S. von Moos, 'Charles Edouard Jeanneret', 1995, pp.59–82. At p.77, von Moos suggested that the project for Mme Meyer 'is soaked with Bonnard', whereas the drawings for the *Ville Contemporaine* 'seem to re-frame Poussin for the modern age'.

15. See, for example, R. Wittkower, *Architectural Principles*, 1962, pp.57ff.

16. The full title of the work is *I quattro libri dell'architettura, ne' quali, dopo un breve trattato de' cinque ordini & di quelli avertimenti, che sono piu necessarii nel fabricare; si tratta delle case private, delle vie, dei ponti, delle piazze, dei xisti e de' tempii.*

17. Palladio, *I quattro libri*, preface (Ware's translation).

18. Palladio, op. cit., II.xii; in Ware's translation, p.46; cited by C. Rowe, 'The Mathematics of the Ideal Villa', 1947, p.101. Cf. Alberti's description of the ancient villa: 'Meadows full of flowers, sunny lawns, cool and shady groves, limpid springs, streams and pools … none of these should be missing, for their delight as well as their utility'; *De re aedificatoria*, trans. J. Rykwert et al., 1988, p.295.

19. C. Rowe, loc. cit.

20. *Eclogues* 1.1.

21. *Eclogues* 1.3, and 1.68, trans. E. V. Rieu, *Virgil*, 1949.

22. *Georgics* 4.566, trans. C. Day Lewis, 1940.

23. ibid., 4.559–60.

24. ibid., 4.18–24. *Contra* the view expressed here see J. Ackerman, *The Villa*, 1990, p.41, where Virgil 'draws together the two traditions of Roman writing on country life, that of the farmer-agronomers and that of the city dweller seeking and praising *otium* in a country estate'.

25. *Epistles* 1.14.35.

26. ibid., 1.14.29–30.

27. *Odes* 2.18.1–5.

28. Pliny, *Epistles* 2.17 and 5.6 respectively.

29. ibid., 2.17.5.

30. ibid., 5.6.20–23.

31. ibid., 5.6.34–5.

32. *I quattro libri*, II.xvi, trans. R. Tavernor and R. Schofield, 1997.

33. Pliny, *Epistles* 5.6.13, citing *Iliad* 18.475ff. and *Aeneid* 8.620ff.

34. *Georgics* 4.176.

35. Horace, *Epistles* 1.16.1–4.

36. ibid., 1.16.5–8.

37. ibid., 1.16.12.

38. *Silvae* 1.3 and 2.2; see B. Bergmann, 'Painted Perspectives', 1991, pp.49–70.

39. *Silvae* 1.3.35–7; cf. Horace's *Odes* 2.18.1–5, note 26 above.

40. *Silvae* 2.2.52 and 73–5.

41. A. M. Guillemin, *Pline et la littéraire*, 1929, pp.141ff, discusses in detail the theme 'description de villa', citing Cicero, Seneca, Horace, Ovid and Statius. See also A.N. Sherwin-White, *The Letters of Pliny*, 1966, p.187: 'verbal echos, especially of Statius, may be detected … But the differences far outweigh the resemblances overstressed by Guillemin, whose scepticism about the factual value of these letters is exaggerated … Pliny's systematic description of layout and his passion for exact detail are all his own.'

42. Pliny, *Epistles* 2.14.9.

43. Quintilian, *Institutio oratorio* 11.2.18–20.

44. A.M. Guillemin, *Pline et la littéraire*, 1929, pp.141ff.

45. Pliny, *Epistles* 2.17.27. For the continuing work at Castelporziano see the ongoing *Castelporziano* series, Rome: 1985–.

46. See P. du Prey, *The Villas of Pliny*, 1994.

47. Reconstructions are collected in H. Tanzer, *The Villas of Pliny the Younger*, 1924; *La Laurentine et l'invention de la Villa Romaine*, 1982; and P. Du Prey, *The Villas of Pliny*, 1994.

48. J. Pinto, 'Piranesi at Hadrian's Villa', 1993, pp.465–77.

49. *Scriptores Historiae Augustae*, 'Hadrian', xxvi.5.

50. P. Grimal, *Les Jardins Romains*, 1943, p.335.

51. Vitruvius, *De architectura*, 7.5.2.

52. F. Bugden, *James Joyce*, 1934, p.15.

53. T. S. Eliot, 'Ulysses, Order and Myth,' *Dial* (Nov. 1923); reprinted in S. Givens, ed., *James Joyce*, 1948.

54. R. Ellman, *James Joyce*, 1982, p.616 note.

55. S. Gilbert, *James Joyce's Ulysses*, 1931; cf. Ellmann, ibid., p.521.

56. Ellmann, ibid., pp.441–2.

57. ibid., p.702.

4

Illustrating Horace's Villa: Allan Ramsay, Jacob More and Jakob Philipp Hackert

Patricia R. Andrew

Higher up among the mountains, Horace had his little farm which he seemed to enjoy so much … This Country, like that of the Latin's seems formed in a peculiar manner by Nature for the Study of the Landscape-Painter.[1]
Thomas Jones, 1777[1]

The energies of Hackert, Jones, and Moore, were employed in realising on canvas the scenery of those places, once the delight of Horace, Cicero, Pliny and Lucullus.[2]
Sir John Soane, 1815

In September 1755, during his visit to Horace's villa, Allan Ramsay made his first sketches of the site, comprising several landscape views and a map now in the National Gallery of Scotland (Catalogue: Ramsay 1)[3]. In November of that year he wrote to Sir Alexander Dick: 'the particulars of this jaunt and my observations upon the ground compared to the passages that relate to it in the Poet I will defer till I can communicate to you at the same time the plan of the situation and some of the principal views, without which any descriptions by words must remain obscure and defective'.[4] Ramsay appears at this stage to have made no attempt to work the sketches up into finished drawings; indeed, there is no firm indication of a plan to use them as illustrations to any potential publication.

By the time Ramsay returned to Italy in 1777, interest in the villa had grown considerably. Thomas Jones's remark that year (quoted above) demonstrates how familiar the theme had become, for although Jones had received a grounding in the classics, his interests in Rome were not those of an antiquarian. By now several individuals had made their way to the site, and books had been produced by De Chaupy and de Sanctis (see pp.81ff below). Ramsay's own thoughts now turned to publication, and it seems that in the first instance he commissioned the Edinburgh landscape painter Jacob More (1740–93)[5] to produce a series of watercolour paintings, some taken from Ramsay's own preliminary sketches. These were to be the basis for engraved illustrations.[6]

It is worth noting that both the scholarly Allan Ramsay and the completely unscholarly Jacob More came from Edinburgh, a major centre of Enlightenment thought.[7] The idea of the classical landscape had also long been current in the minds of Scottish artists, an idealized 'norm' even for those who had never left Scotland. For them, Italy was a visual concept, the artistic equivalent of the intellectual attainment that scholars perceived in the classical world. This concept was allied to the idea of the landscape retreat discussed above by John Dixon Hunt and realized in the idea of the 'English' landscape garden. As Nicholas Philipson has noted:

It is important to realise how well attuned the Scots were to the cultural demands of the English Garden. For much of the eighteenth century Edinburgh remained the focal point of the collective life of men of rank and property in central and lowland

Scotland. The literati of that centre of enlightenment taught modern-minded men to follow the principles of Shaftesbury and Addison, to lead lives which were in harmony with nature and geared to principles of moderation.[8]

Principles such as these were developed by the Edinburgh philosopher David Hume in his writings, and by others, including Adam Smith, Hugh Blair and James Beattie. The most notable realization of these theories was the construction of Sir John Clerk's garden at Penicuik in Midlothian, near Edinburgh, in the 1720s and 1730s: 'His [Sir John' Clerk's] views about the virtues of a well-planned country retreat are conventional and the influence of Milton, Pope, *The Spectator* and, above all, Horace are everywhere apparent.'[9]

But Allan Ramsay did not study the Licenza landscape solely as an eighteenth-century antiquarian attempting to trace the footsteps of Horace; he was also studying the landscape as he found it. The empiricism of Hume insisted that the artist be true to evidence, and as Duncan Macmillan has pointed out,

like Hume's science of human nature, Ramsay's [portraiture] is wholly empirical. What distinguishes him from almost all of his contemporaries is his use of drawing. It is for him an instrument of analysis that he used with the greatest precision to define the only evidence that his painting admits, the physical.[10]

Although the portraitist Ramsay may have been capable of turning his hand to landscape, he perhaps felt it more appropriate to employ an artist who specialized in this field. Jacob More was just such a landscape specialist, who had recently produced the first paintings to capture a real sense of place and atmosphere in Scotland's landscape.

Jacob More

Jacob More lived and worked entirely in Edinburgh until 1771, training first as a goldsmith, then as a house-painter. He worked as a designer and painter of theatre scenery, and travelled widely in the lowlands of Scotland, making plein-air sketches of the local landscape (Fig.4.1). He made his name with a series of innovative, atmospheric depictions of the *Falls of Clyde*, which he took to London and exhibited to great acclaim in the early 1770s.[11] While Allan Ramsay seems to have been more at home with scholars than artists, and probably longed to be recognized as one himself (on this see chapter 1 above), Jacob More was an artist who showed remarkably little antiquarian interest in the landscape he depicted; Italy simply confirmed him in the style of landscape painting he had already adopted before his arrival there (Fig.4.2). Allan Ramsay may well have known More in Edinburgh, and it would be reasonable to assume that they had met in London, where More studied under the landscape painter Richard Wilson in the early 1770s. Wilson had spent some years in Rome, returning to paint the British landscape in the style of Claude Lorrain, whose idealized views of the Roman campagna and interpretation of classical mythology became the model for British landscape artists (Fig.4.3).

After a couple of years in London More himself went out to Rome, where he settled and became known to his British contemporaries as 'More of Rome'. Major recognition came by the mid 1780s, as he produced increasingly large and dramatic landscape paintings, principally for the British Grand Tourists; they feature many of the stock elements of Claude Lorrain's compositions but show great originality in their glowing colours and emphasis on aerial perspective. More's status was assured in 1781 with his election as Accademico di Merito of the Accademia di San Luca, the official Roman academy of art. This was followed in 1783 by an invitation to contribute his *Self-Portrait* to the collection of artists' self-portraits in the Uffizi (see Fig.4.7);[12] it shows him at work in the Grotto of Neptune at Tivoli, which lies on the route from Rome to Licenza and was a favourite haunt of British travellers. More's achievements were unusual for an artist working almost exclusively in landscape, and recognition of his specialized status led to two commissions for the Villa Borghese in the mid 1780s, first for a landscape painting for the refurbished Gallery, then for the creation of an 'English landscape garden' in the grounds, much of which still survives.[13] More continued his plein-air sketching all his life, as his informal studies in Rome and elsewhere in Italy clearly demonstrate, for example his *View of the Vatican* (Fig.4.4) and *Catania and Mount Etna* (Fig.4.5). Despite having ostensibly classical subjects, landscape elements always dominate the compositions, as in the large *Cicero's Villa* (1780), painted for his principal

4.1. Jacob More, *Salisbury Crags, Edinburgh*, brown and grey wash over pencil, 32.8 x 51.2 cm (15.00 x 20.25 in), signed 'Jacob More f.', National Gallery of Scotland

4.2. Jacob More, *Classical Landscape*, scene painting for Edinburgh's Theatre Royal, ink and brown wash heightened with white over prepared ochre paper, 31.0 x 24.5 cm (12.25 x 10.50 in), National Gallery of Scotland

4.3. Claude Lorraine, *Landscape with Apollo and the Muses*, 1652, oil on canvas, 186 x 260 cm (74 x 114 in), National Gallery of Scotland

4.4. Jacob More, *View of the Vatican*, watercolour over pencil, 21.3 x 28.5 cm (8.50 x 11.25 in), National Gallery of Scotland

patron the Earl of Bristol, Bishop of Derry, which serves to show how current was the 'villa' theme in the mental landscape of the period (Fig.4.6).[14] Like so many British artists working in Rome at this time, More was bringing to Italy a far less academic but very fully formed British vision of Italy learnt through the eyes of Claude Lorrain and Richard Wilson, which he proceeded to reinterpret in the land of its origin.

In June 1777, Ramsay arrived in Licenza with his wife and daughter, taking a suite of rooms in Count Orsini's palace. Jacob More joined them there, with the task of translating Ramsay's sketches of the sites into finished watercolours from which an engraver could work. There was a basic difficulty in the production of illustrations: in over twenty poems that include references to his villa, Horace never defined the actual locations and

4.5. Jacob More, *Catania and Mount Etna*, grey wash over pencil, 24.3 x 37.3 cm (9.25 x 14.75 in), National Gallery of Scotland

4.6. Jacob More, *Cicero's Villa*, 1780, oil on canvas, 142 x 198 cm (56 x 78 in), signed and dated 'Jacob More, Rome 1780', Ickworth, the Bristol Collection (The National Trust); painted for More's principal patron, Lord Bristol; one of several versions

there were no visible ruins in the landscape. Ramsay thus concentrated on the nature of the landscape as much as the specific location of the villa, and rather than commissioning a draughtsman who would simply delineate local landmarks or the topographical layout of landscape features, he chose an artist who was sensitive to the landscape's essential character.

A group of four drawings in the National Gallery of Scotland demonstrates that the two artists drew together on the spot. Ramsay worked on a landscape 'map' which is inscribed: 'View of Horace's farm from the window of Count Orsini Villa at Licenza, drawn exactly be me A.R. by the help of pack thread squares, June 21 1777' (Catalogue: Ramsay 2). This relates to three drawings by More, all of the same composition: a general sketch (Catalogue: More 1), a worked up version, including clearer features of Ramsay's map (More 2), and a final, squared version finished for the engraver (More 3). In the final version a wall has been added in the foreground for local interest. Both More 2 and More 3 bear inscriptions on the reverse, probably in Ramsay's hand, as the information is too detailed for More's knowledge. Normally, More's work tends not to have great clarity of detail, but the final version of this set is executed with a precision, and on a scale, that gives an engraver sufficient detail from which to work.

More produced a second set of views of Licenza the same year, all in preliminary states. Two are long-distance views, both now entitled *View of Licenza* (Catalogue: More 4 and More 5). A third view exists in two states and suggests that More was adding Ramsay's own topographical notes to his composition: *View near Licenza* (More 6) and *A View near Horace's Villa* (More 7, Pl.5).

The repetition of More's compositions and the various titles assigned to them over two centuries – for example, *Horace's Villa*, *Licenza*, *Valley of Igentia*, *Digentia*, *Tivoli*, *Italian Landscape* – tend to make identification and chronology very confusing.[15] For example, a watercolour that appeared on the art market in 1972, signed and dated 'Jacob More Rome 1778' and inscribed in More's hand 'A VIEU OF HORAC'S VILLA taken near the MILL OF LICENZA' (Catalogue: More 8) shows a view from exactly the same spot as a version in the Paul Mellon Collection, Yale (More 11). Both appear to be based on one of Ramsay's five sketches pasted into his 'Enquiry' (see below), which would suggest that Ramsay's sketches are contemporary with his text, though the very wavering hand with which they are drawn makes this uncertain. A further, even larger version of the same view appeared on the art market in 1976, sold as one of a pair with a signed *Italian Waterfall*. When it was produced is unknown, but its highly toned bodycolour attempts to portray the richness of colour and depth of aerial perspective of More's oil paintings (Catalogue: More 9, Pl.VI). This in turn is similar to yet another *View of Licenza* in the National Gallery of Scotland, which does not in fact depict Licenza, but another town (More 10). The five drawings and accompanying notes by Allan Ramsay attached to the National Library of Scotland's version of his 1777 'Enquiry' are executed in a very shaky hand, suggesting that they might have been added during his last visit in 1783. More worked up these

sketches, accompanied by inscriptions, to a size of approximately 28 x 40 cm
(11 x 16 in), and numbered them (Catalogue: More 11, More 12, More 13,
More 14 (Pl.VII) and More 15).

As the British Museum version (More 15) fails to follow the composition of
the equivalent Ramsay sketch as faithfully as the others, and is larger and
more finished and bears no number, it may be taken from another set that has
been lost, or it may have been produced independently by More. There are
no doubt other finished watercolours still awaiting discovery. A second,
signed version of the *Rocca Giovane* composition appeared on the art market
in 1976, thought at the time to show Hadrian's Villa (Catalogue: More 16). It
was one of a pair with a *Mountain Landscape*, both the same size as More 15.

More's rendering of the Licenza valley is a faithful translation of the pale,
rounded hills with their patterns of olive groves, depicted in limpid greens,
yellows and ochres that suggest the heat as well as light in the landscape.
Unfortunately, some of the watercolours are now in a faded condition, and
only the heavy foreground additions suggest the variety and strength of the
original colour. All the topographical elements, though sketched in
apparently casual style, are reasonably accurate. Also shown without
embellishment is the simplicity of rural life, in marked contrast to the posed
and decorative peasants that crowd the foregrounds of paintings produced
by Jakob Phillip Hackert three years later. Of the two artists, More's work
most fully accords with Ramsay's own appreciation of the inhabitants of the
Licenza area, whom he consulted in the course of his research. Like Horace,
he was pursuing a rustic retreat away from the bustle of life in contemporary
Rome: 'Having mentioned the country people, I should not do them justice if
I did not take notice of them amongst the antiquities of the place … they seem
to be of the same stamp with those who, according to the poets and
historians, inhabited that country in the days of Numa Pompilius'.[16]

A word should be said about attribution. One of the most frequently
reproduced of 'More's' watercolours is the *View of Vicovaro* in the National
Gallery of Scotland (Catalogue: Labruzzi, Pl.VIII), which is inscribed verso,
'*Vicovaro in the Valley of Aniene above Tivoli – Italy*'. The clarity of delineation
and bright colours make it ideal for modern reproduction, but it has nothing
of More's drawing or colouring, nor is it even a view of Vicovaro, but of San
Cosimato. Hackert included the scene in his series of gouaches and
engravings (Catalogue: Hackert 1.2). It is probably the work of Carlo
Labruzzi, one of the few Italian artists in Rome who worked extensively as a
landscape painter at this time. He and More were colleagues, and the two
artists had British and Italian patrons in common.[17]

What Ramsay's final intentions were regarding the illustration of his
'Enquiry' can only be a matter of conjecture. More's drawings found their
way back to Britain and it is possible that Ramsay still intended them to
illustrate the publication. But Ramsay's encouragement of Hackert's
engraving enterprise and its evident success suggests that he may have
required More's work for reference purposes alone, or indeed for their
intrinsic value as watercolours.

Jakob Philipp Hackert

No progress was made with either the publication of Ramsay's 'Enquiry' or the illustrations after his return to Britain in 1779. However, between Ramsay's departure from Italy and his third visit in 1782–4, the Prussian artist Jakob Philipp Hackert produced a series of detailed drawings and gouache views of the Licenza area and began work on an ambitious series of engravings. This ongoing project rendered Jacob More's intended illustrations redundant, though it is possible that some of More's work was prepared for Ramsay at this period to complement rather than compete with Hackert's series.

Jacob Philipp Hackert (1737–1807) trained at the Berlin Academy and arrived in Rome in 1768 via Sweden and Paris, accompanied by Johann Gottlieb, one of his younger brothers. Recognition came quickly, with a major commission from Catherine the Great in 1771. Hackert travelled widely in Italy and Sicily, finally settling in Naples in 1786 as Court Painter to Ferdinand IV, accompanied by his engraver brother Georg Abraham and by the Farnese sculpture collection, the transfer of which he supervised from Rome.[18] Self-publicity was his forte, and it was combined with a keen business sense. He worked as a tutor to young Grand Tourists and published several instructive works on the practical aspects of painting. He was notably gregarious, becoming a confidant of men of influence such as Goethe, and he is frequently recorded in the diaries of Grand Tourists of every nationality. His numerous artistic relations travelled widely, and their work is to be found in collections all over Europe. Although he worked principally as a painter, he is now best known for the highly successful engraving business he developed in Rome and Naples with his brother Georg Abraham.

Although Jakob Philipp Hackert was More's main rival as the chief landscape painter of Rome in the 1780s, the two artists' careers ran in parallel rather than in competition, and they seem to have enjoyed a cordial relationship. Both arrived in Rome in the 1770s, attracting the patronage of Grand Tourists with their idealized visions of the Italian landscape, which feature many subjects in common. By the late 1780s they were sharing patrons and competing for commissions. The Earl of Bristol, who became More's principal patron, bought pictures of similar size and theme from both artists in 1780.[19] More mentioned Hackert in a letter to his patron Lord Cowper in 1782, justifying a rise in the price of a painting as it was now 'the Price Mr Hackert had for that Size'.[20] The two artists made such a natural pair that numerous Grand Tourists referred to them as such: the (anonymous) diary of one British visitor noted that More and Hackert were recognized as the two foremost landscape painters in the city,[21] though it was perhaps More's success in Rome that prompted Hackert's later move to Naples. Neither artist was much of a theorist. More's style was self-consciously 'Claudian' – 'My Countryman More comes the nearest to Claude of any painter I know' said George Irvine in Rome in 1781[22] – and Hackert was sometimes described in these terms as well.

4.7. Jacob More, *Self-portrait*, 1783, oil on canvas, 198 x 147.5 cm (78 x 58 in), signed and dated 'Jacob More pinxt/ Roma 1783', Galleria degli Uffizi, Florence

But while Hackert became increasingly studio-bound, More retained his love of outdoor sketching and the image that went with it. Two portraits (Figs 4.7 and 4.8) serve to show how each artist saw himself: More, carefully posed as a solemn and slightly pompous *plein-air* painter, and Hackert, full of bourgeois bonhomie in a studio busy with domestic activity – though, interestingly, working on a landscape painting that features recognizable elements of the 'English' landscape garden that More had laid out in the Villa Borghese some years before. Hackert's large *capriccio* compositions are a complete contrast to More's, built up as a busy assemblage of individual elements, each of which is delineated with the precision of a cartographer

II. Villa of Horace looking north-east, showing the remains of the
imperial baths in the foreground and the residential wing beyond,
with Licenza in the background

PREVIOUS PAGE
I. Villa of Horace looking north, showing the remains of the so-
called *vivarium* with Licenza in the background

III. Villa of Horace looking west along the east–west axis between
the north residential wing and the garden, with mosaic-floored
cubicula to the north and Colle Rotondo in the background

IV. (above) Teatro Marittimo at Hadrian's Villa, Tivoli, AD 117–138
(below) *Assault of the Lestrygonians*, scenes from the *Odyssey* on a
Roman wall painting

V. Jacob More, *View near Horace's Villa*, 1777, National Gallery of
Scotland

VI. Jacob More, *View of Horace's Villa*, National Gallery of Scotland

VII. Jacob More, *Rocca Giovane*, National Gallery of Scotland

VIII. (?)Carlo Labruzzi, *San Cosimato*, National Gallery of Scotland

IX. Jakob Philipp Hackert, *Licenza Series no.1: View of Vicovaro*,
1780, Düsseldorf, Goethe-Museum

X. Jakob Philipp Hackert, *Licenza Series no.4: View of Cantalupo and Bardella*, 1780, Düsseldorf, Goethe-Museum

XI. Jakob Philipp Hackert, *Licenza Series no.6: View of Licenza*, 1780,
Düsseldorf, Goethe-Museum

XII. Jakob Philipp Hackert, *Licenza Series no.9: View of Fonte Bello on Mons Lucretilis*, 1780, Düsseldorf, Goethe-Museum

4.8. Augusto Nicodemo,
*Jakob Philipp Hackert in his
Studio, 1797*, oil on wood,
55.8 × 42.1 cm (22.0 × 16.5 in),
signed and dated 1805,
Nationalgalerie, Berlin

(e.g. *River Landscape*, Fig.4.9). While More found it tiresome to insert buildings and other specific features of the landscape into his compositions, Hackert was incapable of painting a landscape as a unified whole. Most of the German-speaking visitors to Rome favoured his precise work, finding More's compositions too formless, while British visitors preferred More's style with its atmospheric passages and aerial perspective. Count Stolberg wrote, 'We have visited two painters. Jacob More, the first, is a Scotchman; and one of the good landscape painters of our times,' but 'the trees and foliage of this painter, however, do not wave and breathe, with that pure life of nature, which Hackert has the art to communicate.'[23]

4.9. Jakob Philipp Hackert, *River Landscape*, 1795, oil on canvas, 120 x 165 cm (47 x 65 in), signed and dated, Attingham Park, the Berwick Collection (The National Trust)

Goethe was enthusiastic about the merits of British artists, noting in his journal that as young man he had sometimes indulged a daydream of being accompanied to Italy by an educated Englishman. In 1786 he lavishly praised the work he saw in More's studio; some years later he compared the achievements of the two artists, concluding that More had on the whole a milder, more gentle colouring and, in general, more visual harmony: 'Ein denkender Kunstler, mit schönem Geist und Talent begabt, war der Engländer More. Er liebte, studierte und ahmte die Natur nach, aber wie Claud Lorrain'.[24] Goethe, however, remained a keen admirer of Hackert, publishing his posthumous biographical notes in 1811,[25] and like many visitors from continental northern Europe he found the crowded and detailed foregrounds of Hackert's paintings particularly attractive. Thomas Jones had less kind things to say: 'He [Hackert] was pleased to pay many Compliments on my progressive Improvement in paying due attention to the *Detail* – that is to say, minute finishing, which by the bye, was more congenial to his own taste, who like most German Artists, study more the *Minutiae* than the grand principles of the Art.'[26]

Hackert had British patrons and knew their interests well. In 1777, while Ramsay and More were busy in Licenza, he was employed, along with one of his British pupils Charles Gore, to illustrate an antiquarian project in Sicily organized by the young English dilettante Richard Payne Knight. The three men set off for Sicily, where they recorded and measured temples and climbed Mount Etna, returning to Rome in July. Like Ramsay, Payne Knight had intended to publish the resulting journal, *Expedition into Sicily, 1777,* as an authoritative guide, using illustrations based on the drawings of Gore and Hackert, but the project never reached publication. Goethe found Payne Knight's manuscript text among Hackert's papers after the artist's death and published it in German over thirty years later. The original English manuscript he worked from was presumed lost until 1980, when it was rediscovered in the Goethe–Schiller Archive, Weimar, and finally published in 1986.[27] Was Hackert aware of Ramsay's similar interest in a publication at this stage, and did he begin to produce his series of Licenza prints soon after with a view to offering them to Ramsay for his use? Despite Hackert's sharp business sense, he had the misfortune to undertake two commissions connected with antiquarian publications by British authors, both of which are dated 1777 and both of which have taken over 200 years to reach publication.

Jakob Philipp Hackert and his brother Johann had first been to the Licenza area as early as October 1769, when the brothers undertook a walking tour with Johann Friedrich Reiffenstein. Reiffenstein was a friend of Winckelmann and an expert on classical antiquity and modern art, later Director of the Russian Academy in Rome and to a large extent the unofficial leader of the German artistic community in the city. The 1769 trip was made entirely on foot, with a servant accompanying them as a cook, their paper and provisions carried by a donkey; they visited Licenza itself and the sites associated with Horace's Villa, then went on to Subiaco and returned to Rome via Paliano and Palestrina after completing a considerable amount of illustrative work.

Hackert was a prolific painter, and in 1780 he produced a large number of works, including the *Licenza* series of ten landscape views (Catalogue: Hackert 1.1–1.10 and Pls IX–XII), and started work on a major series of engravings of the same compositions. Each very detailed painting in this series is signed and dated 1780, and each measures only 33 x 44 cm (13.5 x 7.5 in). This suggests that they were either the basis for the engravings, which are approximately the same size, or that they were produced after them (as suggested by one contemporary reviewer in *Giornale delle belle Arti*). They depict the Licenza area of the 1770s but with a decidedly artificial air, despite accurate and detailed architectural features and considerable 'local interest' in a large population of idealized, decorative peasantry, visited by a few rather more authentic tourists. Nothing could be farther from the delicacy and fluidity of Jacob More's sketches, but these small-scale pictures do show Hackert at his best. The tight handling and small scale make for better compositional integrity than the usual crowded *capriccio* landscapes, and the restricted palette and dramatic shadow effects are enhanced by the use of highlights in red, a feature probably taken from the work of Claude-Joseph Vernet, whom Hackert had met in Paris.

One of the series shows eight tourists who have climbed to find Fonte Bello and to consult a guidebook and a map on a rock (Pl.XII) that Ramsay mentions it in his 'Enquiry': 'The source of this stream is from a hole in a rock, about three quarters of a mile high in the valley.'[28] He was apparently far from a rare visitor by this time.

The series of gouaches were acquired by the Queen of Naples, Maria Carolina, and sent to Brussels as a gift for her sister, the Arch-Duchess Maria Christina. The ship that was carrying them was wrecked, and for two centuries it was assumed the whole series had perished, as stated in Goethe's biographical notes on Hackert published in 1805. The series was, in fact, recorded in a Royal Palace inventory in 1820, and in 1982 the pictures reappeared on the art market. They were acquired by the Federal Republic of Germany, and are now on permanent loan to the Goethe-Museum in Düsseldorf.

Engraved reproductions of landscape paintings were enjoying huge popularity at this period, particularly with British collectors. By the 1780s engraving had become a large-scale business in Rome, following the success of Piranesi and then Volpato, whom More mentions several times in his correspondence. With customary business acumen, Jakob Philipp Hackert set up a print business with his brother Georg in the Piazza di Spagna, the centre of international artistic activity in Rome. Jakob took overall charge of the business side, while Georg ran the studio and saleroom. Most of their prints were published in sets or pairs, suggesting that they were intended for display rather than merely portfolio collections. In producing a major series of engravings of the Licenza area, despite the considerable investment it entailed, Hackert knew he could hardly go wrong.

Recent developments in engraving, combined with etching, enabled oil paintings to be translated to prints while increasingly retaining much of the depth and atmosphere of the originals. William Woollett's numerous prints after Claude, Wilson, Vernet and others, and Earlom's publication of Claude's *Liber Veritatis* in 1777, had made printmaking a buoyant industry and prints a fashionable medium for British buyers. In particular, William Woollett, with his prints after Claude and Wilson, had raised both the popularity and status of engraving. When Jacob More planned engravings to be made after his paintings in Rome in 1786 (possibly spurred into action by Hackert's success) he made it clear he wanted them to be considered a continuation of Woollett's series[29] – an intention well appreciated if one compares More's stock compositions with one of Woollett's interpretations of Claude, for example the *Temple of Apollo* published by John Boydell in 1760 (Fig.4.10).[30] The necessary detailing of composition was not More's forte, however, while for Hackert it was a selling point. Not surprisingly, More's only engraving venture was as spectacular a failure as Hackert's were successful.[31]

The Hackerts' Licenza series is dated 1780, though this was only the start of four years' work on the ten prints and accompanying map (Catalogue: Hackert 2.1–2.10 and map – see Fig.6.3). The plates were etched by Dunker and Eichler[32] and finished off by Georg Hackert and others in Rome.

THE TEMPLE OF APOLLO.
From a Picture of Claude le Lorrain in the Altieri Palace at Rome.

Balthasar Anton Dunker was one of the Hackerts's chief collaborators for some years, though he never actually visited Rome but undertook all his work from Berne. Jakob Philipp Hackert recorded ongoing progress in a letter to his Dutch patron Johann Meerman of 5 July 1780: 'Je fais graver actuellement par Duncker 10 vues des environs et situations où la maison de campagne d'Horace a été dans la Sabine, aujourd'hui Licenza. Le texte original d'Horace sera cité dessous les estampes, quand il a parlé des situations, et l'estampe sera expliquée en français.'[33]

At least two sets of drawings must have existed, the second for use by the engravers in Rome and as advertisements; indeed, Hackert showed a set to Allan Ramsay in 1782 (see below), though none of these are now known. In the autumn of 1784 the prints enjoyed a series of enthusiastic reviews in the Roman art journal *Giornale delle Belle Arti*,[34] and although there is little specific detail, the reviewer lavishly commends the work and praises the gouaches as well, comparing them favourably with the best productions of London and Paris.[35] The prints are technically impressive, with a depth and variation of tone far more developed than in the Hackerts's previous prints of similar

4.10. William Woollett, after Claude Lorrain, *Temple of Apollo*, 1760, etching and engraving, image 40.9 × 57.0 cm (16.0 × 22.5 in), National Gallery of Scotland

size. They retain the same coherence of composition and liveliness of local
detail that are such a feature of the paintings. The sense of distance is
emphasized by accentuating the device already used in the gouaches of
combining sunshine and shadow, for example in No.II, *View of the Convent of
San Cosimato* (Catalogue: Hackert 2.2) and No.IV, *View of Cantalupo and
Bardella* (Hackert 2.4). In No.III of the series, *View of the Bridge and Ruined
Aqueduct near San Cosimato* (Hackert 2.3), the drama of the narrow bridge
over the fast-flowing river is emphasized by the darkness of the space
beneath. The engravers could be playful too: in No.VII, *View of the Site of
Horace's Villa* (Hackert 2.7), the birds that serve to enliven the top right of the
composition are repeated outside the main image, below the inscriptions.[35]

By the time Ramsay returned for his final visit to Italy in 1782, Hackert's
engraving project was well underway. There is no evidence of any previous
meeting between the two men, but the artistic world of Rome was small, and
when Ramsay returned they were both probably eager to meet and discuss
the progress of their respective projects, about which they were no doubt
already well informed. We are indebted to Ramsay's schoolboy son, the
future General John Ramsay, for recording events in his manuscript diary.
Soon after their arrival in Rome, on 12 February, the Ramsays visited 'Mr
Hackert who showd us several of the drawings he had made near Horace's
Villa, of all which he was making prints to which my father subscrib'd'. Two
days later 'the two Hackerts' visited Allan Ramsay, who advised on
identification of locations in the prints. On 8 April at breakfast 'Mr Hackert
brought us the drawings from which he means to make his prints & my
father assisted him very much in adjusting their titles and motto's'. The
Ramsays then left for a three-month visit to Naples, where Hackert called on
them again (26 April). A few days after their return to Rome on 1 July,
Hackert visited, bringing 'a map he had made of Horace's country house and
the country adjacent' (see Fig.6.3). The caption to the map acknowledges 'Mr
de Ramsay', and a scaled drawing of the mosaic fragment found at the villa
site was added as an inset. This map accompanying the series was begun
only in 1782, but from its title, 'Carte generale … suite de dix Vües …', it is
clear Hackert intended it to head the set. The idea of adding the map appears
to be have been Hackert's, as Ramsay stated in his 'Enquiry':

To make all this description perfectly intelligible I am sensible that a map becomes
necessary: and, in Spring 1783 I was actually in search of a land-surveyor for that
purpose, when, happily, I was relieved from that task by a person much more
capable than myself to see it duly performed. This was Mr Philip Hackert the
Landskip painter at Rome.[36]

Luigi Sabatelli and other artists

By 1787 the Hackerts had moved to Naples, where they issued further
examples of their series of Licenza prints. However, they were not well
served by the publication of another series of Licenza views produced back
in Rome by Luigi Sabatelli. Tantalizingly, the Hackerts have apparently left

4.11. Louis Ducros, *Site of Horace's Villa*, c.1793–4, pen and black ink and watercolour, 54.8 x 75.5 cm (21.50 x 29.75 in), Goethe-Museum, Frankfurt

no personal references to this production, and Sabatelli's undated prints have been assigned dates as far apart as 1784 and 1850, though they were most probably produced in the late 1780s or early 1790s, cashing in on the popularity of the first set. Luigi Sabatelli was a Florentine who worked in Rome from 1788/9 to 1794, concentrating on pen drawings and engravings; he subsequently moved back to Florence and then settled in Milan as Professor of painting at the Accademia. The publisher was Agapito Franzetti, who acknowledged the origin of the compositions – 'Peint par J. Ph. Hackert' – and perhaps had the Hackerts's blessing for the project, since the engraving was undertaken by Francesco Morel, a pupil of Volpato, and one of the Hackets's own employees, who worked with the Hackerts in the 1780s (Jacob More also employed Morel on his only engraving project). However, the assertion that the Hackerts oversaw this instance of Morel's work is unfounded.[37]

The format of the prints was much reduced in the Sabatelli series, to approximately 14.0 x 18.5 cm (5.0 x 7.5 in), and the execution relatively crude, with a simplified version of the accompanying map (Catalogue: Sabatelli, title page, map and 1.1–1.10). Horace's landscape is now peopled by dramatically posed figures in classical dress, 'le figure allegoriche al Poeta su[d] d'invenzione e disegno di Luigi Sabatelli'. To the modern eye the near-

4.12. Jakob Philipp Hackert,
*Landscape with the Young
Horace*, 1805, oil on canvas,
74.8 x 106.5 cm (29.5 x 50.0
in), Kunsthalle, Karlsruhe

histrionics of the characters inhabiting this mythical landscape appear quite
comic, though they are typical of Sabatelli's elevated dramatic style.[38] The
basic elements of the landscape views are faithfully reproduced from the
originals, though very much simplified. Contemporary buildings are
retained: Horace is now visiting the eighteenth century rather than inviting
the viewer back to his own contemporary landscape. One plate, however,
View of the Bridge and Ruined Aqueduct near San Cosimato, copies Hacket's
figures in eighteenth-century dress and thus provides a comparison of
compositional detail (Catalogue: Sabatelli 1.3). At least two sets of prints were
made from unfinished plates.[39] The most successful compositions are the
least dramatic, such as the *View of Cantalupo and Bardella* and *View of Fonte
Bello* (Sabatelli 1.4 and 1.9).

Jacob More and Philipp Hackert were not the only artists to record the
landscape and location of Horace's villa. They appear to be the sole artists
with whom Allan Ramsay worked and the only individuals to produce any
explanatory illustrations of the area, but other artists made their way to the
Licenza valley, Jacob More's Swiss colleague Louis Ducros among them.
Ducros arrived from Switzerland in 1777 with one of the Hackerts's
engravers. He produced a typically precise yet atmospheric view across the

valley, the *Site of Horace's Villa*, probably around 1793 or 1794 (Fig.4.11). Related works exist (two drawings, one squared for transfer; a pen and ink drawing also squared for transfer; and an engraving), suggesting that a larger picture was produced.[40] Ducros frequently stayed at Tivoli between 1780 and 1793. Jacob More was a close colleague, and in March 1783 Allan Ramsay and his son accompanied More on a visit to 'Mr de Cros who shewd us some of his works which were very pretty but particularly those in aqarelle which surpass any thing I ever saw of it.'[41] Several of Ducros's drawings and watercolours of the Licenza area are now in the major collection of his work in the Musée Cantonal des Beaux-Arts, Lausanne.

Scholarly pilgrimages continued. Robert Bradstreet wrote in his *Sabine Farm: a Poem* (1810) of his 'Poetical Pilgrimage, by an excursion from Rome to Licenza',[42] noting that 'The ground is all strewed with fragments of various marbles … I have picked up some specimens which I hope to bring you home'.[43] The illustrations to Bradstreet's publication are crude and amateurish, but he makes the point that no formal illustrations can ever be a substitute for visiting in person:

If these antiquarian proofs were less strong, the place itself would bear no feeble testimony to its having been the seat of Horace, as there is not any one of the numerous descriptions he has left of it, to which it does not at this day perfectly answer. Of these I was better enabled to judge by reading Horace upon the spot, and it will, probably, as you are so fond of reading him at home, be the pleasantest method I can take of describing the modern appearance of the place, to refer you to his own descriptions of it in its ancient state.[44]

Hackert himself produced at least one later painting inspired by Horace, the *Landscape with the Young Horace* (1805) now in the Kunsthalle, Karlsruhe (Fig.4.12),[45] which illustrates a passage from Horace, quoted by Allan Ramsay in his 'Enquiry':

    Fatigu'd with Sleep, and youthful Toil of Play,
    When on a Mountain's Brow reclined I lay
    Near to my natal soil, around my Head
    The fabled woodland Doves a verdant Foliage spread; ...
    That thus, in dewy sleep, unharm'd I lay.[46]

Notes

1　T. Jones, *Memoirs*, 16 November 1777.

2.　D. Watkin, *Sir John Soane*, 1996, p.614 (Lecture IX).

3.　Sketchbook, 20.5 x 14.2 cm, NGSD 4878; map fols 15–16.

4.　Ramsay to Dick, 12 November 1755, NAS, Dick Cunyngham of Prestonfield Muniments, GD331/5/18.

5.　See P.R. Andrew, *Jacob More: Biography*, 1993, for a full account of Jacob More's career and list of recorded work.

6.　Two previous publications discuss Jacob More's illustrations to Ramsay's 'Enquiry': J. Holloway, 'Two Projects', 1976, accompanied by the National Gallery of Scotland's *A Villa in the Hills* in 1977; and P.R. Andrew, 'Rival Portraiture', 1989, Checklist, B.11.i–xvi. The listing in chapter 8, Catalogue, is a revised and abbreviated version of that published in P.R. Andrew, 'Jacob More: Biography', 1993, in which details of provenances and references are given. Most of More's extant sketches come from the collection of the Edinburgh antiquarian David Laing and are now in the National Gallery of Scotland.

7. For background see I. G. Brown, *Poet and Painter*, 1984.

8. Phillipson, 'The English Garden in Enlightened Scotland', 1978, pp.22–3.

9. ibid., p.25.

10. D. Macmillan, 'The Scottish of Scottish Art', 1984.

11. See P. R. Andrew, 'Jacob More's Falls of Clyde Paintings', 1987.

12. Described in P. R. Andrew, 'Rival Portraiture', 1989; see also Andrew, 'Jacob More; Biography', 1993, Checklist B.34.

13. Detailed in P. R. Andrew, 'An English Garden in Rome', 1981.

14. See P. R. Andrew, 'Jacob More and the Earl-Bishop of Derry', 1986; and 'Jacob More: Biography', 1993, Checklist B.28.i., B.28.ii.

15. Identification has been clarified as far as possible in P. R. Andrew, 'Jacob More: Biography', 1993, updating J. Holloway, 'Two Projects', 1976.

16. A. Ramsay, 'Enquiry', p.66 (Ramsay's pagination).

17. P. R. Andrew, 'Rival Portraiture', 1989, p.140, and Checklist C.2.vi.

18. For details of the Hackert family of artists see P. Chiarini, *Il Paesaggio Secondo Natura*, 1994; W. Krönig, *Hackerts Zhen Aussichten*, 1983; C. Nordhoff & H. Reimer, *Jakob Philipp Hackert*, 1994. See also A. Griffiths and F. Carey, *German Printmaking*, 1994, for an account of Hackert's career as a printmaker and his place in the developments of German printmaking.

19. P. R. Andrew, *Jacob More, 1740–1793*, 1981, p.178.

20. Hertfordshire Record Office, Panshanger Papers, D/EP 310/85, More to Lord Cowper, Rome, 30 November 1782.

21. East Riding Record Office, Arundell Papers (unlisted), DD EV-6-6.

22. BL, Add MSS 36493, Cumberland Papers III, fol. 128, J. Irvine to G. Cumberland, Rome, 10 February 1781.

23. F. L. Stolberg, *Travels through Germany*, vol.2, 1797, p.250.

24. Visit described in J.W. von Goethe, *Italienische Reise*, 1961, p.129, 7 November 1786; comparison in Goethe, *Winckelmann und sein Jahrhundert*, 1969, pp.183–4.

25. Goethe, *Jakob Philipp Hackert: Biographische Skizze*, 1811.

26. T. Jones, *Memoirs*, p.117, 2 December 1782.

27. R. P. Knight, *Expedition into Sicily*, ed. Claudia Stumpf, 1986, pp.7–17. A brief account is given in A. Wilton and I. Bignamini, *Grand Tour*, 1996, cat. no.190.

28. A. Ramsay, 'Enquiry', p.14.

29. J. More's MS Letterbook, fols 14–15, [26 September–28 October 1786], EUL, Laing MSS IV 25. For details of his engraving see P. R. Andrew, 'Rival Portraiture', 1989, pp.125–7.

30. William Woollett, *Temple of Apollo*, image 40.9 x 57.0 cm (16.0 x 22.5 in), inscribed: THE TEMPLE OF APOLLO/From a Picture of Claude le Lorrain in the Altieri Palace at Rome./Five Feet Four Inches high. Seven Feet Four Inches wide./J. Boydell excudit, London/Claude Gelée Le Lorrain pinxt/William Woollett Sculpt,1760'.

31. P. R. Andrew, 'Jacob More: Biography', 1993, Checklist C.1.ii. The one print produced by More as a sample (engraved by Francesco Morel, who later worked on the second version of Hackert's Licenza series) demonstrates all too well that his atmospheric skies and foliage do not translate easily to the medium of engraving.

32. Dunker accompanied Jakob Philipp Hackert to France in 1765, then settled in Berne in 1773. He maintained a long distance collaboration with Jakob Philipp Hackert and his brother Georg for some years, producing etched plates that he sent to Rome for finishing in the Hackerts's studio. By the mid 1780s Georg Hackert's developing business in Rome seems to have ended the need for such collaboration. See A. Griffiths and F. Carey, *German Printmaking*, 1994; and H.M. Aluffi, *Balthasar Anton Dunker*, 1990.

33. See [J. P. Hackert], *Breiven van Jacob Philipp Hackert*, 1988, p.31.

34. *Giornale delle belle Arti* (1784), various issues: no.47, pp.385–6 first refer to Horace's Villa, and there are fuller reviews in no.48 (p.380), no.49 (p.399), no.50 (p.406), no.51 (pp.412–14) and no.52 (pp.419–21). The reviewer states that the gouaches were copies of the finished engravings, repeated 'in colori in dieci quadri'.

35. The engravings are to be found in various public collections. The British Map Library holds a set in particularly good condition (K.Top.82.18); the British Library holds a set pasted into an edition of Horace published in Parma in 1791 (BL 682.K.4), which has led to this date being given erroneously to the engravings.

36. A. Ramsay, 'Enquiry', p.56.

37. C. De Seta, *Philipp Hackert*, 1992, p.92, confuses the Hackert/Dunker sets with the later Sabatelli/Morel set, assuming that a set of engravings were made under Hackert's direction by Sabatelli and Morel after the ship carrying the gouache paintings sank.

38. L. Sabatelli, *Pensieri diversi*, 1795. Sabatelli's work was briefly surveyed in an exhibition in Florence in 1978: *Luigi Sabatelli (1772–1850): Designi e Incisioni*, Gabinetto Designi e Stampe degli Uffizi. The British Library's Sabatelli/Morel series is listed as 1840, hence this date has been attributed to it.

39. Damage includes a scratch on the plate of No.IX, *Vue de Fonte Bello*, and unfinished figures in No.VII, *View of the Site of Horace's Villa*, and No.X, *Vue de la grotte des Chèvres*.

40. For a survey of this artist's career and work see *Images of the Grand Tour: Louis Ducros, 1748–1810*; also J. Zutter, ed., *Abraham-Louis Ducros*, 1998.

41. National Library of Scotland, MS 1833, diary of John Ramsay, 29 March 1783.

42. R. Bradstreet, *The Sabine Farm: a Poem*, 1810, Preface.

43. ibid., pp.7–28.

44. ibid., pp.23–4.

45. Jakob Hackert, *Landschaft mit dem Knaben Horaz*, inscribed 'Horaz Lib III. Od. IV/Phi: Hackert 1805', and verso 'Me Fabulosae Vulture in Appeulo/Albricis extra limen Apuliae,/Ludo, fatigabumque Somno/Fronde nova puerum Palumbes/Texere./Horaz Lib.III Od. IV. Philipp Hackert pinx. 1805'.

46. 'Enquiry', p.27.

5

Ramsay's 'Enquiry': Text and Context

Bernard D. Frischer

Besides, we may observe, in every art or profession, even those which most concern life or action, that a spirit of accuracy, however acquired, carries all of them nearer their perfection.
David Hume, *An Enquiry Concerning Human Understanding*, 1748

The first issue of *Archaeologia, or Miscellaneous Tracts, Relating to Antiquity. Published by the Society of Antiquaries of London*, appeared in 1770.[1] Among its sixty-one articles, two stand out both because of their authors' renown and because of their diametrically opposed views of archaeology: Martin Folkes's 'On the Trajan and Antonine Pillars at Rome'; and William Stukeley's 'The Sanctuary at Westminster'. Stukeley was the eighteenth century's most distinguished scholar of Stonehenge. Folkes was President of the Society of Antiquaries and one of Stukeley's most vocal critics.[2] Ramsay had been a fellow of the society since 1743.[3] To appreciate his 'Enquiry into the Situation and Circumstances of Horace's Sabine Villa' we do well to position Ramsay between the two poles in British antiquarianism represented by Folkes and Stukeley. These might be characterized as the pole of quantitative empiricism, championed by Folkes; and the pole of high-flying speculative rationalism, associated with Stukeley.

Folkes's article is purely descriptive and quantitative – a relentless accumulation of numbers and measurements without interpretation or commentary. The tone is set at the very beginning: 'The Trajan column at Rome, is all of white marble, and consists of 30 stones, whereof 8 make the pedestal, 19 the pillar, and 3 the basis of the statue that stands on top. The side of the lowest plinth of the pedestal contains 20 English feet and three inches'.[4]

Stukeley's essay is quite different. In six short pages it covers not only the little church (seventy-five feet square) known as The Sanctuary, which was being torn down when Stukeley visited it in 1750, but also ranges discursively over an amazing range of issues, including a catalogue of stone buildings before the Conquest[5] and the origin of architecture itself:

Our church at Westminster is of the ... sort ... we may call Roman–Saxon ... from whence I infer it is later Saxon work, when there was and had been many years, perhaps, as now, too much intercourse between us and France; and when our builders began to conform to that later sort of architecture, with pointed arches.

How this later manner of pointed arches prevailed in Europe, over the former manner of semicircular arches, I cannot otherwise account for, but in supposing we had it from the Saracens ... they brought it from Africa, originally from Arabia; and from the southern parts of Asia ...

When I have thought on the origin of architecture, I persuade myself, this Arabian manner, as we ought to call it, is the most antient of all ... The original of all arts is deduced from nature; and assuredly the idea of this Arabian arch, and slender pillars, is taken from the groves sacred to religion, of which the great patriarch

Abraham was the inventor. The present Westminster Abby, and generally our cathedrals ... present us with a true notion of those verdant cathedrals of antiquity; and which our Druids brought from the east into our own island, and practised before the Romans came hither.[6]

For Stukeley, the little building of his study was a synecdoche for vast themes and contexts. On the other hand, Folkes' essay – though written about monuments of far greater cultural import to the learned readers of his age – is couched in a tone so dry as to be dessicated. One almost wishes that Folkes and Stukeley could have exchanged topics: it is Stukeley whom we would like to read on Trajan's Column, and Folkes on the Sanctuary at Westminster.

To assess Ramsay's achievement in the 'Enquiry' we must apply the standards both of his day and of our own. There is, in fact, much more to praise in the 'Enquiry' than to criticize. Ramsay's essay is the first compendious presentation of the Licenza site conventionally known as Horace's Villa, and the range of information synthesized exceeds anything until Mazzoleni (1891) or Lugli (1926). Ramsay knew the key works of earlier scholars, and he was intimately familiar with the villa site and the valley in which it is situated. He presented most of the passages about the villa that occur in Horace's poetry, relating the poet's descriptions to the topography of the Licenza valley. Observing standards set by *Archaeologia* and by British antiquarians such as Robert Plot and John Aubrey in the previous century, he apparently planned at one stage to provide illustrations of the valley, commissioned from Jacob More. He also wished to include a relief map, commissioned from Jakob Philip Hackert, and to present his own drawings of architectural details and small finds. Hackert's map was printed separately, and even today it is a useful aid for understanding the topography of the Licenza valley (see Fig.6.3).

The 'Enquiry' stands the test of time well, not simply because it offers several precious verbal and visual descriptions of archaeological remains not otherwise available for study, but also because it integrates so well the very different themes of a Stukeley and a Folkes. Methodologically, it succeeds because it represents an application of the 'mitigated scepticism' of Ramsay's friend, David Hume. 'To be a Humean, precisely, is to take no system as final, nothing as ultimate except the spirit of enquiry.'[8] Ramsay's treatise, entitled with the very Humean word 'Enquiry',[9] shows that its author was as critical of himself and his views as he was of his predecessors and their theories, and that he knew full well that the investigation in which he was engaged would continue long after his death. He even concluded with a modest disclaimer about the finality of his results and sketched a future plan of research for finding the Temple of Vacuna near Rocca Giovine that is still valid today:

[I] shall conclude these remarks by observing that though they contain all the lights I have been able to acquire, I am far from thinking that the subject has received all the light that may be possibly thrown upon it. Something more certain and precise may still be learnt concerning the particular situation of Mandela and the extent of the Massa Mandelana by an examination of the title deeds of the family of Orsini, anciently Lords of all this territory; or of those of Nuñez and Borghese who derive from them; and still more from the Archives of the Vatican, and of the Church of St. John Lateran, if they happen to be accessible. Much, likewise, may be still learnt concerning the true situation of the Fanum Vacunae, and other particulars of this interesting valley, if any man of classical curiosity with 20 or 30 spare sequins in his pocket would employ the country people to dig upon Colle Franco, and other places already mentioned by me in these remarks.[10]

The enquiry into Horace's Villa is organized into two parts. Ramsay began with the 'situation,' or location, of Horace's estate (pp.1–5 in Ramsay's pagination), examining the arguments of such earlier scholars as Biondo, Cluverius, Holstenius and Volpi.[11] Comparing their views with Horace's own hints about where his country house was located, he found that everyone except Holstenius is contradicted by passages in Horace's poetry, by geographical features or by both. Holstenius, the great geographer and Vatican librarian of the mid seventeenth century,[12] had implicitly placed Horace's villa in the valley of the Licenza River, several kilometres to the north of Vicovaro.[13] Ramsay agreed, as have most scholars down to the present day.[14] As we will see, this reflects Ramsay's Folkesian side of careful measurement and observation.

In the much longer second part of his treatise (pp.6–67), Ramsay considered the 'circumstances' of the villa. This term covers a large number of topics, including the hydrology, agriculture and flora of the Licenza valley; the probable size of Horace's estate; the exact location of the dwelling and its unexpectedly large scale; the later owners and subsequent history of the estate; and the characteristics of the valley's inhabitants. Throughout, Ramsay showed himself competent at handling a surprisingly wide range of disciplines, including archaeology and architectural history, literary and textual criticism, cartography, epigraphy, geography, linguistics and even Church history. He also displayed admirable warmth toward the humble *comunisti* of Licenza. Here, then, we see Ramsay working in a more expansive, Stukeleyan mode.

Unfortunately, Ramsay did not organize his treatment topically but according to the order of poems in the edition of Horace he was using.[15] Since the poems are not arranged in chronological order, it was awkward for Ramsay to treat the historical evolution of the villa or the poetic development of the villa theme.[16] Then, too, the poems are to some degree repetitive in their presentation of the villa. To solve this problem, Ramsay made good use of cross-references, but he did not entirely avoid the trap of repetitiousness.[17] Finally, while the structure of the 'Enquiry' might have made sense had Ramsay been pursuing the villa theme as an element in Horace's poetry, it is rare that he stopped to consider the role played by a villa passage within the overall context of the poem in which it appears.[18] Similarly, he did not pay attention to the effects of the various genres (satiric, lyric, and epistolary) on Horace's descriptions of his villa, although this is a topic to which the structure of his essay would have been well suited.

Of course, Ramsay's approach to organizing his material had the virtue of being straightforward and, whatever its flaws, does not detract from the

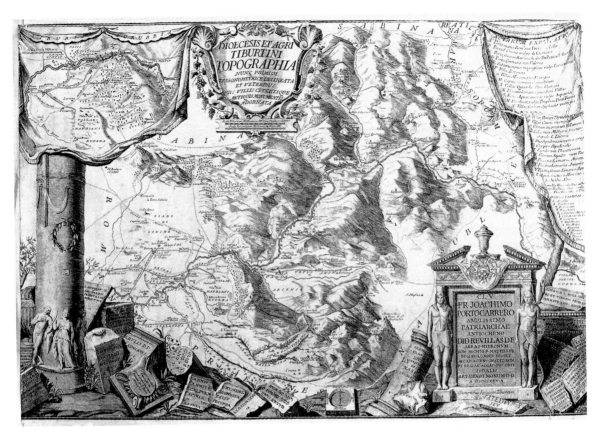

5.1. Map of the Diocese of
Tivoli, from D. G. De Revillas,
Dioecesis et agri tiburtini, 1739

material itself and his methodology. It is to these that we will turn after
setting the stage for Ramsay's essay by reviewing work on the villa by other
antiquarians in the period 1440–1770.

The Antiquarian Context: Situating Horace's Villa, 1440–1770

Not surprisingly, in over twenty poems mentioning his villa Horace never
had occasion to locate the place with any precision. That is not what poets
generally do. Horace did, however, note several places that were near his
villa. Locating the villa, at least in a general way, has thus always entailed
finding the modern places that correspond to the ancient sites in Horace
since, as was well known by the mid sixteenth century, if not before, place
names in Italy quite frequently had changed beyond recognition from
antiquity to modern times.[19] The places appearing in Horace's villa poems
include the Digentia River (*Epistles* 1.18.104), the Fanum Vacunae (*Epistles*
1.10.49), Mandela (*Epistles* 1.18.105), the Mons Lucretilis and Valley of Ustica
(*Odes* 1.17), and Varia (*Epistles* 1.14.3).[20] None of these names survived intact
to modern times.

There were old local traditions at Tivoli, Vicovaro and Licenza placing
Horace's villa near these towns.[21] Such folklore was at first ignored or

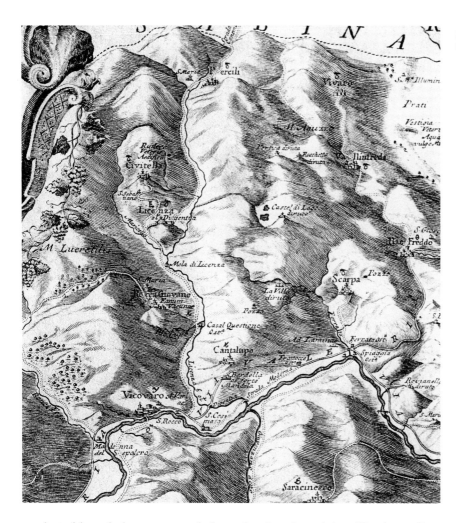

5.2. Detail of Fig.5.1, showing the Licenza area

neglected by scholars concerned about the situation of the villa, the earliest of whom was Flavio Biondo. Biondo's influential *Italia Illustrata*, written in the mid fifteenth century, put the villa near Farfa.[22] This view was adopted by such important sixteenth-century Horatian commentators as Cruquius.[23]

In 1624, Cluverius's *Italia Antiqua* put the villa near Montelibretti on the basis of the similarity of the modern place name with Horace's Mons Lucretilis. This was soon challenged by Cluverius's student, Lucas Holstenius, in posthumously published notes on his teacher's book.[24] Holstenius was librarian of the Vatican Library until his death in 1661 and an acknowledged expert on ancient geography. His views were thus taken very seriously, and his new placement of Horace's Villa in the Licenza valley quickly received important support from the cartographers Mattei and Ameti[25] as well as from Fabretti in his influential work on the Roman aqueducts.[26]

Holstenius's identification rested on Cluverius's equation of Vicovaro with Varia;[27] on an etymological derivation of Licenza from Digentia; and on a religious-historical syncretism of the Roman goddess Victoria with the Sabine goddess Vacuna. Holstenius knew of a Roman inscription mentioning Victoria at Rocca Giovine,[28] and he inferred from this that since Rocca Giovine was in Sabine territory, this might reflect a pre-Roman cult of Vacuna. While this is certainly possible, it should be noted that the Romans equated Vacuna with several Roman goddesses, not just with Victory,[29] and that no other evidence has come to light in Rocca Giovine of a cult of Vacuna, whereas since the Renaissance much evidence of such cults has been discovered elsewhere in the Sabina, particularly in the area around Rieti.[30] Thus, Holstenius's thesis required additional support. It also needed to be made more precise, since it did no more than situate the villa somewhere in the valley of the Licenza, which is over eight kilometres long. Kircher, Fabretti, Mattei and Ameti in their maps of the valley differed about where Horace's villa should be situated and made mistakes that show they were only vaguely familiar, at best, with the valley's principal features.[31]

Precision in locating the villa required, first of all, an accurate map, and this was still a desideratum for the Licenza valley at the beginning of the eighteenth century. The first map of the area, made with the aid of trigonometry and containing a scale, was that of Diego de Revillas in 1739 (Fig.5.1).[32] Though considered accurate for its day, its quality should not be overestimated, for if we superimpose a scaled version of Revillas's map over an accurate contemporary map such as the Carta Tecnica Regionale of the Regione Lazio, Sezione 366110 (Licenza), we can see that Revillas's map is distorted. For example, Rocca Giovine is one kilometre farther north than it should be, and the Licenza River and adjacent land extend too far to the east. At any rate, Revillas's map caught the attention of antiquarians because he followed Holstenius in identifying Licenza as Digentia and Rocca Giovine as Fanum Vacunae. Though he did not, in his first edition, include Horace's Villa, he was apparently eager to take this next logical step, and in the posthumous second edition of 1767 we find the first indication of 'ruins of Horace's Villa' on a map. When Allan Ramsay made his first trip to find Horace's Villa in 1755, we know that he used a sketch he made of Revillas's 1739 map (Fig.5.3).[33]

Finally, in 1755, the Jesuits Cristoforo Maire and Ruggero Giuseppe Boscovich published their highly praised maps of central Italy, including one of the Papal States undertaken at the request of Pope Benedict XIV.[34] On this map we find few ancient sites or place names, and none in the Licenza valley. But the location of modern sites was determined with a scientific exactness that easily surpasses anything found earlier.[35] The Maire–Boscovich map of Latium was republished and reused many times in the later eighteenth century and became the basis for modern maps of the area. Ramsay knew it and referred to it in the 'Enquiry', using it to criticize the map of De Chaupy (Fig.5.4; on De Chaupy, see below), which was a throwback to the days of unscientific mapmaking, in which the position of Mandela, Vicovaro, Rocca Giovine and Licenza could shift about unreliably from one cartographer to another.[36] Maire–Boscovich provided antiquarians with a critical new tool that they would need if further progress was to be made.

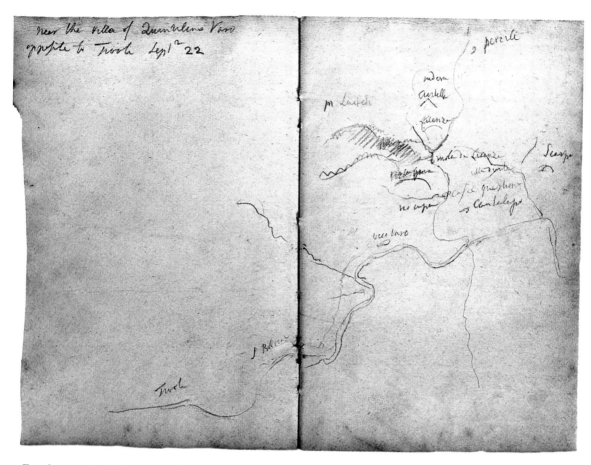

Employment of this new tool required a task that it could help discharge, and though (as Ramsay's first trip to Licenza shows) there was a perennial interest in visiting Horace's Villa among learned people of all European nations, only a handful actually did so. Ramsay's account, in fact, is the earliest to survive. It is interesting because it shows Ramsay turning to a country man near Licenza for help in finding the Fons Bandusiae. This implies that local tradition located the villa near the site where the Roman remains now known as Horace's Villa were excavated from 1911 to 1914 by Angiolo Pasqui. Within ten years of Ramsay's visit, several other British travellers were to come, including James Boswell and Andrew Lumisden. We know from them that there were no ruins visible above ground in the 1750s and 60s.[37]

For their part, antiquarians felt no special urgency to focus on Horace's Villa, since there were hundreds of sites and monuments available for study in Rome, in the Roman Campagna, on the Bay of Naples and elsewhere. The eighteenth century was a period of intensive archaeological exploration and discovery, and attention was naturally directed to the new artifacts that came out of the ground and to exploring sites which, judging from the ruins visible above ground, might yield spectacular finds.[38] The relative neglect of Horace's Villa is thus not surprising.

5.3. Map of the Licenza area based on De Revillas, sketched by Allan Ramsay in 1755

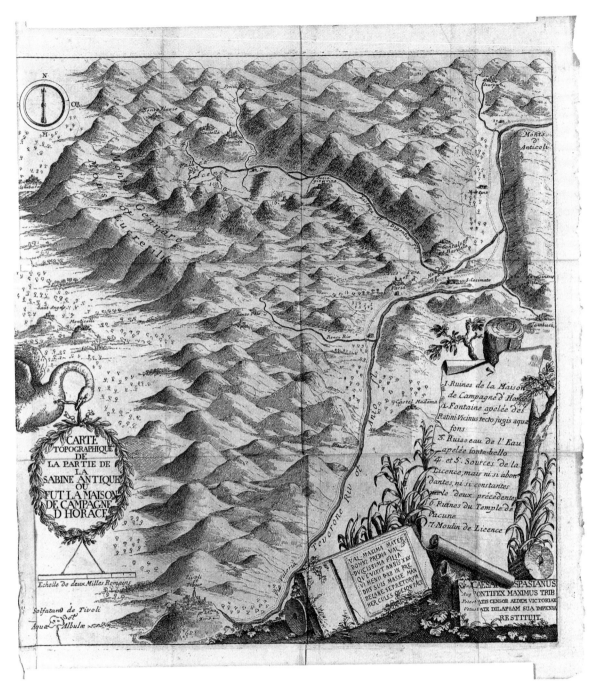

5.4. Map of the Licenza area, from Abbé C. De Chaupy, *Découverte de la maison*, 1769

In 1757, the situation changed somewhat when the Vicovaro notary Giuseppe Petrocchi found an ancient inscription giving an important clue about the location of another place name mentioned by Horace in his villa poetry. The inscription (*CIL* XIV.3482; Fig.5.5) is an epitaph mentioning Valeria Maxima, the proprietor of a large group of properties (*massa*) known as Massa Mandelana. *Massae* were often named after a nearby town, and a

'Massa Mandelana' should thus be an estate near a town called Mandela. Horace says in *Epistles* 1.18.104–105 that his country estate is near the Digentia River, 'the cool stream from which Mandela drinks'.

Petrocchi recognized the importance of the inscription, finding suggestive, too, the fact that it was found near a town called Bardella. Bardella, he concluded, is the modern name for Mandela; a new piece of the puzzle about the location of Horace's Villa had been found. Of course, the new piece resembled Varia and Fanum Vacunae in simply indicating in a general way where the villa had been built. However, the fact that another Horatian place name had been located raised anew the old problem of finding the exact spot.

None of the leading antiquarians in Rome seems to have been inspired by Petrocchi's find to grapple with the problem. Winckelmann, for example, made no contribution to the study of Horace's Villa. All we know about his views is that he placed the Fons 'Blandusiae' near Tivoli.[39] It may or may not be coincidental that the few people known to have been interested in Horace's Villa were (like Revillas before them) members of the Accademia degli Arcadi: the Dutch physician and poet George Nicolaus Heerkens and a priest of Tivoli, Domenico de Sanctis. Heerkens gave a talk to the Arcadians about his visit to Horace's Villa.[40] The talk does not survive, nor is there a trace of it in the Archives of the Arcadians at the Biblioteca Angelica in Rome, though the date would appear to be in the period 1757–58. A few years later, in 1761, de Sanctis wrote a short tract on Horace's Villa, and he began by saying that it was Petrocchi's discovery of the Massa Mandelana inscription that made him eager to see if the site itself could be found.[41]

De Sanctis's little book is less important for its author's own account of the Licenza site – which is in fact minimal, since most of the book concentrates on the villa passages in Horace's poetry – than it is for the light it throws on another pair of colourful figures who in c.1760 undertook the first known excavations of the Licenza site: the Baron de Saint'Odile and the abbot Bertrand Capmartin De Chaupy. The nature of the Saint'Odile–De Chaupy partnership is complex and has been treated more fully elsewhere.[42] Born Mathieu-Dominique Charles Poirot de la Blandinier at Blamont (Lorraine) in the early 1700s, Saint'Odile came to be one of the leading diplomats of mid-eighteenth century Rome.[43] Though mainly concerned with his diplomatic duties, he was typical of his age in also cultivating antiquarian interests. He enjoyed touring the Roman Campagna, and we hear of one trip he made to the Tivoli area, during which he travelled far and wide and stayed at Count Fede's villa, which stood on the grounds of the Villa of Hadrian. He himself wrote that Tivoli was his 'customary place to breathe fresh air'.[44] On another trip he travelled up the Anio Valley, eventually reaching Ancona before returning to Rome.[45] An unconfirmed source tells us that Saint'Odile even corrected the map of the Campagna published in 1711 by the great French cartographer Guillaume Del'Isle.[46] This map was not noticed by Frutaz in his comprehensive collection of the maps of Lazio,[47] and no trace of it remains in the cartographical collections in Washington, DC, London and Rome. One wonders whether it might not correspond to the map published in De Chaupy that was criticized by Ramsay.

As will be seen, Saint'Odile promoted the explorations at Horace's Villa. De Sanctis, our best informant about the De Chaupy–Saint'Odile project, describes their work as follows:

I will conclude by making honoured mention of the further lights shed by the most praiseworthy care and diligence of the Baron de Saint'Odile, the Plenipotentiary to the Holy See of his Majesty the Emperor and Grand Duke of Tuscany, a man who in the midst of his duties nourishes a strong love for learning and literature. He, too, completely persuaded that Horace's Villa was located in Licenza, did not neglect to investigate the truth of the matter in a more certain way. Since having observed the remains of an ancient structure not far from the site I have indicated, and under a spring from which without doubt the stream of the Licenza takes its name, he imagined that Horace's house once stood here, and he undertook its excavation [scavamento]. There he discovered well-built foundations and a cellar, which may be signs of a dwelling that – if not magnificent and luxurious – was at least proper and comfortable. There a pipe is also seen bringing water from the spring to the house both for domestic use and also, perhaps, for the convenience of a domestic bath complex.[48]

De Sanctis's short book was first published in 1761, which provides a *terminus ante quem* for Saint'Odile's excavations in Licenza. We can also establish a *terminus post quem* of 1756, the year in which the Abbé Capmartin De Chaupy arrived in Rome in exile from his native France.[49] As De Chaupy's acquaintance Joseph Jérôme La Lande wrote in 1769:

All the antiquarians placed the house of Horace at Tivoli because he often speaks of Tivoli in his works. But the Abbé Chaupy having thoroughly discussed this matter,

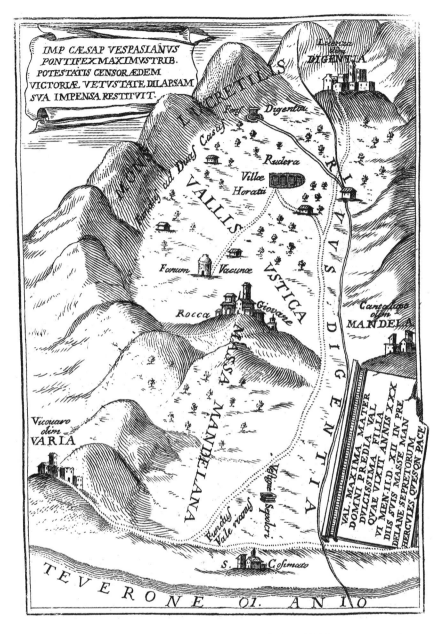

5.6. Map of the Licenza valley, from D. de Sanctis, *Dissertazione*, 1784; the two Roman inscriptions were also recorded by Ramsay

and having combed the whole area with the Baron de Saint'Odile, wrote a work in several volumes in which he strongly argued the view that when Horace speaks of Tivoli, he refers to the house of Maecenas or of someone else; but when he speaks of his own house, he speaks of the Digentia [River], the Mons Lucretilis, or the Sabine valleys, which is therefore where one has to find its location.[50]

Thus, by dating the beginning of De Chaupy's work at Horace's Villa, we can also date the excavations of Saint'Odile. De Chaupy wrote that he began exploring the villa 'a few years after the discovery' of the inscription now referred to as *CIL* XIV.3482, which, as noted, was found in 1757 near

Mandela.[51] Elsewhere, he explained that he arrived at his first sketch of the idea that the Licenza villa was Horace's a few months before the publication of de Sanctis's *Dissertazione*, which could not have happened before mid April of 1761.[52] Putting these two passages together, we may infer that De Chaupy and Saint'Odile were exploring the countryside sometime in late 1760 or early 1761.[53]

De Chaupy presented two lengthy and consistent descriptions of the finds in the third volume of his book. To summarize, he reported finding two separate structures, both in *opus reticulatum*, which he dated to the first century BC and took as evidence that the villa was Augustan. The first structure, he wrote, occupied the ruined church of St Peter. Because of its small size, the water pipes found leading to it and its low position, he conjectured that it was probably a bath complex. The second building was located in a more open position and was much larger, implying to De Chaupy that it was the residence. Also found scattered around the site were *tesserae* of mosaics – some polychrome – as well as fragments of columns and entablatures.[54] Near these structures was a garden, which, from De Chaupy's description, corresponds to the area below what today is called the Nymphaeum of the Orsini, several hundred meters to the west of the archaeological site known from Pasqui's excavations in the period 1911–14. In this area the local winegrowers found fragments of lead pipes inscribed T. CLAVDI BURRI and TI. CLAVDI B. These were destroyed later in the eighteenth century when the Archpriest of Licenza, to whom they had been entrusted, used them for birdshot, as Allan Ramsay recounted several years later.[55]

That Saint'Odile published no account of his excavations is certain; but it is less clear that he wanted his important discoveries to remain completely unknown. In favour of the hypothesis that Saint'Odile meant to keep silent about his finds is not only the lack of publication but also the odd fact that De Chaupy never explicitly mentioned his partner, or sponsor, Saint'Odile, in his publication of Horace's villa. Instead, Saint'Odile is named only by de Sanctis, a man who was to become De Chaupy's bitter rival in a dispute about who could rightly claim priority in identifying the Licenza site as Horace's Villa. Yet, the excavations at Licenza, if made known to the world, could only have raised the Baron's standing in the eyes of the cultural and political élite of Europe in this age of the Grand Tour. In this context we may compare Robert Adam's archaeological publication of Diocletian's palace at Split, which was begun in the late 1750s and was intended to be, in Adam's memorable words, 'a great puff, conducive to raising all at once one's name & character'.[56]

If Saint'Odile consciously chose to forego the glory of being known as the discoverer of the site (as opposed to having been deliberately omitted from the story of the excavations by De Chaupy), this may have been a necessary consequence of his failure to obtain an excavation permit: publishing a report would have been a *de facto* admission of flouting the law.[57] Another reason may have been that Saint'Odile felt his project was not yet finished and hence not ready for publication. The end of the first printing of de Sanctis'

Dissertazione of 1761 reads: 'thus continuing the enterprise he [Saint'Odile] has begun – as is most desirable for the Republic of Letters – one can hope that some more singular monument can be found, which will make the identification of Horace's Villa in Licenza ever more secure.'[58] At the end of the third and final printing of de Sanctis' study in 1784, this expression of hope has been changed into a statement of disappointment that 'well-known events have prevented [Saint'Odile] from completing the enterprise he began'.[59] The allusion is undoubtedly to Saint'Odile's abrupt dismissal from office in 1774 for improper behaviour and to Archduke Pietro Leopoldo's order that his erstwhile ambassador never again set foot in Rome or Florence.

What motivated the Tuscan ambassador to Rome to excavate Horace's Villa in the first place is still a mystery, though in view of his reputation as an intriguer, the scandalous end to which he came and the eighteenth-century view of archaeology as a business the purpose of which was to find salable treasure,[60] we may well suspect that Saint'Odile's motives were more mercenary that scientific. Be that as it may, at least we know from de Sanctis that it was the Baron de Saint'Odile who first had the idea of digging at the Licenza site and of initiating the long project, still alive today, of empirically testing the thesis that the Roman villa located there was Horace's *Sabinum*.

As for De Chaupy, the fact that he never mentioned the Baron by name in his book may have been a deliberate attempt to rob his partner of any credit due him for the project at Horace's Villa.[61] This was typical of the abbé, who also felt compelled to belittle the contribution of de Sanctis and to claim priority in discovering the villa site, even though (as de Sanctis and others noted) it was really Holstenius who deserved to be considered its discoverer. De Chaupy's quarrelsomeness was perhaps less of a problem than his prolixity: his book on Horace's Villa ran to three stubby volumes. Contemporaries noted this with disapproval or amusement. Ramsay, in the 'Enquiry', wrote: 'at least one half of his book is employed upon subjects which, though very interesting in themselves and very learnedly and ingeniously treated, have little or no relation to the general title of the work.'[62]

Immediately upon completion of his three-volume *Diverse maniere d'adornare i cammini*, in 1769, Ramsay's friend Piranesi mocked the poor abbé with a scatological satirical engraving (Fig.5.7) serving as the tailpiece to the book's 'Apologia'.[63] Although Piranesi makes no reference to it and does not express his motives in printing it, the engraving is self-explanatory. It depicts a work in three volumes, on the spines of which the author is given variously as Cap Martin Chaupy and Capo confuso ('Muddle-Head'). At the top of the engraving is an inscription with the exclamation, 'A dry spring and a few broken walls have brought forth three big volumes. What do you have to say about this, o my Baretti! Where is your goad?' Giuseppe Marco Antonio Baretti was the author of an Italian–English dictionary, a traveller's guide to Italy and, more to the point, a book of literary criticism called *La frusta letteraria* ('The Literary Goad'). Below the inscription is a large map with a real place name, Licenza, but also with such imaginary places as Corrupt Passages and the Academy of Fanatics. Dominating the centre of the map are

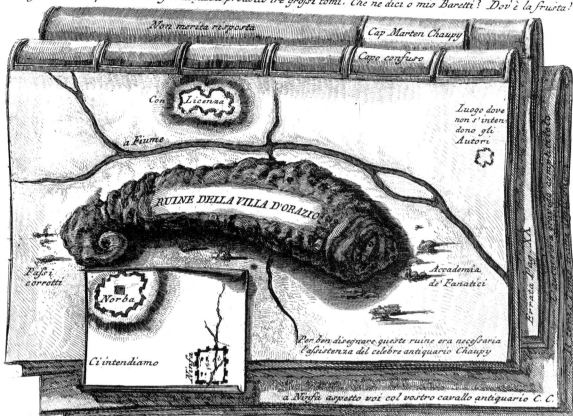

Una fonte secca, e pochi muri infranti hanno prodotto tre grossi tomi. Che ne dici o mio Baretti? Dov'è la frusta!

Non merita risposta

Cap. Marten Chaupy

Capo confuso

Con Licenza

a Fiume

Luogo dove non s'intendono gli Autori

RUINE DELLA VILLA D'ORAZIO

Passi corrotti

Norba

Accademia de' Fanatici

Errata Libero XX XX in niverso al complemento

Ci'intendiamo

Ninfa

Per ben disegnare queste ruine era necessaria l'assistenza del celebre antiquario Chaupy

a Ninfa aspetto voi col vostro cavallo antiquario C.C.

Vi avverto a prender consiglio prima di stampare.

5.7. Engraving by Piranesi satirizing Capmartin De Chaupy's *Découverte de la maison,* from *Diverse maniere d'adornare i cammini,* 1769

the 'Ruins of Horace's Villa,' and the turd-like shape these take leaves very little doubt about Piranesi's opinion of their worth.

Such satirical engravings were Piranesi's characteristic mode of attacking important antiquarian adversaries.[64] His satire also reflects more profound disagreements with De Chaupy, the man and the scholar. We do not know if the two ever met, but if they did, they must have found very little in common. Piranesi was a member of Monsignor Giovanni Gaetano Bottari's anti-Jesuit circle of antiquarians.[65] Bottari and his followers believed in the necessity of preserving, interpreting and publishing Rome's pagan and Early Christian monuments, and they viewed a reformed and enlightened Church as the institution best suited to undertake this enormous task. De Chaupy – who at the beginning of the French Revolution was to publish a long attack on Voltaire[66] – upheld the *ancien régime* and had been exiled from France in 1756 for publishing an attack on the Parliament of Paris. Beyond their ideological differences, Piranesi and De Chaupy held strongly divergent views about the purpose of antiquarian research. For Piranesi, study of the past served to provide creative sources of inspiration for new architecture.[67]

For De Chaupy, the study of Horace's villa was an end in itself, justifiable by the importance of Horace's poetry. Piranesi was influenced by Bottari's view that the archaeologist should modestly serve the public, not promote himself. Bottari even went so far as to leave his name off the books he published.[68] De Chaupy's egotistical boasting about his priority in discovering the true site of Horace's Villa must have been highly offensive to Piranesi and other members of the Bottari circle. Finally, where Piranesi revelled in providing detailed technical diagrams and (often fanciful) architectural renderings and reconstructions of the sites he studied, De Chaupy's text is wholly unillustrated. That De Chaupy's verbal approach to archaeological description would have displeased Piranesi is clear from the title page to Piranesi's *Osservazioni sopra la lettre de M. Mariette* (1765). Two insets contrast Mariette's one-and-only tool, the pen, with the well-stocked toolkit of an architect such as Piranesi, which included a compass, a palette with brushes for illustration, a hammer and chisel, etc.[69]

With Piranesi, we come to the end of the period leading up to Ramsay's 'Enquiry'. It is apparent that the problem of Horace's Villa never engaged the leading Italian antiquarians at any period, except in passing. The remains on the surface were too spare in comparison with other sites closer to Rome or Naples. In the eighteenth century, excavations were often undertaken to find treasure such as statues, and both the condition of the Licenza site and Horace's descriptions of his villa as a humble farm must have made it seem unlikely that digging there would repay the investment. When excavations finally did occur, they did not result in significant finds that anyone could or would talk about. To make matters worse, the site had become the focus of a distasteful and pitiful *baruffa* in which, from the Italian point of view, the aggressor was a foreigner and an egotistical bully. By 1769 the Licenza site almost seemed to suffer from 'guilt by association' with De Chaupy, whom, as Piranesi's engraving shows, Italian scholars understandably found disagreeable.

Ramsay's 'Enquiry': Composition, Characteristics, Significance

Ramsay was an old friend of Piranesi, though they, too, had their public disagreements, especially about the relative merits of Greek and Roman art (see pp.12–13 above).[70] Ramsay's decision to write about Horace's Villa shows that on the matter of its importance, he also took leave to differ from his friend. For Ramsay, the villa was important not for the height of its walls, nor for the art treasures to be found there, and certainly not for the fame that a book about it might bring to its author, but for its literary and sentimental associations and for the scientific discoveries that could still be made there. As the son of a poet who had been a long-time admirer of Horace (see pp.7–10 above),[71] a wealthy and successful portraitist and a Fellow of the Society of Antiquaries, whose journal, *Archaeologia*, shows that there was practically no antiquity, no matter how humble, that was not worthy of a serious publication, Ramsay approached the Licenza site with very different goals and expectations from a Piranesi, a De Chaupy or a Saint'Odile. Moreover, we should not neglect a purely personal motive for Ramsay's decision to persist with the writing of the 'Enquiry': he found the related travel and study a fillip to his spirits, if not to his health, which was failing in the period of his fourth and final visit to Italy (1782–4). What Ramsay wrote to his friend Archibald Hamilton about his visit to Naples in June of 1783 is valuable testimony of this: 'Here my infirm body is relieved by the gentleness of the climate; and my spirits kept up by the company of my son, and the variety of objects which a country, uncommonly interesting, daily presents to me.'[72]

But even before the infirmity of his old age, Ramsay did not need Petrocchi's 1757 discovery of the Massa Mandelana inscription or the de Sanctis–De Chaupy controversy to draw his interest to the site. This is clear from the fact that he had already visited Licenza looking for Horace's Villa during his second trip (1754–7) to Italy;[73] indeed, he is the first person on record to have visited. Sketches and a crudely drawn map (cf. Fig.5.3) survive, showing us where he went and what he saw.

Ramsay journeyed to the site in September of 1755 with his wife and an English lady friend of hers. In a letter to Sir Alexander Dick, Ramsay described the trip as a pleasant jaunt of two days, during which time he saw the Fons Blandusiae and some other things that he sketched on a map and in some views he made. These survive and show that Ramsay put the villa up the Licenza Valley north of Vicovaro, between Rocca Giovine and Licenza. He placed the site to the west of the town mill, which is not shown on his map but in a drawing preserved in Edinburgh.[74]

When the idea of writing the 'Enquiry' occurred to Ramsay is not known with certainty; it is, however, likely that the project began to form in his mind during his first visit to Licenza in 1755. We know only that he began the book during travels through Italy in 1775, as the title indicates. The manuscript was not finished when Ramsay returned to England in 1777, and Ramsay appears not to have touched it again until he went back to Rome in 1782. By the time he died in Dover on 10 August 1784, the text was almost finished,[75] and Ramsay had commissioned an unknown amanuensis to copy his second draft, making what was possibly a fair copy by incorporating the various changes of the draft of 1782–3 and by the addition of finished drawings of the illustrations he planned to use. Judging from this third copy, now at the University of California, Los Angeles, Ramsay decided in the end not to use the watercolours he had commissioned from Jacob More, which he perhaps planned originally to have converted into engravings. The appearance in 1783 of Jakob Philipp Hackert's ten engravings of the Licenza valley, supplemented (with Ramsay's knowledge and encouragement) by the publication of a map showing the valley, doubtless made Ramsay see that publishing his own views would be superfluous. At pages 55–6, Ramsay added a note in which he mentioned Hackert's ten views and praised his map.

The deliberate pace at which Ramsay let his project develop, despite the enthusiastic encouragement to publish quickly, which he received as early as 1778 from such friends as Boswell, Gibbon, Sir Joshua Reynolds and Samuel Johnson, shows that Ramsay was operating in the careful spirit of a scientist-antiquarian, not that of a self-promoting writer on the make. Of course, this is hardly surprising, since his reputation had already been made by the time he started his project on Horace's Villa.[76]

The diary of Ramsay's son, John (*b* 1768), gives us some precious glimpses into Ramsay's work on the 'Enquiry' from late 1782 to 4 October 1783, when he and his father were living in Rome.[77] Despite Ramsay's failing health,[78] he had enough good days to enable him to make progress on his project. We can easily imagine that he was determined to finish the 'Enquiry' before dying. From the diary, it is clear that Ramsay still had an impressive range of acquaintances among the artists and antiquarians of Rome, including James Byres, Jacob Philip Hackert, Gavin Hamilton, Angelica Kauffman and Jacob More.[79] Unfortunately, our diarist was only a youngster when observing the events and personages he covered, and he had a tendency to write about his father's meetings without conveying anything about their content, giving the reader the impression of watching fascinating encounters behind soundproof glass. Thus, despite John's record of several meetings between Ramsay and More, we have no idea what the two discussed.[80]

Luckily, there are some important exceptions. For example, on 12 February 1783, John and his father 'called upon … Mr Hackert who showd us several of the drawings he had made near Horace's Villa, all of which he was making prints to which my Father subscrib'd.' Two days later John returned home to find Hackert talking with his father. On 8 April Hackert visited the Ramsays, and John wrote that he showed his father 'the drawings from which he means to make his prints my father assisted him very much in adjusting their titles and motto's.' From 9 April to 27 June the Ramsays travelled south through Albano, Nemi and Velletri to the Pomptine Marshes, Terracina and ultimately to the Bay of Naples. On 1 July, a few days after their return to Rome, Hackert spent an evening with Ramsay, bringing with him 'a map he had made of Horace's country house and the country adjacent' (see Fig.6.3), about which Ramsay wrote in the 'Enquiry'.[81] Ramsay obviously had maps on his mind, for John wrote that on 8 July, 'In coming home we stopped at the Calcografia and bought the map of the Sabine country as also that of Latium by Ametio.' These are the Revillas and Ameti maps to which Ramsay refered several times in the 'Enquiry'. Meanwhile, there are several more visits with Hackert, on 2 and 9 July, and finally, after these preparations, John and his father set out for Tivoli on 17 July.

At this point, John's strengths as a diarist, such as they are, came to the fore, since he and his father then retreated to the countryside more to tour and observe than to socialize and converse. They used Tivoli as a base from which to explore the area up to Licenza, staying at Signor Cochimara's house, where the garden covered the site of the Temple of the Sibyl – 'the most beautiful elegant thing I ever saw,' wrote John. Work related to the 'Enquiry' began in earnest on 30 July; John described the day as follows:

Set off from Tivoli at 7. The country all the way betwixt Tivoli and Vico Varo is very picturesque the road being all by the side of the Anio whose banks are famous for their beauty. Arrived at Vico Varo at 10. Went to Sig.a Camilla whose house we found in a very quiet disorder. … Went to the Villa Bolognetti where I copied some inscriptions and particularly that one of Abbé Chaupy in which [is indicated] the situation of the ancient town of Mandela. Dined at 2. At 4, we ordered the chaise & went to San Cosimato a convent in a most charming picturesque situation. From it you have a very fine view taking in Licenza, Cantalupo, Vico Varo, Castel Madama &c. From there, we came home straight to Tivoli … Arrived at Tivoli at 8.

A few days later, on 4 August, the Ramsays and a fellow hotel guest whom John calls 'the Frenchman,'[82] and some *ciceroni* set off on asses for Vicovaro at three o'clock in the morning. They reached the town in time for breakfast. John continued:

I went to the Arciprete who gave me a letter of recommendation to the Arciprete of Rocca Giovane. Travelling for almost an hour in the most delightful country we arrived at Licenza where we found that my father could get good lodgings at the Arciprete's. From thence we set out for Rocca Giovane. Rocca Giovane is situated upon the top of a high rock to which the ascent and descent is very difficult. The arciprete of Rocca Giovane told us that this town was so miserably poor; that there were not a house that had a window in it; that it was utterly impossible to find a lodging of any sort. Going out of the gate of Rocca Giovane I copied an inscription which said that Vespasian had restored the temple of Victory which was going to ruin. Set out from Rocca Giovane at 11. Arrived at Sig.a Camilla's at Vico Varo about 12. Dined at 1. After dinner we took a walk about the town in which there is nothing very remarkable … Set off from Vico Varo at 5 … Arrived at Tivoli at 8.

The purpose of this visit appears to have been to find a place to lodge near Horace's Villa and to record the Victory inscription (*CIL* XIV.3485) in the town. Having failed to find a place to stay, the Ramsays returned to Tivoli, presumably somewhat disappointed. In the days that followed, John Ramsay took short trips in the Tivoli area, visiting the villa of Quintilius Varus, the Lago della Solfatara (that is, Bagni di Tivoli), and churches in Tivoli itself. John sat for his portrait, which his father worked on for several hours at a time over a period of several days. Ramsay *père* remained in his room, reading and making sketches of the landscape. Finally, on 18 August, the Ramsays returned to Rome. On 22 August Allan Ramsay received a letter from Count Orsini giving him permission to use the palace at Licenza, and by the next day he had returned to Tivoli with his son. By the 27th, the Ramsays were settled in the Orsini Palace in Licenza. John wrote:

Arrived at Licenza about 9 where we got very good lodgings in the Palace of Count Orsini out of each of the windows we had a most beautiful view of the valley of Licenza which reached down to San Cosimato & of Horace's country house which was just under our windows. The arciprete & Sig. Antonio dined with us. After dinner we went all together to see Horace's country house of which there is very few remains. They dug for us and opened us up a piece of marble which was in this form [here follows in the manuscript a drawing of the arrowhead mosaic in Lugli room G1; see Fig.5.8 below]. Near this there is a great piece of antient wall. From thence we went up to the Cascada which is a little artificial fountain pretty enough. Came home at 7.

On the next day, John read de Sanctis's *Dissertazione* to his father, undoubtedly to refresh his memory, since Ramsay already shows familiarity with the book in the 1777 manuscript of the 'Enquiry'. On the 29th the Ramsays went to the Fonte Ratini, where they drank the water 'with a great zeal and found it to be most excellent water tho' very cold'. Next, they visited the little church between Horace's Villa and Rocca Giovine known as S. Maria delle Case. After having a 'pleasant repast' at Rocca Giovine, the Ramsays returned to Licenza. On 31 August the Ramsays went to Percile, where Ramsay *père* wished to see 'Theresa a young girl of Licenza married to the surgeon of Percile and who had been the companion of my sister Amelia when she was in this country. She was exceedingly happy to see my father again and inquired a great deal about my sister.' This recalls the ending of the 'Enquiry', where Ramsay, after making a rather disparaging remark about the superstitiousness of the 'country people' of Licenza, concluded by saying of them:

they seem to be of the same stamp with those who, according to the poets and historians, inhabited that country in the days of Numa Pompilius, with the same laborious manner of living, the same contented poverty, and the same innocence; so that when my wife, my daughter Amelia, and I took our leave of them upon the 28 of June, 1777, we did it with much regret.[83]

For the next twelve days, Allan Ramsay seems to have stayed in the town of Licenza, continuing his work on the portrait of his son, who read to him from Cellini's autobiography in the evenings. It is a fair guess that he also worked on the text of the 'Enquiry'. Meanwhile, John Ramsay explored the area, taking walks to Colle Franco, Riocupo, Percile etc. On 7 September the myserious Frenchman came to Licenza from Tivoli, paying the Ramsays a visit and being shown Horace's Villa by John. Allan Ramsay felt strong enough on the 12th to travel in his chaise to Colle Franco to see the view of Horace's Villa visible from that vantage point. He also visited the local apothecary, who had an ancient seal found at Horace's Villa, which close inspection showed to be Christian. The next day, Ramsay *père* travelled by chaise to Civitella. By the 14th, the Ramsays felt that they had completed their researches in the Licenza area and started their return to Rome via Vicovaro and Tivoli.

Ramsay lived almost one more year before dying on 10 August 1784 at Dover, where he had sailed in order to be reunited with his daughter Amelia, who had returned to England from Bermuda, where her husband was stationed. At the time of his death, his manuscript of the 'Enquiry' was all but complete. It is to an assessment of this that we now turn.

Ramsay's account of previous work on the situation of Horace's villa is solid and reliable. He knew the work of his predecessors, omitting only two of any importance.[84] He was *au courant* about the recent publications on the site by de Sanctis and De Chaupy, though he never showed awareness of the driving force behind their researches, the shadowy Baron de Saint'Odile. He even consulted an unpublished manuscript by the Vicovaro notary, Abate

Giuseppe Petrocchi.[85] In treating the work of previous scholars, he was fair and balanced, just as likely to assign praise as blame. After the nasty and absurd battle that had broken out in the previous decade between de Sanctis and De Chaupy, Ramsay's dispassionate objectivity is a welcome relief. For example, although he criticized De Chaupy for the incorrect orientation of his map and other errors,[86] he praised the abbé for his work in identifying the Fons Bandusia near Horace's birthplace of Venusia (Venosa) and for his publication of an inscription important for locating the ancient site of Mandela.[87]

In method, Ramsay showed himself to be firmly committed to empiricism and autopsy. For centuries, he believed, scholars had fallen into error because they allowed their prejudices or 'prepossessions' to dictate their beliefs about Horace's Sabinum.[88] This was as true of the ancient commentators (or, 'scholiasts') as of contemporaries such as De Chaupy. Thus, writing about the latter, he stated, 'but in [the map] of the Valley of Licenza drawn by Abbé De Chaupy … the good Abbé has suffered his pencil to be guided rather by his prepossessions than his eyesight and has moved heaven and earth in order to make the actual situation of things correspond with what he believed to be Horace's description of them.'[89] Similarly, he penned the following complaint against one of the ancient commentators on Horace's poetry:

But here our Scholiast is of very little authority, as he appears to have no knowledge of the place [ie, Ustica; cf. *Odes* 1.17.11] or its circumstances beyond what he had picked up from passages of Horace and Virgil, which were they sufficient, lie at this time as open to us moderns as to him. … The best commentary upon this passage in Horace is to be found in the present Valley of Licenza.

It should be noted that Ramsay was prepared for just such an attack on ancient and modern authorities by papers printed by the Society of Antiquaries in the 1770s. In 1770, Smart Lethieullier published a letter showing that Stukeley's speculative reconstruction of the route of the Icening-street between Newbury and Old Sarum was fanciful. In 1772 Daines Barrington argued that Caesar was mistaken in identifying the Medway River as the Thames. Thus, in questioning the authority of the scholiast and in suspecting that his identification of Ustica is an unreliable back-formation from the poetry, Ramsay was a product of his age. This form of criticism has gathered strength in recent years, anticipating the trend to doubt the veracity of many of the biographical details reported by the scholiasts.[90]

For Ramsay, the corrective to such prepossession was accurate observation of the 'present Valley of Licenza.' He encouraged the successful engraver Jacob Philipp Hackert to prepare a new map of the valley (see Fig.6.2), and he struggled through various attempts to identify the site of Ustica by reconciling Horace's descriptive passages about the place with several possible hills in area. We can follow Ramsay's mind at work in the 1777 version of the 'Enquiry' in the National Library of Scotland, wherein his first idea was that 'perhaps Ustica might have been the name anciently given to the sloping ground to the west of Licenza'. But a moment's reflection told him that this spot did not particularly correspond to Horace's description, and so he crossed out this passage and wrote: 'To say the truth, there is nothing in the appearance of this piece of ground that is very distinguishing, or deserving of any epithet at all, and Horace's *curiosa felicitas* in the choice of his terms ought to make us suspect that none of them are employed idly.'[91]

So Ramsay had second thoughts about equating the slope to the west of the town of Licenza with Ustica, and he set off in a new direction, trying to find a feature that could fairly be described in the words Horace uses in *Odes* 1.17 as being *cubans* ('reclining') and as having *levia saxa* ('smooth rocks'):

What if the present Rocca Giovane was the ancient Ustica? It is a singular situation to which the word *cubans* and *levia Saxa* will very well apply. For here is a village built upon the top of a bare rock in most places perpendicular [see Pl.VII]. The whole of this rock lies in a hollow, shaped like a cradle, and on every side, except to the east, is surrounded by ground higher than itself; particularly to the west. All this is in the straight part which gives entrance into the Valley, and one afternoon in my return from Horace's farm, I had occasion to hear a remarkable echo in this place, by one country man bawling to another, on the other side of the Digentia.

But Ramsay was not satisfied with this conjecture, and so he again cancelled his text, writing instead: 'Some inscription may be hereafter found, or some charters of the neighbouring lands, able to give us light into this matter; in the mean time it would be shutting the door against future discoveries if we were to mention things as certain, which have no better support than loose conjectures.' Ramsay knew that others would rely on his accuracy of thought and observation and that if he put forward an identification as certain that was merely speculative, it might 'shut the door against future discoveries'. Moreover, if documentary evidence should emerge from which the location of Ustica could be inferred, and if his guess was wrong, then he would open himself to the kind of criticism that Stukeley had to endure from his critics.

In 1777, then, Ramsay decided to play it safe, noting that Horace's Valley of Ustica could not be securely identified and that his readers should be so apprised. But, as the final draft of 1783 shows, Ramsay continued to ponder the question, and in the end decided that he was on the right track in his initial supposition but had wrongly limited his survey to the western slope of the hill of Licenza. Thus, in the final draft, he wrote:

In reading the words *levia saxia* which resounded with the pipe, I had, all my life, formed an idea of living rocks of considerable magnitude; which by the help of valleys, or recesses, adjoining to them performed this mimic function. Accordingly upon coming into the middle of the Valley of Licenza I looked about for some place which might correspond to the image I had formed in my mind and soon observed at the north end of the valley some rocky ground, and particularly one rock, perpendicular on the east side, upon which is built the little village called Licenza … I observed likewise other deep recesses to the west of this rock and was satisfied that this rock was the Ustica, and these recesses the valleys mentioned in the ode, as uniting to produce the echo.

With regard to the *Usticae cubantis*, the old Scholiast does not seem to have accurately performed his function of grammarian in assigning the same meaning to *jacens* and *cubans*, as the one means in the best authors 'lying', and the other 'reclining'. The epithet of 'reclining' may tolerably well suit the hill of Licenza which

slopes all the way to the top on that side which looks towards Horace's house; and
the whole hill, though high with respect to the plain, is low with respect to the hills
behind, and on each side of it, to a degree that will surprise any one who views it
from Civitella.[92]

Ramsay's ultimate solution to the puzzle of where Ustica was located may
not be completely compatible with the one immediately preceding it, but we
must at least grant that Ramsay did not present the identification as
unproblematically as he did in his first suggestion or as speculatively as he
did in his third idea. In navigating between the overly optimistic speculation
of Stukeley and the overly cautious empiricism of Folkes, Ramsay may even
have hit upon the correct solution, since two important twentieth-century
topographers have independently arrived at the same conclusion: that Ustica
is the hill on which the town of Licenza sits.[93] The key factor enabling Ramsay
to reach the solution of 1783 was his autopsy of the Licenza valley from the
top of Civitella, which he first visited on 13 September 1783, just when he was
writing the final passage.[94] Observing Ramsay struggling to identify Ustica,
we are reminded of Hume's 'doctrine of belief': 'the sentiment of belief is
nothing but a conception more intense and steady than what attends the
mere fictions of the imagination, and … this manner of conception arises
from a customary conjunction of the object with something present to the
memory or senses'.[95]

Ramsay's methods included excavation, at least to a modest extent. He
recorded two specific dates on which he had the country people dig in the
Vigne di San Pietro to expose a mosaic in the room labelled G1 on Lugli's
plan of 1926 (Fig.5.8).[96] Although on the first occasion, 27 June 1773, he
incorrectly inferred from the layout of the mosaic that the building of which
it was a part was orientated to the cardinal points of the compass (it is
actually oriented NW–SE), Ramsay was right to attempt to raise this issue.
He also tells us that he had 'at other times been shown parts of this mosaic
composed of flowering foliages'. The mosaic in room G1 was completely
exposed in Pasqui's excavations of 1911–14, and it cannot be described as
having 'flowering foliages'. Some of the nearby rooms and passageways are
lacking a pavement. Perhaps what Ramsay saw (but, unfortunately, did not
draw) was part of a mosaic in one of these other parts of the building. Be that
as it may, Ramsay gave no sign of planning to undertake large-scale
excavations of the site; nor did he show any of Thomas Jefferson's grasp of
how stratigraphy could be used to illuminate the history of a site. When
Bernardo Pomfili, a local farmer, brought to Ramsay's attention the remains
of *cubilia* in his field,[97] Ramsay did not bother to dig the site but was satisfied
to indulge in some speculation that the gatehouse to Horace's Villa might
have been located there. His goal in writing the 'Enquiry' appears to have
been simply to provide a stimulus for someone else to undertake the task of
thoroughly digging and publishing the villa.

Turning from Ramsay's method to his results, the first thing to note is that
he raised some issues that were far ahead of his time. This is, doubtless, not
because he was farsighted but because he had a Stukeleyan breadth of vision

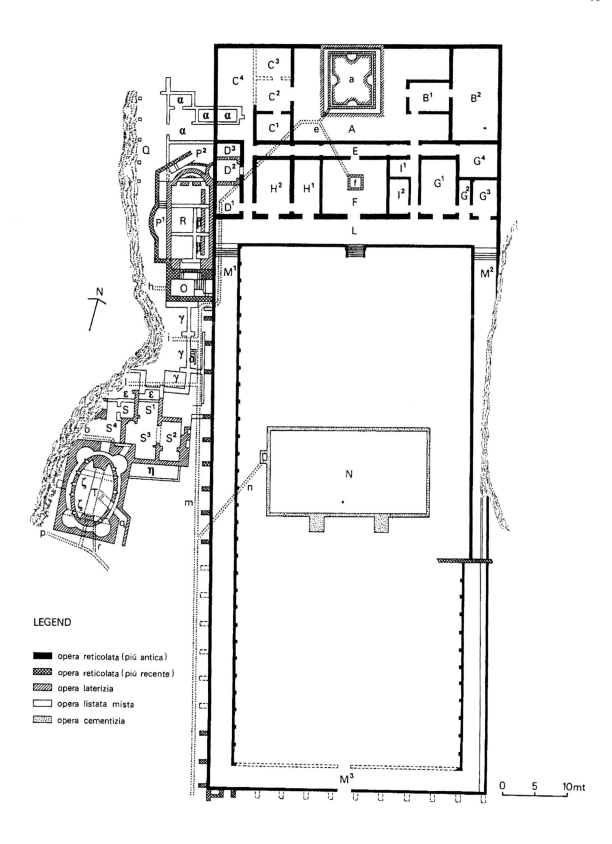

LEGEND

- █ opera reticolata (piú antica)
- ▨ opera reticolata (piú recente)
- ▨ opera laterizia
- ▢ opera listata mista
- ▨ opera cementizia

of the scope of antiquarian research, which went far beyond the quantitative aspects of a monument to its real-life uses and its cultural significance. Like recent scholars, for example, he wondered about the size of the estate, speculating that it was very large.[98] He had a panoramic view of the history of the property, differentiating the various ancient periods from each other, antiquity from the Middle Ages, and the Middle Ages from his own day. He realized that understanding the Horatian phase of the site required peeling away layers from his day back to the first occupation of the area. His ideas about dating the various phases have held up remarkably well, considering how slight the evidence was on which they were based. For example, he was right to conjecture a major rebuilding in the mid imperial period, though he was wrong in identifying the person responsible as Sextus Afranius Burrus.[99] He was also probably correct in imagining that the property was donated by Constantine to the church of St Peter and Marcellinus, remaining largely in Church hands until his own day.[100] Among students of Horace's Villa to the present day, he is unique in wondering how often and at what times of the year Horace used the place.[101]

Also quite progressive is Ramsay's survey of the ancient remains all around the Licenza valley. He was interested not only in standard questions such as the identification of Horatian place names, but also in such new problems as whether Horace had any neighbours and, if so, where their properties might be located. In giving the results of his survey, he reported finds not otherwise known, such as an inscription on an altar at the door of a peasant in Licenza.[102]

Ramsay's sympathy for the country people enabled him to track down places and objects that other investigators missed, perhaps because they did not stay at Licenza as long as he did and because they were not nearly so open to intercourse with the uneducated inhabitants of the valley. Bernardo Pomfili (whom Ramsay familiarly calls 'Bernardo') showed him the ruins of an important structure in *opus reticulatum* on his land not far from the villa site.[103] Ramsay's informant thought that the *cubilia* on his land were used as pavement for a road, but Ramsay preceptively noted that the Romans never used this construction technique for laying causeways. He was quite right, too, to ponder the still unresolved question of how the villa site was reached by a *diverticulum* from the main Roman road through the valley. Another man in Rocca Giovine invited Ramsay into his house to see a missing piece of the Victory inscription over the door (Fig.5.9), and Ramsay went beyond previous students of the inscription by probing the circumstances that may have surrounded Vespasian's restoration of the temple of the goddess.[104] Other natives told him about various place names (Il Sainese, Il Pomario etc) that gave him leads (albeit possibly false) about the ancient identity of the areas.[105] At least once he appeared to have misunderstood what his informants told him when he reported the find of a 'marble chariot' instead of 'a cartload full of marble', though in general his Italian was quite good.[106] Ramsay's most significant discovery was the mosaic in room G1 on the Lugli plan. It is easy to imagine that it was Ramsay's interest in the inhabitants of

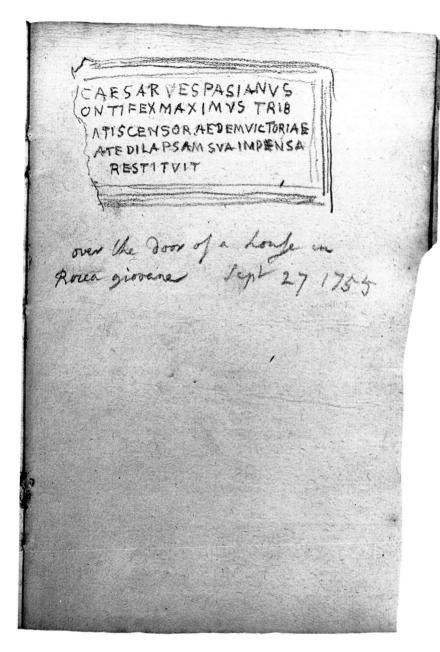

5.9. The so-called Victory inscription from Roccagiovine, sketched by Ramsay in 1755

the Licenza valley that enabled him to be the first scholar on record to see this pavement; in his description of how he came to view the mosaic, he wrote as though it had long been known to 'the master of the vineyard' and did not imply that it was found through his own independent efforts.[107] Even if we might wish that Ramsay had dug more extensively on the site, he must be praised for garnering as much information as possible from local peasants. Here, Ramsay looks forward to the Romantic antiquarians of the nineteenth century.[108]

Of course, for all his virtues, Ramsay suffered both from the general limitations of his age and from his own personal shortcomings. While he was generally effective in linking Horace's descriptions of places in the valley to likely sites on the map, he sometimes went too far, as when he thought he could find the spot mentioned in *Odes* 3.18, where 'the peasants play/on the grassy-matted soil,/round their oxen, free from toil.'[109] His description of the villa site as covered with 'thousands of stones' is precious, but even more valuable would have been various views of the site. The one long view he made from a window in the Orsini Palace is, for its time, uniquely informative but cannot substitute for a series of close-ups in and around the Vigne di San Pietro.[110] Likewise, we are grateful for his illustrations of the mosaic in room G1 but wish he had also left a drawing of the apothecary's Christian seal or of the mosaic, now vanished and never otherwise recorded, with 'flowering foliages'.[111] Undoubtedly, the poor state of his health – particularly during his last visit to the site – prevented him from making as many illustrations as he might have liked.

Ramsay's sense of the topography of the valley was very strong and reliable, but he too blithely assumed an uninterrupted continuity from antiquity to his own day. For example, he thought that the modern place name 'Il Pomario' marked the spot of Horace's garden, and he believed that 'La Romana' applied to the site of an ancient Roman structure.[112] In the last example, he may be faulted for violating his own principle of autopsy, since he relied on the hearsay of the country people for the report that there were ancient walls on the site. In general, when he most went astray it was because he digressed or neglected his own policy of sceptical enquiry.[113]

Nevertheless, Ramsay's strengths outweigh his weaknesses. What most differentiates him from many of his contemporary antiquarians in Italy is the honesty with which he conducted his research and the purely scientific aims that he pursued.[114] He viewed digging as a tool for ascertaining the truth of archaeological conjecture, not as a means of finding treasure that could be sold for self-enrichment. Indeed, he realized that excavation undertaken on behalf of the advancement of knowledge will certainly cost more money than it will return. But, whatever the costs, Ramsay knew from personal experience that digging would bring sufficient satisfaction to 'men of classical curiosity' to justify the expense.[115]

Ramsay's plan for an extensive excavation of the Vigne de San Pietro site took over a century to be realized. Throughout most of the nineteenth century, the Licenza site was unquestioningly accepted as Horace's in the guidebooks,[116] but it was occasionally challenged by scholars.[117] In 1891 Mazzoleni published a magisterial article re-arguing the case in favour of the site in the Vigne de San Pietro, and after repeated official requests by the town of Licenza to the government in Rome, the first scientific excavations were undertaken from 1911 to 1914 by Angiolo Pasqui on behalf of the Ministry for Public Instruction. Pasqui died before completing his work, and in 1926 his preliminary results were published by Giuseppe Lugli,[118] who was to become

been of consequence for shewing that Horace's
ground extended at least so far south; and the
more conclusive that at the remains of the Villa
itself, which is about three quarters of a mile off, there
are thousands of stones to be gathered exactly formed
like this pretended pavement, But as these stones
are formed precisely, very proper for causewaying, like those made use of in
the Opus reticulatum to be found in the Mausoleum
of Augustus, and almost all the buildings of the first
Emperors as far down as Caracalla, thus,

a.
a. Opus reticulatum
   for walls
b. head or surface
   of the Stone
c. depth of it.

We must suspend our believe concerning the alledged
pavement till it is actually uncovered, and seen in its unbroken
state.

———— habitatum quinque focis

Et quinque bonos solitum Variam dimittere patres.

Here Horace means to shew his Villicus that his
farm could not be very contemptible, as it had been sufficient
for the maintenance of five families of distinction. In the
common editions the abovementioned town is called Baria
by a change very usual in the lower times of the Roman Empire
the inscriptions of which often present us with BIXIT and
SE BIBO instead of Vixit and Se vivo, but Dr Bentley
gives us Variam upon the authority of the most ancient
manuscripts. It is now called Vico Varo, standing upon

one of the twentieth century's leading scholars of Roman topography. In 1930–31, Thomas Drees Price, a Fellow in Landscape Architecture at the American Academy in Rome, reopened the excavations in collaboration with Lugli, continuing work on the east side of the quadriporticus where Pasqui had stopped digging fifteen years earlier.[119]

By 1932 the foundations of the villa on the San Pietro site had largely been revealed. The core of the site was a structure orientated NW–SE and measuring *c*.110 x 40 m. The structure consisted of three parts (Fig.5.8): a two-storey residence to the north, with an atrium and peristyle and well-preserved floor mosaics in several rooms; a garden and quadriporticus to the south; and a bath complex to the west. Four phases were identified but only vaguely dated to the pre-Horatian period, the Horatian period, the mid imperial period and the early medieval period. The significant remains from the site were placed in a local museum in the Palazzo Orsini in Licenza. These included some statuary from the quadriporticus, statuettes from the residence, and wall painting dating to various building phases from an undetermined part of the complex. No hard evidence was found proving or disproving the identification of the site as Horace's. Occasional archae-ological surveys of the Licenza valley have found no other villa occupied during Horace's lifetime, and so the latest authority agrees that, *faute de mieux*, it is probable that the San Pietro site was the one owned by Horace.[120]

Notes

1. On the creation of the journal, see J. Evans, *Society of Antiquaries*, 1956, pp.134–47.

2. On Stukeley see S. Piggott, *William Stukeley*, 1985; on Martin Folkes and his quarrel with Stukeley, see ibid., pp.115–17, and Evans, loc. cit., pp.91–2, 126 (citing Stukeley's diary entry on the death of Martin Folkes in 1754, that 'most miserable object of dereliction').

3. A. Smart, *Allan Ramsay*, 1992, p.30.

4. M. Folkes, 'Trajan and Antonine Pillars', 1770, p.130

5. W. Stukeley, 'Sanctuary at Westminster', 1770, p.47.

6. ibid., p.44.

7. On archaeological illustration, see S. Piggott, *Antiquity Depicted*, 1978.

8. J. A. Passmore, *Hume's Intentions*, 1952, p.159.

9. The term 'enquiry' appears only once in a title in *Archaeologia* during the period 1770–80, when over 175 articles were published. On Ramsay's close personal and intellectual relationship with Hume, see D. Macmillan, *Scottish Art*, p.104.

10. 'Enquiry', pp.65–6 (Ramsay's manuscript pagination, here and elsewhere).

11. For the identification of these scholars, see pp.152–3 below, notes 3, 4, 5 and 7.

12. See R. Almagià, *L'opera geographica*, 1942.

13. See L. Holstenius, *Annotationes*, 1666, p.106. On this page, Holstenius equates modern Rocca Giovine with the Fanum Vacunae and the hilltown of Licenza with Digentia, both places stated by Horace to be near his villa (cf. *Epistles* 1.10.49 [Vacuna] and 1.18.104 [Digentia]). Holstenius does not explicitly discuss Horace's Villa.

14. For recent years, cf. F. Coarelli, *Lazio*, 1984, pp.109–13; Z. Mari, 'La valle del Licenza', 1994, pp.66–8; E. A. Schmidt, *Sabinum*, 1997.

15. Bentley's; cf. 'Enquiry', p.22 ('Doctor Bentley, whose text I generally follow') and p.6 ('I shall therefore, according to the order in which they commonly stand in Horace's works, select all those passages which relate to his farm, accompanying them with such explanations and remarks as my reading upon the subject, and my attentive inspection of the ground itself have enabled me to make').

16. Scholars had begun working out the chronology of Horace's poems before Ramsay wrote the 'Enquiry'; see A. Dacier, *Oeuvres d'Horace*, 1733; J. Masson, *Q. Horatii Flacci Vita*, 1708.

17. See, for example, 'Enquiry', p.47: 'Following the Colle Franchisi, or Francolisi, westward, up the Lucretilis, and along the north side of the Fossa Sainese, this ground has the name 'Il Sainese,' that is the Sabinenses, as I learnt from several of the country people'; and p.60: 'The Digentia anciently divided the Sabina from the country of the Marsi, and the country people to this day call part of the ground on the west side of it the Sainese, that is the Sabinensis.'

18. The exception to this comes at p.59 in his discussion of *Epistles* I. 16, where he writes, 'Upon a general review of this Epistle, I suspect that it has come down to us mutilated and confused, and very different from what it was when sent out by Horace to his friend, if ever it was sent. He begins it with a number of questions concerning the produce of his farm, all which he promises to answer *loquaciter* or in a very particular manner. But we look in vain for those answers, and after sixteen lines of general and desultory hints, fall all at once into a string of moral precepts, very good in themselves, and very much in the spirit of Horace, but as little connected with one another, as with the proposed subject of the epistle. The whole is probably made up of memorandums left unfinished at the author's death, or of fragments of his finished works picked up afterwards by his admirers, and stuck together in the best way they could.'

19. cf. G. di Gastaldi, *I nomi antichi*, 1564, in which over 300 ancient places in Italy are listed with their sixteenth-century Italian equivalents.

20. I omit mention of the *Fons Bandusiae* (*Odes* 3.13), which may not have been near Horace's Villa.

21. For the tradition linking the Convent of St Antonio in Tivoli with Horace, see A. Del Re, *Dell'antichità tiburtine*, 1611, p.116; J. Landucci, *Voyage de Rome*, 1792, p.45. The most recent study of the subject is G. D'Anna, 'È veramente esistita', 1994, who argues that Horace had only the Licenza villa until *c.*17 BC, when he seems to have come into possession of a property at Tivoli. For the popular tradition of the villa of Horace near Vicovaro (in the area called San Giovanni in Camporaccio), see L. Torrentius, *Q. Horatius Flaccus*, 1608, p.679: 'Atque adeo nunc quoque inter Tibur et Praeneste locus est non incelebris, qui Italis Vicovaro appellatur: quo fit, ut facilius credam Horatii villam ad octavum ultra Tibur lapidem fuisse ... Quin et incolas affirmantes audivi, extare adhuc eius vestigia in campo, quem hodieque Horatium vocant' ('and now there is a place, not unknown, between Tivoli and Palestrina, which the Italians call Vicovaro, where [as I can easily believe] the villa of Horace was located near the eighth milestone beyond Tivoli ... Indeed, I have heard the inhabitants state that there are still remains of it in a field that today is called 'Camporaccio'). Cf. also 'Mr T—' in J. Spence, *Observations*, 1966, vol.2, p.674 (no.34): 'Horace's villa was in the hilly country of the Sabines, not far from Vicovari.' I am indebted to Iain Gordon Brown for this reference. As for Licenza, when in 1755 Allan Ramsay, the first visitor in modern times to record his visit to the Licenza site, turned up in the area asking to be taken to the Fons Blandusiae, he was immediately taken by a country man to a spring in the vicinity of the town, which must have been known to him and others for quite some time; see Ramsay's letter to Sir Alexander Dick, NAS GD331/5/18, and I. G. Brown, *Poet and Painter*, 1984, p.39.

22. See F. Biondo, *De Roma*, 1527; see also p.100 above, note 3.

23. J. Cruquius, *Q. Horatius Flaccus*, 1579.

24. L. Holstenius, *Annotationes*, 1666; see also p.152 below, note 7.

25. I. Mattei, *Nuova et esatta tavola*, 1674, on which see A.P. Frutaz, *Le carte del Lazio*, 1972, vol.2, tav. 157 (xxx.2.b); G. F. Ameti and D. de Rossi, *Il Lazio*, 1693, on which see Frutaz, loc. cit., vol.1, p.xxxii, vol. 2, map xxxiii.2.

26. R. Fabretti, *De Aquis*, 1680.

27. Cluverius emended the text of Strabo, *Geography* 5.3.11, from Valeria to Varia.

28. *CIL* XIV.3485.

29. See Porphyrio and Ps.-Acro on Horace's *Epistles* 1.10.49 (quoted in Ramsay's 'Enquiry', p.42).

30. See *CIL* 1.1844=*CIL*IX.4636=*ILS* 3484; *CIL* IX.4751=*ILS* 3486; *CIL* IX.4752=*ILS* 3485; *ILS* 9248; *L'Année Epigraphique*, 1907, no.212; 1981, no.199; 1990, no.332.

31. R. Fabretti, *De Aquis*, 1680, in his third map bound before p.3, puts Licenza and Cantalupo on the wrong sides of the Licenza River; I. Mattei, *Nuova et esatta tavola*, 1666, has Percile and Civitella in the wrong places with respect to Licenza; and although he puts the Fons Blandusiae near Licenza, he (like Ameti, following his lead) puts Ustica and the Villa Horatii too close to Palombara Sabina. A. Kircher, *Latium*, 1669, and G.F. Ameti and D. de Rossi, *Il Lazio*, 1693, put Rocca Giovine north of Licenza, an error that can be traced to Pirro Ligorio's 1551 map, which was the first map of Latium to include the Licenza Valley.

32. On Revillas see M. Pedley, 'Diego de Revillas', 1991; A. P. Frutaz, *Le carte del Lazio*, 1972, vol.1, pp.xxix–xxx.

33. Ramsay's map can be linked to Revillas's through a number of features the two share that are not common on other eighteenth-century maps. These include the Rio Cupo south of Rocca Giovine; Casal Questione at the junction of the Rio Cupo and the Licenza River; and 'La Villa

diruta' on the east side of the valley. Ramsay wrote an account of the trip in a letter to Sir Alexander Dick; above, note 21.

34.   A. P. Frutaz, *Le carte del Lazio*, vol. 1, pp.xxix–xxx, 90–92; ibid., vol.2, carta XL c; M. Pedley, ' "I due valeutuomini" ', 1993.

35.   Maire and Boscovich, *Carta geografica*, 1769 (whose map is at a scale of *c.* 1:100,000), place Licenza 0° 29' east of Monte Mario, while the I.G.M. map of 1940 puts it 27' east of Monte Mario; Maire and Boscovich place Licenza at about 42°4' of latitude, not far different from the 42° 4' 3'' of the I.G.M. map.

36.   See Ramsay, 'Enquiry', p.54.

37.   C. De Chaupy, *Découverte de la maison*, 1767–9, vol. 1, p.xxxvii, reported that he was told that the first visitors to Licenza in living memory were two Englishmen who arrived in 1755. George Nicolaus Heerkens, a Dutch physician and poet, states in a book published in 1765 that he visited Licenza during the pontificate of Benedict XIV (*d* 1758). Heerkens is vague about the exact date of his visit, stating only that he arrived in Rome in the first days of December of a year he does not mention. His dedication, on the other hand, is dated to 14 November 1755, but this is an oddly early date for a book not published for ten years and may represent a typographical error. On Lumisden's visit, see A. Lumisden, 'Letter to John MacGouan', 1765; on his and Boswell's visit see also pp.16–17 above. I am indebted to Iain Gordon Brown for this reference.

38.   For an overview see C. Pietrangeli, *Scavi e scoperti*, 1983.

39.   cf. Erdmannsdorf's diary for 3 April 1766 in J. J. Winckelmann, *Briefe*, 1957, p.246; also Ermannsdorf's letter to Huber dated 3 April 1766, ibid., p.255.

40.   See G. Vichi, *Gli Arcadi*, 1977.

41.   D. de Sanctis, *Dissertazione*, 1784, p.ix.

42.   See B. Frischer, 'First Excavation of Horace's Villa', 1998.

43.   On Saint'Odile's birth name see R. B. Litchfield, *Emergence of a Bureaucracy*, 1986, p.268. In eighteenth-century sources and in modern scholarship his name is spelled variously as Sainte-Odile, S. Odill, Saint-Odile, St. Odil, St. Audil, Saint-Odill, di Santedille, Saint Odyle, Santodile, Sant'Odile.

44.   Archivio di Stato Firenze, Fondo Affari Esteri, Filza 2284, in a dispatch to Count Piccolomini dated 31 July 1773.

45.   On Saint'Odile's trip up the Anio Valley to Ancona, see the dispatches to the Council of the Regency sent in October 1757 by Saint'Odile's secretary, Antonio Valentini, in Archivio di Stato Firenze, Fondo Affari Esteri, Filza 2278.

46.   See G.C. Moroni, *Dizionario*, 1846, vol.36, p.195. For Del'Isle's map see G. Del'Isle, *Tabula Italiae*, 1711, on which cf. A.P. Frutaz, *Le carte del Lazio*, 1972, vol. 1, pp.81–2.

47.   Frutaz, op. cit.

48.   D. de Sanctis, *Dissertazione*, 1761, p.43.

49.   On the Abbé Capmartin De Chaupy, see *Biographie universelle*, vol.8, pp.45–6; E. Galletier, 'L'Abbé Capmartin de Chaupy', 1935; N. Mathieu, 'Capmartin de Chaupy', 1987.

50.   J.J. La Lande, *Voyage d'un François*, 1769, vol.5, pp.385–6.

51.   C. De Chaupy, *Découverte de la maison*, 1767–9, vol.3, p.249.

52.   ibid., vol.1, p.xxxix. The earliest de Sanctis's book could have been printed is after he received permission from the Holy Office to publish it on 18 April 1761 (p.[v]).

53.   The preface to de Sanctis's third printing of his book in 1784 makes the date of early 1761 more probable, since there (at p.x) we read of De Chaupy that he 'accidentalmente con un Personaggio di qualche rango capitò nel 1761 in Vicovaro.' The 'Personaggio di qualche range' was presumably Saint'Odile.

54.   De Chaupy, op. cit., vol. 3, pp.10, 352–4.

55.   ibid., pp.356–7. The inscriptions are *CIL* xiv.3487 and xv.3897b. For the story about the Archpriest, see Ramsay, 'Enquiry', p.39, note. De Chaupy, op. cit., vol. 3, p.10, confirms Ramsay's statement that the fragments inscribed with Burrus' name were entrusted to the local priest.

56.   Cited in I. G. Brown, *Monumental Reputation*, 1992, p.11.

57.   One may compare Saint'Odile's similar failure in 1769 to obtain a licence to export the Niobe group and Apollino from the Villa Medici to Florence. M. Maugeri, 'Il trasferimento a Firenze', speculates that this failure resulted from the Baron's unsuccessful attempt to export the statues through legal means and his resort to corrupting the relevant authorities. On Papal edicts concerning excavation permits in the eighteenth century, see A. Emiliani, *Leggi*, 1996, pp.66–83.

58.   *Dissertazione*, p.44.

59. ibid., p.62.

60. See the brief but pertinent remarks of I. Bignamini and I. Jenkins, 'The Antique', 1996 (with bibliography).

61. See B. Frischer, 'First Excavation of Horace's Villa', 1998, p.287.

62. 'Enquiry', p.5.

63. See J. Wilton-Ely, *Piranesi: The Complete Etchings*, 1994, vol.2, p.890 (no.817); H. Lavagne, 'Piranesi', 1985, p.267). I am indebted to Iain Gordon Brown for bringing Piranesi's joke to my attention.

64. cf. J. Wilton-Ely, *Piranesi as Architect*, 1993, pp.35–61.

65. See A. Monferini, 'Piranesi e Boltari', 1985.

66. See B. Frischer, 'First Excavation of Horace's Villa', 1998, p.281.

67. cf. J. Wilton-Ely, *Piranesi as Architect*, 1993, p.35.

68. A. Monferini, op. cit., p.222.

69. For an illustration of the title page see Wilton-Ely, *Piranesi as Architect*, 1993, fig.51.

70. Piranesi wrote *Della magnificenza ed architettura de' Romani* partly in response to Ramsay's *Dialogue on Taste* (1755); see I. G. Brown, *Poet and Painter*, 1984, pp.40–41; A. Smart, *Allan Ramsay*, 1992, pp.123, 147.

71. cf. Brown, op.cit., passim.

72. cf. the letter to Archibald Hamilton, quoted below at n.78.

73. See A. Smart, *Allan Ramsay*, 1992, p.126.

74. Smart, loc. cit., the letter to Dick (GD 331/5/18) is quoted in part.

75. It only lacked a few minor details such as the measurements of the capitals Ramsay saw in front of a blacksmith's shop in Licenza; 'Enquiry', p.38.

76. For Boswell's remarks see the Introduction. Ramsay's attitude towards his project contrasted with that of Robert Adam towards Split; see pp.19–20 and 84 above.

77. National Library of Scotland, MSS 1833–4.

78. cf. Ramsay's letter to Archibald Hamilton, Esq., Naples, 14 June 1783 (National Library of Scotland, MS 10782, f.156).

79. On James Byres see B. Ford, 'James Byres', 1974; B. Skinner, *Scots in Italy*, 1966, pp.16–17; on Gavin Hamilton see S. Q. Hutton in N.T. de Grummond, *Encyclopedia*, 1996, vol. 1, pp.562–6; on Angelica Kauffman see O. Sandner, *Angelika Kauffmann*, 1998. On Jakob Philipp Hackert and Jacob More see chapter 4.

80. cf., for example, the entries for 5, 8, 10, 13, 21, 29 and 30 March, 7 April, and 2 and 8 July. On 10 March More showed the Ramsays his picture of Cicero's villa, which, John Ramsay opined, 'was very well painted.'

81. 'Enquiry', pp.55–6.

82. This is not (as one might be tempted to speculate) the French–Swiss painter Louis Ducros, who was a friend of Ramsay and who painted views of the Licenza valley; cf. [Ducros], *Images of the Grand Tour*, 1985, pp.75–6 (note 54). From John Ramsay's diary we know that the Ramsays first met 'the Frenchman' on 17 July 1783 in Tivoli. From the diary (see entries for 29 March and 7 July 1783) it is clear that the Ramsays already knew Ducros before that date.

83. 'Enquiry', pp.66–7.

84. A. Kircher, *Latium*, 1669; R. Fabretti, *De Aquis*, 1680.

85. cf. 'Enquiry', p.8; on Petrocchi, see Petrocchi, *Orazio*, 1958, p.36, note 6.

86. cf. 'Enquiry', p.54.

87. op. cit., pp.24, 61–2.

88. The term 'prepossession' has a Humean ring; cf. D. Hume, *Enquiry*, 1975, p.151: 'It seems evident, that men are carried, by a natural instinct or prepossession, to repose faith in their senses; and that, without any reasoning, or even almost before the use of reason, we always suppose an external universe, which depends not on our perception, but would exist, though we and every sensible creature were absent or annihilated … But this universal and primary opinion of all men is soon destroyed by the slightest philosophy, which teaches us, that nothing can ever be present to the mind but an image or perception, and that the senses are only the inlets, through which these images are conveyed, without being able to produce any immediate intercourse between the mind and the object.'

89. 'Enquiry', p.54.

90. See N. Horsfall, *Companion*, 1995, p.1.

91. NLS, MS 730, f.10.

92. EUL, La.III.492, p.14.

93. G. Lugli, 'La villa sabina', 1926, col.484; Z. Mari, 'La valle del Licenza', 1994, p.20.

94. cf. the entry for that date in the diary of John Ramsay, NLS, MS 1834, p.145.

95. D. Hume, 'Enquiry', 1975, p.50.

96. Ramsay, 'Enquiry', p.53. Note that when Ramsay dates the second occasion to 27 September 1783, he is mistaken. John Ramsay's diary entry (cf. p.90 above) shows that the correct date was 27 August and that by 14 September the Ramsays had left Licenza to return to Tivoli and Rome.

97. Ramsay, 'Enquiry', p.46.

98. ibid., pp.45–6; see also Z. Mari, 'La valle dell'Aniene', 1995, p.33.

99. 'Enquiry', p.36, note 39.

100. ibid., p.6.

101. ibid., p.40.

102. ibid., p.38.

103. ibid., p.46.

104. ibid., p.42.

105. ibid., pp.34 and 48.

106. ibid., p.38, note 40.

107. ibid., p.57.

108. See S. Piggott, *Ruins in a Landscape*, 1976, p.129.

109. cf. 'Enquiry', p.52.

110. ibid., p.46. For the long view, see Ramsay's *View of Horace's Farm* (Catalogue: Ramsay 2) and More's *View near Horace's Villa* (Catalogue: More 2). See also I. G. Brown's essay in *Archives and Excavations*, forthcoming.

111. 'Enquiry', p.57.

112. ibid., pp.34 and 48.

113. The best example of this is his irrelevant digression on the etymology of Cotiso; see ibid., p.21, note 29.

114. One might contrast the 'sharp and seductive practices' of a Thomas Jenkins; cf. S. Howard in N. T. de Grummond, *Encyclopedia*, 1996, vol.1, pp.619–20.

115. cf. 'Enquiry', p.66.

116. See B. Frischer, 'Shifting Paradigms', 1991, p.80, note 104.

117. cf. P. Rosa, 'Notizie intorno', 1857.

118. See G. Lugli, 'La villa sabina', 1926.

119. See T. D. Price, 'A Restoration', 1932.

120. cf. Z. Mari, 'La valle dell'Aniene', 1995.

6

A Note on the Text of Ramsay's 'Enquiry'

Bernard D. Frischer and Iain Gordon Brown

Three versions of Ramsay's 'Enquiry' survive. They are located in the National Library of Scotland (hereafter NLS); the Edinburgh University Library (EUL); and the Library of the University of California, Los Angeles (UCLA). All three manuscripts make reference, in their titles, to Ramsay's travels in Italy between 1775 and 1777: in no case has the title been changed to indicate that on his later visit in the early 1780s Ramsay continued to pursue the project. The manuscripts represent work done largely in the 1770s, although it is evident that they must comprehend also the results of Ramsay's topographical explorations and his thinking about the subject during his final visit to the region. Indeed, additions in Ramsay's hand in the Edinburgh University Library manuscript are dated 1782 or 1783 and refer to the personal observations on the site, or reflections on the topic in general, made in those years.

The earliest of the manuscripts, and the least polished, is the version in NLS, MS730. It is largely in Ramsay's hand and in that of his wife, who acted as amanuensis. The earlier portion of the manuscript is more or less a fair copy in her hand. Later folios indicate that she had been allotted the task of copying quotations which appear between passages of commentary or argument in her husband's autograph. Mention on f. 29 of an event in June 1777 (cf. 'Enquiry,' p. 67) gives a *terminus post quem* for the composition of at least this portion of the manuscript. Ramsay evidently returned from time to time to this original manuscript, for there are passages or insertions in his later and rather more infirm hand. All in all, it is something of a patchwork of hands and additions of varying dates. The binding is modern blue buckram. Paper size is 18.5 x 24.5 cm. The NLS manuscript was presented to the Library in 1932 by The Hon. Sir Hew Hamilton Dalrymple, sometime Vice-Chairman of the Library's Board of Trustees and Chairman of the Trustees of the National Gallery of Scotland. He had collected a number of manuscripts and sketchbooks relating to the history of Scottish art of the period. The earlier history of the manuscript is not known. The NLS manuscript is primarily interesting for the five landscape sketches by Ramsay which are bound at the end (cf. Catalogue, Ramsay 3).

The next manuscript in date is that in EUL, MS.La.III.492. It is more complete and more polished, being later than the NLS version. On the title page, the author's name was originally given as 'A.R.' At an indeterminate later date, someone added 'Allan Ramsay.' It is almost wholly written in the hand of Ramsay's wife, who died in March 1782. Ramsay later added some passages in his own hand. The manuscript retains its original grey paper-covered boards. Paper size is 19 x 23 cm. The EUL manuscript was presented to the Library under the bequest of the distinguished bookseller, librarian and collector, David Laing, who died in 1878. Laing also owned (and bequeathed to the Library) a number of important manuscripts of the elder Ramsay and the autograph life of his father by the painter, as well as drawings and sketchbooks of Allan Ramsay the Younger and Jacob More, which he bequeathed to the Royal Scottish Academy. From there these graphic works passed to the National Gallery of Scotland. All the manuscripts had been bought by Laing at the sale of the library of Sir John Murray of Henderland, Lord Murray, a Scottish judge who was the heir of General John Ramsay, the painter's son. The 'Enquiry' can be identified as lot 1527 in the Dowell and Lyon sale catalogue, Edinburgh, February 1862. From a collation of the NLS and EUL copies, we can see that from 1777 to 1783 Ramsay continued to struggle with difficulties such as the identification of the Valley of Ustica, and he also moderated his tone and degree of assertiveness on problematic points. Thus in 1777 he wrote: 'Volpi's opinion is still more foolish' (NLS ms., f. 5); but by 1783 this had become the more diplomatic 'Volpi's opinion is more foreign' (EUL ms., p.30). At first Ramsay attempted to date the composition of Odes I.17 to 'about the beginning of August' on the basis of when strawberries become available in the Licenza Valley; but in the EUL version he wisely dropped this piece of speculation.

The third, latest, and by far the best version of the text is the UCLA copy. Purchased in 1965, it has been catalogued under 'Anonymous' since then because, unlike the NLS and EUL manuscripts, it lacks Ramsay's name or initials on the title page. The shelfmark is: Bound Manuscripts, Collection 170/376, Department of Special Collections, Charles E. Young Research Library, UCLA. The manuscript contains 67 pages, which are numbered. The paper size is 29 x 23.25 cm. It is bound in half-calf over pink papered cardboard. The binding is 30 cm. high, 24.2 cm. wide, and 1.3 cm. thick. There are head- and footbands. The spine is tooled with seven compartments. "M.S." is blocked on the second compartment, and there are fleurons in the other compartments. The end-papers are of the same paper as was used for the text, as can be determined from one watermark which is just barely visible (on the paper and watermark, see below), making it all but certain that the binding (which UCLA Rare Books Librarian P. G. Naiditch independently dated as 'late eighteenth-century') and manuscript are contemporary. The provenance of the manuscript is unknown. It was accessioned by UCLA in October 1965 and attributed to Ramsay by Bernard Frischer in October 2000, immediately after it was brought to his attention by P. G. Naiditch.

Examination of the UCLA version shows that it was written by an amanuensis and fitted out with finished drawings of the illustrations he intended to use. We do not know who was responsible for the drawings, nor the identity of the amanuensis. The close association of the UCLA manuscript with Ramsay is demonstrated by two facts. There are two corrections written in pencil, very probably in the unmistakable infirm hand of Ramsay's old age. Secondly, the UCLA version is written on the same paper as the EUL copy: the Turkey Mill paper of James Whatman II, whose paper was considered the finest in England (see A. H. Shorter, *Paper Mills and Makers in England 1495–1800*, *Monumenta Chartae Papyraceae Historiam Illustrantia*, vol. VI

[Hilversum 1957] pp. 58-9, 187-88; and for the watermark [crown, horn, fleur-de-lis, and the initials GR] see nr. 198 [p. 378 with p. 268]). In view of the foregoing, we have based our text of Ramsay's 'Enquiry' on the UCLA manuscript. We thank P. G. Naiditch for bringing it to our attention; and Anne Caiger for granting us permission to publish it. Conceivably, the UCLA manuscript was Ramsay's final copy, but definite proof is lacking.

The changes between the EUL and UCLA manuscripts are few and not substantive. The UCLA version incorporates corrections to the EUL manuscript, and so is later. The UCLA copy enabled us to ensure that the text we present corresponds to Ramsay's last wishes; and it also confirms our earlier suspicion that Ramsay did not, in the end, intend to use Jacob More's views to illustrate his text.

The UCLA copy was still incomplete with respect to a trivial detail when Ramsay died: at p. 38 he has left blank the measurement of a pillar. Since the pillar in question is no longer to be found in Licenza where Ramsay saw it, the editor has had perforce to retain the blank. Ramsay's Latin was excellent, and Latinity was universal among the educated public for whom he wrote. There is no indication that he would have translated the Horatian passages and other Latin quotations. To help the modern reader who may well have little or no Latin, extended passages from Horace have been quoted in the original, followed by the English versions of Philip Francis, the most popular British translator of Horace in Ramsay's day. Translations of shorter passages and other Latin texts have been furnished by the editor. Spelling, punctuation and capitalization have been modernized. The editor's additions are indicated by square brackets. The text has been equipped by the editor with endnotes which explain points that might be obscure to the non-Classicist; and the attempt has been made to provide an update on several of the most important topics discussed by Ramsay such as, for example, the location of the Fons Bandusiae of Odes 3.13. Ramsay's own notes are printed as footnotes. Since the UCLA manuscript is thought to be Ramsay's last, we have given its pagination in the margins of the 'Enquiry', and this pagination has been used throughout in all references to the 'Enquiry' in this volume. In illustrating the 'Enquiry', we have used the UCLA drawings, wherever possible.

7

An Enquiry into
the Situation and Circumstances of
Horace's Sabine Villa
Written during travels through Italy
in the years 1775, 76, and 77

[By Allan Ramsay]

Advertisement

After writing the following Enquiry, the author, to alleviate his bodily infirmities by change of climate, and to dissipate the melancholy occasioned by the loss of one valuable part of his family, and the dispersion of others, undertook a fourth journey to Italy, Sept. 4, 1782, accompanied by his only son.[1] In the course of these wanderings, which went as far as Paestum, he passed almost the whole month of September 1783 in Count Orsini's Villa at Licenza, visiting all the places in the neighbourhood, and making new observations upon them, some of which he has incorporated with his former remarks, and others he has added, by way of notes.

Horace, the prince of the Roman lyric poets was possessed of a villa or farm   1
in the Sabina, a province more remarkable for the purity of its air, than the
fertility of its soil; and therefore not an unfit place for the residence of a man
who was both a philosopher and a poet; one who sought for health and
repose; and who found in the exercise of his genius, that pleasure which
wealth endeavours in vain to procure for its possessors. Accordingly his
fondness for this rural retreat, breaks forth in many of his poems and
particularly in an epistle (Book 1, Epistle 16) to his friend/ Quintius, where   2
he undertakes to give a detailed description of its situation in these words:[2]

> Ne perconteris, fundus meus, optime Quinti,   1
> Arvo pascat herum, an baccis opulentet olivae,
> Pomisne, an pratis, an amicta vitibus ulmo;
> Scribetur tibi forma loquaciter & situs agri.
> Continui montes; ni dissocientur opaca   5
> Valle: sed ut veniens dextrum latus aspiciat Sol,
> Laevum decendens curru fugiente vaporet.
> Temperiem laudes. quid, si rubicunda benigni
> Corna vepres & pruna ferunt? si quercus & ilex
> Multa fruge pecus, multa dominum juvat umbra?   10
> Dicas adductum propius frondere Tarentum.
> Fons etiam rivo dare nomen idoneus, ut nec
> Frigidior Thracam nec purior ambiat Hebrus,
> Infirmo capiti fluit utilis, utilis alvo.
> Hae latebrae dulces, & (jam si credis) amoenae,   15
> Incolumem tibi me praestant Septembribus horis.

Ask not, dear Quintius, if my Farm maintain
With Fruits, or Meadows, or abundant Grain,
Its wealthy Master; ask not if the Vine
Around its Bridgegroom-Elm luxuriant twine,
For I'll describe, and in loquacious Strain,
The Site and Figure of the pleasing Scene.
   A lengthened Chain of Mountains, that divide,
And open to the Sun on either Side:
The right wide spreading to the rising Day,
The left is warm'd beneath his setting Ray.
How mild the Clime, where Sloes luxurious grow,
And Blushing Cornels on the Hawthorn glow!
With plenteous acorns are my Cattle fed,
Whose various Oaks around their Master spread;
For you might say, that here Tarentum waves
Its dusky shade, and pours forth all its Leaves.
A Fountain to a Rivulet gives its Name,
Cooler and purer than a Thracian Stream,
Useful to ease an aching Head it flows,
Or when with burning Pain the Stomach glows.
Or this pleasing, this delicious soft Retreat
In Safety guards me from September's Heat.

But this description although it might very exactly paint the particular
circumstances of his farm, and the situation of its parts relative to one
another, left the reader entirely in the dark with regard to its place in the

Sabine country, which is above 40 miles in extent, nay does not even mention its being in that province. There are, indeed, other passages in his works which tend to give/farther lights; and yet, with all those helps, every writer who, after the revival of letters, undertook to illustrate the ancient geography of Italy, has given us a different opinion concerning it. Biondi, who wrote about 300 years ago, gives us as Horace's Sabine Valley, the valley under the monastery of Farfa;[3] which is, in fact, an extended plain of 15 or 20 miles, interspersed with small hills or villages. He gives the name of Mandela to Poggio Mirteto, without any authority, and that of Digentia to the Rio del Sole, which runs from Poggio Mirteto, although there are within this unbounded valley five or six rivulets which might equally claim that honour. Cluverius a very learned geographer, places this villa near Monte Libretti, which he supposes, from the likeness of the name only, to be the Mons Lucretilis, supposing the Fossa di Corese to be the Digentia, and a fountain that runs into it to be the Bandusia;[4] while Padre Volpi, in his *Latium vetus atque recens*,[5] places all Horace's possessions on the bank of the Teverone[6] directly opposite to Tivoli, and under the spot where now stands the convent of Saint Antonio.

Although the passage already cited from the Epistle to Quintius might not be sufficient to point out in what part of the Sabina this celebrated villa was situated, it was sufficient to put a negative upon all these three opinions. Horace is distinct in describing 'a close valley in the midst of hills', but the ground for many miles round Poggio Mirteto is free of every thing that can be called *continui montes*. The ground mentioned by Cluverius, Cluverius had never seen and had learned his lesson so ill from those who had informed him as to place/Monti Libretti and his Fons Blandusia on the north side of the Fossa di Corese, which in fact stand upon the south side of it, and where I found them in a little journey to that country in summer 1756. Volpi's opinion is still more foreign, for in the place he has found for this farm there is no valley at all, except we can call the deep gully in which the Teverone runs a valley, and of which the banks are in most places too steep for goats to keep their feet upon.

The first who discovered to us the true place of this valley was Holstenius;[7] who, among his short remarks upon Cluverius, has the following:

Cluv: page 672, line 38, post Fanum putre Vacunae] Rocca Giovane locus nunc dicitur. Nam isthic Vespasianus Imperator Victoriae Templum vetustate collapsum restituit, ut testatur lapis ibidem repertus.
Line 43] Nam Digentia vicus, qui nunc *Licenza*, proxima inde sequitur.[8]

without giving any farther reasons for his opinion, but rather treating it as a matter obvious, and generally known. This hint was adopted by Padre Revillas[9] in his map of the Diocese of Tivoli [see Fig.5.1], who was followed by Ameti[10] in his map of Latium and by other modern geographers. The reason that this Sabine valley had been unknown to the learned enquirers before Holstenius is to be found in Horace's own description of it: for in the last line but one, as quoted above, he calls it *latebrae*, or a lurking place; and

3

4

it so truly answers that description that a traveller may pass his whole life in travelling from town to town throughout Italy without seeing the Valley of Licenza, which Holstenius discovered to be the valley of Horace.[11] Volpi alone is inexcusable who, having received information concerning/this valley, was　　5 either so lazy as not to visit, or having seen it, was so stupid as to reject it for the sake of another situation which, with the first glance of his eye, he might have perceived to be nothing at all to the purpose.

The reasons for believing this to be the true place of Horace's Villa, though neglected by Holstenius, have been sufficiently supplied by Abate de Sanctis[12] in his dissertation entitled *La villa d'Orazio* printed at Rome 1761, and still more fully by the Abbé De Chaupy[13] in a work of three volumes octavo, written much about the same time and titled, not very correctly, *La decouverte de la maison de campagne d'Horace*, as the discovery had been made long before he was born, and as at least one half of his book is employed upon subjects which, though very interesting in themselves and very learnedly and ingeniously treated, have little or no relation to the general title of the work.

There is a strong curiosity in mankind to know the personal circumstances of those who have distinguished themselves from the rest, either by arms or by arts. We are anxious to know when and where they were born, when and where they were buried, with every occurrence of their domestic life, however unconnected with those exploits, by which they became famous. Without enquiring strictly into the useful tendency of this sort of curiosity, it is sufficient to say in its defence that it is a part of human nature; that it is most conspicuous in active and informed minds; and therefore an unfit object either for our censure or our ridicule. But the enquiry into the situation of Horace's country house has something more to claim in its favour than a bare indulgence: as it will be found that its true/situation being known, new　　6 lights will be from thence reflected upon his poetry, which has long been the delight of men of the best understandings, and will always be held in the highest esteem while there are charms in the truest pictures of nature, and the most exalted sentiments of morality, conveyed in the best chosen and happiest words.

I shall therefore, according to the order in which they commonly stand in Horace's works, select all those passages which relate to his farm, accompanying them with such explanations and remarks as my reading upon the subject, and my attentive inspection of the ground itself have enabled me to make.

Book 1, Ode 17:

> Velox amoenum saepe Lucretilem　　　1
> Mutat Lycaeo Faunus.
>
> *Pan from Arcadia's Heights descends*
> *To visit oft my rural Seat.*

Upon this passage the ancient Scholiast says, 'Lucretilis mons est in Sabinis' ('Lucretilis is a mountain in the Sabina') leaving us to find its place in the wide country of the Sabines as we may. We must therefore have recourse to other helps. Anastasius the Bibliothecarian, in his life of St. Silvester, mentions amongst the donations made by Constantine to the Church of the Saints Marcellinus and Peter the Exorcist 'possessio in territorio Sabinensi quae cognominatur ad duas Casas, sub monte Lucretio' ('an estate in the Sabine territory which is called "Near Two Houses" on the slopes of Mt. Lucretius').[14] / Cluverius makes no doubt that this Mons Lucretius of Anastasius is the same with the Lucretilis of Horace; and then, upon very slight grounds, finds it to be what is now called Monte Libretti. But it was the misfortune of Cluverius that with a very extensive knowledge of the ancient authors, he was very little acquainted with the modern face of Italy. If he had known that there was a town in it called Percile, he would have found another passage in the same life of St. Silvester, which would have led him to conjecture that the land 'Ad duas casas' and with it the Mons Lucretilis were in a part of the Sabine territory at a great distance from Monte Libretti. For we are told that the same Constantine had before that time built a church at Rome called Titulus Equitii, near the Baths of Domitian, and had endowed it with four different pieces of land which are thus described:

Fundum Valerianum in territorio Sabinensi qui praestat Solidos 40; Fundum Statianum, in territorio Sabinensi qui praestat Sol. 55. Fundum duas Casas, in territorio Sabienensi, qui praestat Sol. 40. Fundum Percilianum, in territorio Sabinensi, qui praestat Sol. 20.[15]

It is not at all probable that Constantine would endow a church at Rome with four pieces of land picked up here and there, in different parts of the Sabine country, which makes it natural to believe that they were all in the neighbourhood of Percile – which is in the most easterly part of the ancient Sabinian territory and about two miles to the north of the Valley of Licenza and consequently that the 'Ad duas Casas', with its Lucretius, or Lucretilis, were there or thereabouts. So far Cluverius might have gone in his knowledge, but he could hardly go so far / without getting farther lights. For there is no way to Percile but through the Valley of Licenza, where he would have heard that the little pleasant rivulet which waters it is called likewise Licenza, a sound which would have called to his mind the ancient Digentia with more ease than the word Libretti did Lucretilis.[16] There has been found within these 18 years near to the Convent of San Cosimato the inscription of a sepulchre belonging to a family called Valeria, and which says it was erected *on their own lands*. This ground then, which is the sort of peninsula formed by the Licenza turning eastward before it falls into the Anio, was probably the *fundus Valerianus*. From San Cosimato going up the river Licenza, we come in about a mile to a piece of ground called Lo Stazio, which Sig. Petrocchi, in an unfinished manuscript which he has left of the history of Vicovaro alleges to be the *fundus Statianus* from a family called Statius which anciently possessed it; and supposes the following inscription[17] now built into the wall of the staircase of the Villa Bolognetti to relate to them.[18]

MVNATIA ST.F
C. MVNATIVS
D. L. PAMPHIL
IN AGR. P. XIIX

I insert it here only because it belongs to Horace's neighbourhood, believing that ST stands for SEXTI, or any other praenomen and not for *Statii*, which is a well known family name.

Continuing our course northward along the west side of the rivulet, we pass for/about a quarter of a mile through a strait formed by the hills near Rocca Giovane, after which we come into a very beautiful valley of an oval form: on the West side of which is a hill, part of Monte Gennaro, higher and more fertile than those on the east side, and which is situated about halfway between Lo Stazio and Percile. So situated, there is great ground to believe that it is the 'Lucretius' of Athanasius; and that the land immediately under it is the 'Fundus ad duas Casas' given by Constantine to the church of Saints Peter and Marcellinus. What helps very much to confirm this conjecture is that this land is now called by the country people 'Le vigne di San Pietro' without their being able to give any reason for the appellation. And there is, moreover, hard by upon the side of this hill (which I will now venture to call the Lucretilis) a little chapel and hermitage which is still called 'La Madonna delle Case'.

We are obliged to the Abbé De Chaupy for this second quotation from Anastasius, which had escaped the diligence of Cluverius – his being so unacquainted with this part of the country that the still existing town of Percile was equally unknown to him with the 'Ad duas Casas.' The Abbé, however has in his turn quoted imperfectly in having omitted the several yearly valuations which Anastasius has given us of the lands – by which omission we are left in doubt whether the Bibliothecarian had not blunderously assigned the same land called 'Ad duas Casas' to two different churches during the same reign. But this doubt vanishes upon looking into the original text, as there we find that besides the one being called a *possessio* or estate, and the other only *fundus* or farm; the *possessio* is rated at 200 solidi, while the *fundus*/is only 40. Horace, indeed, gives his land only the title of *fundus*, a word employed by him in many places of his works to signify a small piece of land. But this must only be understood as a modest expression, as when he says: *mihi parva rura* (*Odes* 2.16.37: 'my small farm') and, *mihi me reddentis agelli* (*Epist.* 1.14.1: 'of the small field that restores me to myself') with other suchlike phrases, which he uses in a comparative view of his own estate with those of the great men of Rome with whom he lived familiarly. Upon another occasion, when he meant to express his contentment with his situation and circumstances, he says that he had only wished for a *modus agri non ita magnus* but that he was in actual possession of what was *auctius et melius'* (*Sat.* 2.6.1–4: 'This is what I prayed for: a measure of land not so very large … The gods have given me something bigger and better') – and such it appears to have been by several circumstances mentioned by him, and which I shall have occasion to take notice of in the course of these remarks. It is

9

10

probable that the whole of this *possessio*, which including the *fundus* was valued in Constantine's time at 240 solidi, had belonged to Horace and had continued to be part of the Emperor's private domain from the time that Horace bequeathed it to Augustus by a nuncupatory will, as we are told by the ancient author of his life. The church built by Constantine to Saints Peter and Marcellinus was built in a place called 'Inter duas Lauros', at the third mile from Rome on the Via Labicana. Bosius[19] finds its catacombs and other remains at a place called the Tor Pignattara, or sepulchre of Santa Helena, now belonging to the Chapter of St. John Lateran. At what time or by what means the Sabine lands were disjoined from this old church, I have not yet learnt. But by a purchase from Count Orsini it now belongs to the/Prince Borghese, except that particular spot called the Vigne di San Pietro, where Horace's house stood, which now pays its rent to the parish church of Licenza.[20]

11

> Inpune totum per nemus   (*Odes* 1.17.5)
>
> *In fearless Safety graze my wandering Flocks,*
> *In safety, through the woody Brake*

This wood is frequently mentioned by Horace's works. I shall defer my remarks upon it till I come to Book 2, Sat. 6.[21]

> arbutos
> quaerunt latentis   (*Odes* 1.17.5–6)
>
> *The latent Shrubs and Thyme explore*

The Lucretilis produces a great variety of shrubs, but, from the word *latentes*, I suppose that Horace means by *arbutos*, strawberries, of which there is great plenty, but which are seldom ripe enough to be eaten till about the middle of July, six weeks after they cease to appear in the market at Rome.

> Utcumque dulci, Tyndari, fistula
> Valles, et Usticae cubantis
> Levia personuere saxa.   (*Odes* 1.17.10–12)
>
> *For when the Vales wide-spreading round,*
> *The sloping Hills, and polish'd Rocks*
> *With his harmonious Pipe resound*

This passage has very much perplexed the modern commentators and geographers. Most of them seem to take Ustica[22] to be the name of Horace's farm, and not knowing what to make of the words *laevia saxa*, when applied to a valley, some have supposed them to mean the smooth hewn stones of which his house might have been built. But we have no instance amongst the ancient Romans of a proper name being/given to any gentleman's country house, which, when not named after the proprietor, always received its title from some district, or known town, in the neighbourhood: such as Villa Tusculana, Villa Albana, Villa Formiana, or else such a one's Tusculanum, Albanum, or Formianum. Nor can we easily conceive that the walls of a small house, such as Horace's is supposed to be, could produce any echo. The ancient Scholiast says:

12

Ustica nomen Montis et Vallis in Sabinis. Cum autem cubantem suaviter dixit ad resupinam regionem attendens. Sic enim in *Epistolis*: Continui montes nisi dissocientur opaca Valle. Cubantis, depressae: ut—'Megarosque sinus, Thapsumque jacentem' [Virgil, *Aeneid* 3.689].[23]

But here our Scholiast is of very little authority, as he appears to have no knowledge of the place or its circumstances beyond what he had picked up from passages of Horace and Virgil, which were they sufficient, lie at this time as open to us moderns as to him. His notion of Ustica being both a mountain and a valley seems to have had its rise from the above words of the ode itself taken up by him with very little grammatical accuracy, as Horace gives us *valles* in the plural number.

The best commentary upon this passage in Horace is to be found in the present Valley of Licenza. In reading the words *laevia saxa* which resounded with the pipe, I had, all my life, formed an idea of living rocks of considerable magnitude; which by the help of valleys, or recesses, adjoining to them performed this mimic function. Accordingly upon coming into the middle of the Valley of Licenza, I looked about for some place which might correspond to the image I had formed in my mind and soon observed at the north end of the valley some rocky ground, and / particularly one rock, perpendicular on   13 the east side, upon which is built the little village called Licenza, probably not its ancient name but taken from the rivulet called Licenza which runs by the bottom of it, and which is no other than the ancient Digentia, a little softened in the pronunciation. I observed likewise other deep recesses to the west of this rock and was satisfied that this rock was the Ustica, and these recesses the valleys mentioned in the ode, as uniting to produce the echo. Of these recesses or valleys there are three. The most easterly is that which is to the east of the rock of Licenza, and through which passes that branch of the Digentia called La Risecca which has its source from Percile. The next is to the west of the hill of Civitella and through which runs another branch of the Digentia called La Maricella. The third is that close valley of Fonte Bello, of which I shall have occasion to treat more particularly.

With regard to the *Usticae cubantis*, the old Scholiast does not seem to have accurately performed his function of grammarian in assigning the same meaning to *jacens* and *cubans*, as the one means in the best authors 'lying', and the other 'reclining'. The epithet of *reclining* may tolerably well suit the hill of Licenza which is of a sloping shape; and the whole hill though high with respect to the plain, is low with respect to the hills behind, and on each side of it, to a degree that will surprise any one who views it from Civitella.[24] /

Hic in reducta valle caniculae   14
Vitabis aestus   (*Odes* 1.17.17–18)

Here shall You tune Anacreon's Lyre
Beneath a shady mountain's Brow ...
Far from the burning Dog-Star's Rage

Of all the various circumstances which concur in pointing out the Vigne di San Pietro to have been the place where Horace's house stood, there is none that appears to me more satisfactory than that of finding at one corner of it a valley which perfectly answers the description given in this ode. His ground is bounded on the north by a clear stream, now called Fonte Bello, which intersects some very pleasant meadow ground after having issued from a deep dark valley or ravine between Mount Lucretilis and another hill almost equally high to the north of it called Monte Cucuzzo. The source of this stream is from a hole in a rock, about three quarters of a mile high in the valley, from whence it falls so plentiful and clear as to have been taken by some learned people for the Fons Blandusiae. It then runs, forming a great number of small cascades, eastward through this valley which is so deep as never to feel the rays of the sun at noon day, except about the summer solstice, leaving a little flat ground, 20, 30 or 40 feet on each side, of which that on the south side of the stream naturally belonged to Horace. It is a most singular spot of ground, and Horace could not have invited his mistress to a more delicious one for this time of year, which appears to be the beginning of August, or to one more retired from disturbance. /

15   Ode 22:

Namque me silva lupus in Sabina,
Dum meam canto Lalagen, & ultra   10
Terminum curis vagor expeditus,
     fugit inermem:

For musing on my lovely Maid
While careless in the Woods I stray'd,
A Wolf – how dreadful – cross'd my Way,
Yet fled – he fled from his defenceless Prey:

Concerning the wood and boundary here mentioned, see remarks upon Satire 6, [Book 2].

Book 2, Ode 11:

Cur non sub alta vel platano, vel hac
Pinu jacentes sic temere, & rosa
     Canos odorati capillos,   15
Dum licet, Assyriaque nardo
Potamus uncti? dissipat Euius
Curas edacis. quis puer ocius
     Restinguet ardentis Falerni
Pocula praetereunte lympha?   20

Thus beneath this lofty Shade,
Thus in careless Freedom laid,
While Assyrian Essence sheds
Liquid Fragrance on our Heads,
While we lie with Roses crown'd,
Let the cheerful Bowl go round:
Bacchus can our Cares controul,
Cares that prey upon the Soul.
Who shall from the passing Stream

Quench our wine's Falernian Flame,
Who the vagrant Wanton bring,
Mistress of the lyric String,
With her flowing Tresses ty'd,
Careless like a Spartan Bride.

There are many rural images in Horace's works which seem to ordinary readers to have been drawn from the general face of Nature, but which upon closer examination, will be found to be only 'studies', as the landscape painters call them, taken from his own estate. The above passage is plainly / one of those. Hirpinus to whom it is addressed, appears to have been at the time his guest, and he is here pointing out certain objects very near, of which he himself was particularly fond. The 'pine' here mentioned[25] is probably the same which he dedicates to Diana, Book 3, Ode 22, and which he tells us was just above his house:

16

Inminens villae tua pinus esto

To Thee I consecrate the Pine
Which nodding waves my Villa round.

and the *lympha* is probably that fountain or stream, said in Satire 6 [Book 2] to be near his dwelling:

tecto vicinus jugis aquae fons (*Sat.* 2.6.2)

and near the house a spring of never-failing water

and which is now called by the peasants Fonte Ratini.

It would be tedious to take notice of all the passages upon which such a remark might be made; but it may be observed, in general, that all his rural images are taken from a country better stored with rocks, trees, and fountains than with more marketable goods. His description of a river in its placid and enraged state, though it will apply to various rivers, applies in every circumstance to the Digentia, with a peculiar propriety.

     caetera fluminis
Ritu feruntur, nunc medio alveo
Cum pace delabentis Etruscum   35
   In mare, nunc lapides adesos
Stirpisque raptas & pecus & domos
Volventis una, non sine montium
   Clamore vicinaeque silvae;
   Cum fera diluvies quietos /   40
Inritat amnis   (*Odes* 3.29.33–41)   17

The rest is all beyond our Power,
And like the changeful Tiber flows,
Who now beneath his Banks subsides,
And peaceful to his native Ocean glides,
But when descends a sudden Shower
And wild provokes his silent Flood,
The Mountains hear the Torrent roar,
And Echoes shake the neighbouring Wood,

Then swollen with Rage He sweeps away
Uprooted Trees, Herds, Dwellings to the Sea.

See remarks upon the word *Digentia*, Epistle 18 [Book 1].

Book 2, Ode 13:

> Illum, ô, nefasto te posuit die   1
> Quicumque primum, & sacrilega manu
> Produxit, arbos, in nepotum
> Perniciem, opprobriumque pagi;

> *Whoever rais'd and planted Thee,*
> *Unlucky and pernicious Tree,*
> *In Hour accurs'd with impious Hand*
> *(Thou Bane and Scandal of my Land)*

Concerning this tree, the fall of which was like to have killed him, see again Ode 16 [Book 2].[26]

Pagus means a district of land composed of several farms and is probably the origin of the Italian word *paese*.[27] The present country people of Italy often use *paese* to express a village, and the French *pais*. It is here put to signify Horace's own estate, and is so used in Book 3 Ode 18 where he promises a festival in celebration of the Faunalia:

> Festus in pratis vacat otioso   11
>   Cum bove *pagus*:

> *When through Winter's Gloom thy Day*
> *Festal shines, the Peasants play*
> *On the grassy-matted Soil,*
> *Round their Oxen, free from Toil.*

see further remarks upon this word, Epistle 18 [Book 1].

Ode 16 [Book 2]:

> mihi parva rura   37

> *gives me a small farm*

18   Horace in this and in other passages mentions his/land property as being small; but it is when he takes occasion to contrast his situation in life with that of very rich men, as in this ode:

> Te greges centum, Siculaeque circum
> Mugiunt vaccae; tibi tollit hinnitum
> Apta quadrigis equa; te bis Afro   35
>   Murice tinctae
>   Vestiunt lanae: mihi parva rura, &
> Spiritum Graiae tenuem Camenae
> Parca non mendax dedit, et malignum
>   Spernere volgus.   40

An hundred bleating Flocks are thine,
Around Thee graze thy lowing Kine;
Neighing the Mares invite the Reins,
Thy Robes the double Purple stains;
To Me, not unindulgent Fate
Bestow'd a rural, calm Retreat,
With Art to tune the Roman Lyre,
To warm the Song with Grecian Fire,
And scorn, in conscious Virtue proud,
The worthless Malice of the Crowd.

Concerning what may be learnt or conjectured about the real extent of his lands, see the remarks upon Sat. 6 [Book 2].

Ode 18 [Book 2]:

     nec potentem amicum
Largiora flagito,
  Satis beatus unicis Sabinis,
Truditur dies die, etc.   15

My Patron's Gift, my Sabine Field
Shall all its rural Plenty yield,
And happy in that rural store,
Of Heaven and Him I ask no more.
  Day presses on the Heals of Day

By these words ['unicis Sabinis', 'my single Sabine estate'] we learn that Horace had as Villa but his Sabine one.

Book 3, Ode 1:

Cur invidendis postibus, & novo/   45
Sublime ritu moliar atrium?   19
Cur valle permutem Sabina
Divitias operosiores?

On Columns, rais'd in modern Style,
Why should I plan the lofty Pile
To rise with envied State?
Why, for a vain, superfluous Store,
Which would encumber me the more,
Resign my Sabine Seat?

Some readers have imagined that the poet was here deliberating whether he should exchange his Sabine estate for a richer one somewhere else; but this I do not apprehend to be his meaning. He seems rather to have formed a project of rebuilding his house in a grand manner, with pillars and other expensive ornaments of architecture, and then checks himself by saying: 'Why should I change the rural simplicity of my Sabine valley for vain magnificence, which would be attended with more trouble than comfort.' The word 'Sabine' seems by several passages in Horace, and other Roman writers to have been employed to convey an idea of honest and industrious poverty.

Odes 4 [Book 3]:

> Vester, Camenae, vester in arduos
> Tollor Sabinos   22
>
> *Yours, I am ever yours, harmonious Nine,*
> *Whether I joy in Tibur's Vale supine;*
> *Whether I climb the Sabine Mountain's Height*

Horace's farm, though in a valley, stood very high with respect to the sea, as may be known by the course of the water. For the Digentia runs through it into the Anio, which runs rapidly till it falls down a very high hill forming the great cascade at Tivoli from whence it finds its course into the Tiber./

20   Ode 8 [Book 3]:

> Martiis caelebs quid agam Calendis,   1
> Quid velint flores – etc.
>
> *What should I, a bachelor, do on the first day of March;*
> *what do the flowers mean*

This ode was written at his country house on the occasion of a sacrifice and feast which he gave annually on the first of March in commemoration of his being divinely preserved, as mentioned in Book 2, Ode 13, from the fall of one of his own trees; and appears to have been presented to Maecenas upon his coming to partake of this rural festival.

> Voveram dulcis epulas, et album
> Libero caprum, prope funeratus
>   Arboris ictu.   8
>
> *When on my Head a Tree devoted fell,*
> *And almost crush'd me to the Shades of Hell,*
> *Grateful I vow'd to him, who rules the Vine,*
> *A joyous Banquet, while beneath his Shrine*
> *A now-white Goat should bleed*

It is somewhat particular that the poet having confessed Book 2, Ode 17, that he owed his preservation to Faunus should here make his thanksgiving sacrifice to Bacchus:

> Me truncus inlabsus cerebro
>   Sustulerat, nisi Faunus ictum
> Dextra levasset, Mercurialium
> Custos virorum.   (*Odes* 2.17.27–30)
>
> *A Tree, when falling on my Head,*
> *Had surely crush'd me to the Dead,*
> *But Pan, the Poet's Guardian, broke*
> *With saving Hand, the destin'd Stroke.*

I know not how to reconcile this seeming inconsistency except by supposing him to have considered Faunus as only an inferior agent to Bacchus, and that by thanking the principal, the business was more completely finished. The

idea of the satyrs and fauns/ being subordinate to Bacchus seems to be   21
expressed in Epistle 19 [Book 1], where he says:

> — ut male sanos,
> Adscripsit Liber Satyris Faunisque poetas   4
>
> *Among his motley Fold,*
> *Satyrs and Fawns, when Bacchus had enrol'd*

> Occidit Daci Cotisonis agmen   (Odes 3.8.18)
>
> *No more let Rome your anxious Thoughts engage,*
> *The Dacian falls beneath the Victor's Rage*

Although it be foreign to the professed subject of these remarks, I cannot take
leave of this ode without observing that the name of this Dacian chief is a
composition of two Teutonic words very common in Germany and England,
Gottes Sohn, or 'son of God'. Nothing is so easy as the change of a G into a C
either in writing or pronunciation, and it is here the only change; for the
Teutons had their genitive in *is* as well as the Latins, so that *Cotisonis agmen*
is in English 'Godson's army'. Suetonius, in his life of Augustus, calls this
northern chieftain King of the Getae.[28]

Book 3, Ode 13:

> O fons Bandusiae, splendidior vitro
> Dulci digne mero, non sine floribus,
>   Cras donaberis haedo;
>   Cui frons turgida cornibus
> Primis & Venerem & proelia destinat,   5
> Frustra: nam gelidos inficiet tibi
>   Rubro sanguine rivos,
>   Lascivi suboles gregis./
>   Te flagrantis atrox hora Caniculae   22
> Nescit tangere: tu frigus amabile   10
>   Fessis vomere tauris
>   Praebes, & pecori vago.
> Fies nobilium tu quoque fontium,
> Me dicente cavis inpositam ilicem
>   Saxis, unde loquaces   15
>   Lymphae desiliunt tuae.

Bandusia, that dost far surpass
The shining Face of polish'd Glass,
To Thee, the Goblet, crown'd with Flowers,
The rich Libation justly pours;
A Goat, whose Horns begin to spread,
And bending arm his swelling Head,
Whose Bosom glows with young Desires,
Which War or kindling Love inspires,
Now meditates his Blow in vain,——
His Blood shall thy fair Fountain stain.
When the fierce Dog-Star's fervid Ray

Flames forth, and sets on Fire the Day,
To vagrant Flocks, that range the Field,
You a refreshing Coolness yield,
Or to the labour-wearied Team
Pour forth the Freshness of thy Stream.
Soon shalt thou flow a noble Spring,
While in immortal verse I sing
The Trees, which spread the Rocks around,
From whence thy pratling Waters bound.

This Ode is addressed to the Naiad of the spring, or, as it is termed by Juvenal, Satire 3, the *numen aquae*.[29] In the common editions of Horace this nymph is called *Blandusia*, the transcribers having been probably misled by the idea that it had some relation to the Latin word *blandus*. But Doctor Bentley, whose text I generally follow has, upon the authority of the most ancient manuscripts, left out the *L*.[30] It was probably a word of Greek origin, and at first Pandosia (all-giving) compounded of πᾶς and δίδωμι, and turned into *Bandusia* by a change in two letters, which is very easy and common.

The ancient Scholiast formerly cited says 'Blandusiae fonte sacrificium promittit in agro Sabino, ubi villam possidebat',[31] an authority which, because it was ancient, has misled every enquirer and made them consider this fountain as one of the marks by which Horace's Sabine villa was to be found, so that where they did not find a copious fountain falling from a hollow rock they concluded themselves/to be upon a wrong scent. But Horace nowhere said that this fountain was in the Sabine country, and a little attention to the several passages in the ancient Scholiasts relative to this villa ought to have convinced the learned that they were mere grammarians, and that they knew nothing at all of the situation or circumstances of those places but what they learned, or conjectured, from the book they had undertaken to explain. The Abbé Chaupy, who had himself been very much puzzled with this difficulty, was the first who found the solution of it by finding the true Fons Bandusia in a place where nobody could ever have thought of looking for it: for he found it in one of the Pope's Bulls. He had been tempted, by meeting with a copy uncommonly cheap, to purchase the *Bullarium*, or collection of Bulls in 30 volumes folio,[32] and before he put them up in his shelves, happening to toss over the leaves of the first volume to see what sort of matter it might in general contain, his eye accidentally caught the word *Bandusium*. This could not fail to raise the Abbé's curiosity, so he sat down attentively to read the page before him, and found that it contained a Bull, or charter of confirmation, from [Pope] Paschal II, AD 1103, to the monastery of S. Maria of Bantium in Apulia, of all their own rights and possessions, among which are specified, 'Ecclesiam S. Salvatoris cum aliis de Castello Bandusii', and a little lower, 'Ecclesiam Sanctorum Martyrum Gervasii et Protasii in Bandusino fonte apud Venusiam'.[33] Here was not only a fountain of the same name with that which had been in vain sought for, but a fountain of such name and consideration as to serve as a landmark, and at the same time so linked in the Bull itself with other places with which Horace/was known to have been connected as to

23

24

leave little or no doubt of its being the same fountain which he had celebrated in his ode. To a man like the Abbé, who, with the vivacity peculiar to the natives of the Garonne, was still more animated by an enthusiastic love of classic ground, this information was sufficient to make him undertake a journey of above 200 miles upon the Via Appia, of which he has given us a very learned account containing many discoveries of his own and many corrections of the writings of other authors upon that subject. Upon his arrival at Venosa, the ancient Venusia, he easily found out that the church of St. Gervasio and the fountain mentioned in the Bull were at a place called Palazzo about 6 miles beyond Venosa upon the Appian Way leading to Brindisi. But, although he found the spot where by the testimony of the people of the country the fountain and the church of St. Gervasio have formerly been, he had the mortification to find that the church was removed from the bottom to the top of the hill; and that the famous fountain had been by sacrilegious hands destroyed, as far as a fountain is susceptible of destruction. It seems the monastery of Bantium had given the ground in which this fountain is situated to a lay proprietor to be held of them by a feu, or perpetual lease; and that the new proprietor finding himself hampered and embarrassed by a servitude which his neighbours had upon this fountain, tried to free himself from the servitude by getting rid of the fountain itself, which he effected by conducting the stream underground out of his own territory and then filling up the basin with the earth of the rising ground, of which the rock made a part. But though this / might be effectual for his purpose in preventing his neighbours from entering his ground, the water still remains, turning the ground through which it formerly ran clear, into a sort of bog, and from thence breaks out at some distance on the highway in a clear and copious spring where it is called by the country people 'fontana rotta', or the broken fountain. What proves the greatness and beauty of this fountain in its original state is that the place is still called by the country people 'Fontana grande', to distinguish it from two other fountains of Palazzo which are very copious and which had been rendered little only by the comparison. The Abbé Chaupy, moreover, tells us that from the traditional idea of this fountain, still fresh in the place, the present proprietor, the Prince of S. Gervasio, was endeavouring to recover it for the purpose of turning a mill which he intended to erect, and he was informed by Michele Lavoro employed by the Prince in this digging – and who cannot be suspected of knowing much about Horace or his odes – that they had met in digging with many great stones and roots of trees which he supposed formerly to have belonged to the fountain. Such has been the fate of the *Fons Bandusiae*, and Horace expressed himself with a truly prophetic spirit when he said:

> Fies nobilium tu quoque fontium
> Me dicente   (*Odes* 3.13.13–14)

> *Soon shalt thou flow a noble Spring,*
> *While in immortal Verse I sing*

For notwithstanding that these illiterate barbarians have rooted out its 'ever-

25

green oak', have levelled its 'hollow rocks', have mutilated every feature by which it was to be distinguished from vulgar fountains, and have – as it were – buried it alive; yet as Addison says, it will:/

26
> — *run forever by the Muse's skill*
> *And in the smooth description murmur still.*

But, although Horace nowhere intimates that this fountain Bandusia made any part of his Sabine farm, yet it is manifest from the general train of the ode that he was particularly connected with it. Let us endeavour to find out how close this connection might be. Horace was by birth a Venusine, that is a native of that district of land which belonged to the Roman Colony of Venusia, as he tells us, Book 2, Sat. 1, and which was neither altogether in Apulia, or altogether in Lucania, but made out of parts of both:

> — Lucanus an Appulus, anceps:
> Nam Venusinus arat finem sub utrumque colonus   35

> *whether Lucania or Apulia claim*
> *the Honor of my Birth, for on the Lands*
> *By Samnites once possest, Venusium stands*

by which word *colonus* is to be understood not barely a husbandman but a colonist.

> Missus ad hoc, pulsis (vetus est ut fama) Sabellis,
> Quo ne per vacuum Romano incurreret hostis;
> sive quod Appula gens, seu quod Lucania bellum
> Incuteret violenta   (*Sat.* 2.1.36–39)

> *A forward Barrier, as old Tales relate,*
> *To stop the Course of War and guard the State.*

Now this Fons Bandusinus not only appears by its situation to be within the Venusian territory but is so expressly said in the Pope's Charter, written at a time when the ancient Roman names of towns and districts were generally well known by the churchmen, the only scholars and lawyers of those days.
  In this neighbourhood likewise our poet passed his infant years:/

27
> Me fabulosae Volture in Appulo,
> Altricis extra limen Apuliae,   10
>   Ludo fatigatumque somno,
> Fronde nova puerum palumbes

> Texere: mirum quod foret omnibus,
> Quicumque celsae nidum Acherontiae,
>   Saltusue Bantinos, & arvum   15
>   Pingue tenent humilis Ferenti:

> Ut tuto ab atris corpore viperis
> Dormirem & ursis; ut premerer sacra
>   Lauroque, conlataque myrto,
>   Non sine Dîs animosus infans.   (*Odes* 3.4.9–20)

> *Fatigu'd with Sleep, and youthful Toil of Play,*
> *When on a Mountain's Brow reclined I lay*
> *Near to my natal Soil, around my Head*

The fabled woodland Doves a verdant Foliage spread;
Matter, be sure, of Wonder most profound
To all the grazing Habitants around,
Who dwell in Acherontia's airy Glades,
Amid the Bantian Woods, or low Ferentum's Meads.
By Snakes of Poison black, and Beasts of Prey,
That thus, in dewy Sleep, unharm'd I lay;
Laurels and Myrtle were around me pil'd,
Not without guardian Gods and animated Child.

All this scene, faithfully painted after the life by Horace, is still to be seen from Palazzo – with the three towns last mentioned still subsisting in a semi-circle to the south, under the names of Acerenza, Banzi, and Forenza. And it is worthy of remark that along with the *Fons Bandusinus apud Venusiam* two of these towns – *Acherontia* and *Bantium* – are mentioned in the Pope's bull already cited.*

The fountain Bandusia being thus situated in a place where Horace must have had frequent occasions of seeing it, and probably of playing by it when a boy, might have been sufficient to have entitled it ever after to his affectionate regard and remembrance. But the ode itself carries us a little farther, for it is there manifest that at the time of writing he had his residence upon the spot of his announcing/the sacrifice to the fountain for the next day:

29

---

*Monasterium Bantinum in Apulia Acherentia
Diocesis sub protectione sedis Apostolicae
recipitur, eique bona omnia confirmantur./
Paschalis Episcopus servus servorum Dei
dilecto in Christo filio Abbate coenobii
S. Maria, quod apud Bantium si[-]
tum est, ejusque successoribus
regulariter promovendis,
in perpetuum.

28

—unde tibi tuisque successoribus ad praedictae Domus regimen auctoritatem concedimus confirmamus siquidem vobis Coenobium ipsum et omnia, quae ad illud pertinent monasteria sive cellas cum suis pertinentiis videlicet Ecclesiam S. Salvatoris cum aliis Ecclesiis de Castello Bandusii: item Ecclesiam S. Nicolai cum casali suo: Ecclesiam S. Mariae de Cacunigio, S. Maria de Sala, S. Maria de Servaritiae cum casali suo, Sancti Petri de Monachis, S. Michaelis de Monte Salvolo cum Ecclesiis et pertinentiis suis, Ecclesiam S. Maria de Calapano, S. Petri in Gennano cum Casali suo, Ecclesiam S. Vitalis in oppido Gentiano S. Michaelis in loco Firminiano cum villanis suis. Ecclesiam Sanctae Anastasiae apud Acheruntam, cum Ecclesiis ad eam pertinentibus; Ecclesiam sanctorum Martyrum Gervasii et Protasii in Bandusino fonte apud Venusiam, Ecclesiam Sancta Luciae, etc.

('The monastery of Banzi in the Diocese of Acerenza in Apulia is received into the protection of the Holy See, and all its possessions are guaranteed to it.*

Bishop Paschal II, servant of the servants of God to our beloved son in Christ the Abbot of the monastery of S. Maria, which is located at Banzi, and to his regularly appointed successors, in perpetuity:

*—To you and to your successors in the administration of the aforesaid religious house we concede authority and we confirm to you the monastery itself and all the monasteries or hermitages that belong to it with their possessions, namely: the Church of S. Salvatore with the other churches of the Castellum of Bandusium; likewise the Church of St Nicholas with its estate; the Church of S. Maria di Cacunigio, S. Maria della Sala, S. Maria de Servaritia with its estate, S. Pietro de Monachis, S. Michael de Monte Salvolo with its churches and possessions, the Church of S. Maria de Calapano, of S. Pietro in Gennanum with its estate, the Church of S. Vitale in the town of Genzano, of S. Michael in the locality of Firminium with its peasants, the church of St. Anastasia in Acerenza with its churches and possessions; the church of the Holy Martyrs Gervasius and Protasius at the Bandusian Spring in Venosa, the church of S. Lucia, etc.')[34]

Cras donaberis haedo   (*Odes* 3.13.3)

Tomorrow you will be presented with a kid.

Nor could this be an accidental residence in a hired lodging or at a friend's house: for, in that case, he must have sent to market to purchase a kid for the promised ceremonies, which is contrary to the nature of them. Sacrifices to rural divinities such as Pan, Bacchus, Ceres, and Faunus were always performed by the proprietors or cultivators of land to obtain the continuance of their protection; and the victims were always furnished out of the herds or other produce of those lands, which were supposed to have prospered by their tutelage. This practice and the religious principle upon which it was founded is very clearly set forth by Horace himself in many places, particularly in his ode to Faunus, the 18th of the Third Book:

> Faune, Nympharum fugientum amator,   1
> Per meos finis & aprica rura
> Lenis incedas, abeasque parvis
>   Aequus alumnis:
> Si tener pleno cadit haedus anno,   5
> Larga nec desunt Veneris sodali
> Vina craterae; vetus ara multo
>   Fumat odore.
> Ludit herboso etc.

> *Faunus, who with eager Flame*
> *Chase the Nymphs thy flying Game,*
> *If a tender Kid distain,*
> *Each returning Year, thy Fane,*
> *If with Wine we raise the Soul*
> *(Social Venus loves the Bowl)*
> *If thy dedicated Shrine*
> *Smoke with odours,—Breath divine!*
> *Gently traverse o'er my Bounds,*
> *Gently through my sunny Grounds,*
> *Gracious to my fleecy Breed,*
> *Sporting oe'r the flowery Mead.*
> *See my Flocks in sportive Vein*
> *Frisk it o'er the verdant Plain*

and in that to Phidyle, the 23rd of the Third Book:

> Caelo supinas si tuleris manus,   1
> Nascente Luna, rustica Phidyle;
>   Si ture placaris & horna/
>   Fruge Lares, avidaque porca;
> Nec pestilentem sentiet Africum   5
> Fecunda vitis, nec sterilem seges
>   Robiginem, aut dulces alumni
>   Pomifero grave tempus anno.
> Nam quae nivali etc.

> *If on the new-born Moon, with Hands supine,*
> *My Phidyle, laborious Rustic, prays;*
> *If she with Incense, and a ravening Swine,*

30

And yearly Fruits her Household Gods appease,
Nor pestilential storm shall smite her Vines,
Nor barren Mildew shall her Harvests fear,
Nor shall her Flocks, when the sad Year declines
Beneath its Fruitage, feel th'autumnal Air.

We find likewise that the country people put themselves as well as their property under the protection of those rural divinities: *Pan curat oves, oviumque magistros.*[35] In Ode 17 of the second book, Horace imputes his preservation from the fall of his own tree to the care of Faunus; and, upon the same account in Ode 8 of the third book, performing a sacrifice to Bacchus with all that festivity which made a principal part of the ancient Roman religion:

Martiis caelebs quid agam Calendis,	1
Quid velint flores & acerra turis	
Plena, miraris, positusque carbo in	
Cespite vivo,	
Docte sermones utriusque linguae.	5
Voveram dulcis epulas, & album	
Libero caprum, prope funeratus	
Arboris ictu.	
Hic dies, anno redeunte, festus	
Corticem adstrictum pice dimovebit/	10
Amphorae, fumum bibere institutae	
Consule Tullo.	
Sume, Maecenas, cyathos amici	
Sospitis centum; & vigiles lucernas	
Perfer in lucem: procul omnis esto	15
Clamor & ira.	
Mitte civilis etc.	

31

In either Language skill'd, my Lord, 'tis thine
To know, in Greece and Rome, the Rites divine;
And well may you these flowery Wreaths admire,
The fragrant Incense and the sacred Fire
Rais'd o'er the living Turf on this glad Day,
To which the married World their Homage pay.
When on my head a Tree devoted fell,
And almost crush'd me to the Shades of Hell,
Grateful I vow'd to him, who rules the Vine,
A joyous Banquet, while beneath his Shrine
A snow-white Goat should bleed, and when the Year
Revolving bids this festal Morn appear,
We'll pierce a Cask with mellow Juice replete,
Mellow'd with Smoke, since Tullus ruled the State.
Come then, Maecenas, and for friendship's Sake,
A Friend preserved, an hundred Bumpers take.
Come drink the watchful Tapers up To-day,
While Noise and Quarrels shall be far away.

But there is a circumstance peculiar to the sacrifice to the Fons Bandusia, which still farther narrows the circle of country worship and brings it nearer the point I have in view. Besides the deities already mentioned which were

worshipped in common by all country people, there were others of a kind
entirely local, and, as we might say *addicti glebae*, ['devoted to the sod'] such
as the divinity of a particular tree or of a particular fountain, known by the
general name of Dryads and Naiads. These were a sort of 'territorial Lares'
which did not, like the gentilitial, descend from father to son but from
proprietor to proprietor, who were consequently the only persons who might
sacrifice to them. Of this sort of worship may be found likewise an example
in Horace Book 3, Odes 22, where after having invoked Diana as 'protectress
of hills and forests' he consecrates to her a tall pine near his house and then
promised *to it* the annual sacrifice of a young boar:

> Inminens villae tua pinus esto,   5
> Quam per exactos ego laetus annos,/
> Verris obliquum meditantis ictum
>   Sanguine donem.

> *To Thee I consecrate the Pine*
> *Which nodding waves my Villa round,*
> *And here beneath the hallow'd Shrine,*
> *Yearly shall bleed a festal Swine,*
> *That meditates the side-long Wound.*

32

Upon a careful consideration of all the circumstances related above I am
impelled to believe that this Fons Bandusinus, now the property of the Prince
di San Gervasio, was once part of the small estate which Horace inherited
from his father, and which he afterwards forfeited by a most unphilosophical
attempt under the conduct of Brutus to preserve the rotten carcase of a
Republic after its soul was departed, and after the nature of things had
manifestly forbid its longer existence. The history of this will be best related
in his own words as we find them in Satire 6, Book 1 to Maecenas, and in his
Epistle to Julius Florus, Book 2, Epistle 2:

> Atqui si vitiis mediocribus ac mea paucis   65
> Mendosa est natura, alioqui recta; (velut si
> Egregio inspersos reprendas corpore naevos)
> Si neque avaritiam, neque sordis, aut mala lustra
> Objiciet vere quisquam mihi; purus & insons,
> (Ut me collaudem) si & vivo carus amicis;   70
> Causa fuit pater his: qui macro pauper agello
> Noluit in Flavî ludum me mittere; magni
> Quo pueri magnis e centurionibus orti,
> Laevo suspensi loculos tabulamque lacerto,
> Ibant octonis referentes Idibus aera: 75
> Sed puerum est ausus Romam portare, docendum/
> Artis, quas doceat quivis eques atque senator
> Semet prognatos   (*Sat.* 1.6.65–78)

33

> *If some few, trivial Faults deform my Soul*
> *(Like a fair Face when spotted with a Mole)*
> *If none with Avarice justly brand my Fame,*
> *With Sordidness, or Deeds too vile to name:*
> *If pure and innocent: if dear (forgive*
> *these little Praises) to my Friends I live,*

My Father was the Cause, who, though maintain'd
By a lean Farm but poorly, yet disdain'd
The Country-Schoolmaster, to whose low Care
The mighty Captain sent his high-born Heir
With Satchel, Copy-book and Pelf to pay
The wretched Teacher on th'appointed Day.
To Rome by this bold Father I was brought
To learn those Arts, which well-born Youth are taught

Romae nutriri mihi contigit, atque doceri
Iratus Graiis quantum nocuisset Achilles.
        Adjecere bonae paullo plus artis Athenae:
Scilicet ut possem curvo dignoscere rectum,
Atque inter silvas Academi quaerere verum.   45
Dura sed emovere loco me tempora grato;
Civilisque rudem belli tulit aestus in arma,
Caesaris Augusti non responsura lacertis.
Unde simul primum me dimisere Philippi,
Decisis humilem pennis, inopemque paterni   50
Et laris & fundi, paupertas inpulit audax
Ut versus facerem   (*Epist.* 2.2.41–52)

It was my Fortune to be bred and taught
At Rome, what Woes enrag'd Achilles wrought
To Greece: kind Athens yet improv'd my Parts
With some small Tincture of ingenious Arts,
To learn a right Line from a Curve, and rove
In search of Wisdom through the museful Grove.
But lo! the Time, destructive to my Peace,
Me rudely ravished from the charming Place;
The rapid Tide of Civil War a-main
Swept into Arms, unequal to sustain
The Might of Caesar. Dread Philippi's Field
First clipt my Wings, and taught my Pride to yield.
My Fortune ruin'd, blasted all my Views,
Bold Hunger edg'd, and Want inspir'd my Muse.
But say, what Dose could purify me, blest
With Store sufficient, should I break my Rest,
To scribble Verse?

The true situation of the Fons Bandusia and its relation to Horace being found, it will not be difficult to ascertain the period in his life at which the ode to celebrate it was composed: for it must have been after he had acquired at Rome a taste for poetry, by the study of the best Greek and Roman poets, and before he went to finish his studies at Athens. It might, not improbably, be when on his way thither, as the fountain I have described is in the straight road from Rome to Brundusium. It could not be after his return to Italy, for by that time, as he informs us he was stripped of his paternal house and land,/ so that his right of sacrificing to the fountain of Bandusia had ceased   34 together with that vanity which usually attends the possession of any thing rare or beautiful and which was probably the inspirer of the ode.

Satire 6, Book 2:

> Hoc erat in votis: modus agri non ita magnus

> *I often wish'd, I had a Farm,*
> *A decent Dwelling, snug and warm,*

Concerning the extent of Horace's Sabine estate see the remarks upon Epistle 14.

> Hortus ubi —   (*Sat.* 2.6.2)

> A garden where

This garden is mentioned in Book 4, Ode 11:

> Est mihi nonum superantis annum   1
> Plenus Albani cadus; est in horto,
> Phylli, nectendis apium coronis;

> *Phyllis, this Alban Cask is thine,*
> *Mellow'd by Summers more than nine,*
> *And in my Garden, for thy Head*
> *My Parsly-Crowns their Verdure spread;*

and again addressing himself to his *vilicus* Book 1, Ep. 14

> — invidet usum
> Lignorum & pecoris tibi calo argutus et horti.

> (*Epist.* 1.14.41–42)

> *While more refined they view with envious Eye*
> *The Gardens, Horses, Fires, that you enjoy.*

It is difficult at this time to determine on what side of Horace's house his garden lay, but I am apt to believe that it was to the northwest, still called 'Il Pomario', where there is another fountain which has been made to fall in an artificial cascade by the former Lords of Licenza. The soil about Horace's house is very good and is particularly famous for what we call the Burgemy pears, which are annually contracted for by the fruitmongers of Rome./

35
> et tecto vicinus jugis aquae fons   (*Sat.* 2.6.2)

> and a spring of never-failing water near my house

It is by this line that we are enabled to discover very nearly the precise station of Horace's house, for it informs us that it was close to a perpetual fountain. Of those indeed there are several in the valley of Licenza but none in a place very proper for houses or gardens except one. This is called by the country people 'Fonte Ratini', very probably from the word *Horati* to which they have added one of those diminutive terminations very common in their language. It rises in the side of Mons Lucretilis, now Monte Gennaro, under the most southerly of the two summits called the *Campanile*, and its situation is at present pointed out from a distance, by the means of two cypress trees, the only ones on the hill, which grow very near it.[36] Running down aslant the hill it passes near the ruins of Horace's house, and crossing the highway it falls into the Licenza about a stone's throw to the north of the mill belonging to the village of Licenza, after being rejoined by another stream, an artificial branch of the same fountain, which issues from the hill a little to the northwest of Horace's house and of which the former Counts Orsini have made a cascade by cutting down part of the rock perpendicular. Besides the general circumstances of the ground, what proves fully its being a fit place for setting down a house or villa is that there are actually still to be found there the ruins of two ancient dwellings, or of two parts of a large one. These were what probably gave the name of *duae Casae* to this place in the fourth century, which is still preserved in the name of an old hermitage or chapel on the hill above it, which is called *L'Ermitaggio delle case*. What further confirms the opinion/ of this being the *Possessio ad duas casas sub monte Lucretio* given by Constantine to the church of Santi Pietro e Marcellino is that the ground where stands these ruins, and through which runs the Fonte Ratini, is still called 'Le vigne di San Pietro', as I have already set forth in my remarks upon Book 1, Ode 17. The two remains of building stand at the distance of about 100 yards from one another. That to the east consists only of a mosaic pavement of very elegant foliage and expensive workmanship beyond what was to be expected from the simplicity professed by Horace. But this we are enabled to account for by a late discovery of leaden pipes, on one of which was to be read T. CLAUDI BURRI and on another TI. CLAVDI B.* and shew that this villa made illustrious by/ the writings of Horace had been afterwards inhabited by a no less famous man, Burrus the Commander of the Praetorian guards, and prime minister to the Emperor Nero; who having inherited this little possession from Augustus had probably either given or lent it to this great officier.[39] Whether these little remains are all the work of Burrus, or if any of them had been inhabited by Horace, will not be easy to determine at this time. But it is most probable that Burrus preserved what had belonged to the famous poet, enlarging and adorning it in a manner suitable to his own fortune, and to the increased luxury of the age he lived in.

36

37

> Et paulum silvae super his foret —   (*Sat.* 2.6.3)
>
> *Besides a little ancient Grove*

---

*We are obliged to the Abbé Chaupy for the knowledge of these inscriptions[37], which would otherwise have been before this time consigned to eternal oblivion. For, after selling the bulk of the leaden pipes, the late Arciprete of Licenza preserved the two bits containing the name of Burrus and would have transmitted them to his successor, had not, unhappily, a want of shot for killing partridges made it necessary to employ them in that service. It were to be wished that an Antiquarian Society were established at Rome, similar to that of London, but under the presidency of the Pope's Antiquary, which having a Secretary, and regular weekly meetings, might receive and register the accounts that might be sent to it of the discoveries daily made in every part of the Pope's dominions. The Pope's Antiquary is generally a learned and ingenious man, such as Sig. Ridolfo Venuti, the Abbé Winckelmann, and the present Sig. Visconti, but there are persons who would be willing to write a letter to the Secretary of a public society, where they are sure it would be read and minuted and preserved, who would not take the same pains for the private information of one single gentleman. Neither, supposing them to be willing to write, is it to be supposed that the Pope's Antiquary would singly take the trouble of reading and recording all their informations in such a manner that the Republic of Letters might, at some future period, receive any benefit from them. The public is greatly obliged to the present Pope Pius VI, and to some of his immediate predecessors for having preserved so many inscriptions in the corridors of the Vatican. But they are few in comparison with the number of those which are daily destroyed or neglected.[38]

The place of the fountain and house being found we can be at no loss to find the wood, which is here described as *above them*; that is to say to the west upon the declivity of Monte Gennaro, and, indeed, supposing the word *super* to have no regard to situation, this is the only place where it could be. In this place there has been within the memory of the persons now living at Licenza a great deal of fine wood, till by an increase of the inhabitants, this wood was mostly cut down to make place for the more profitable culture of oil, wine, and corn, chiefly Indian. In the neighbouring territory of Rocca Giovane, where the same causes have not operated the wood still subsists full of noble trees, chiefly oaks, and it was probably thereabouts that Horace met the wolf mentioned in Ode 22 of Book 1:

> Namque me silva lupus in Sabina,
> Dum meam canto Lalagen, & ultra   10
> Terminum curis vagor expeditus,
>   Fugit inermem:/

> *For musing on my lovely Maid*
> *While careless in the Woods I stray'd,*
> *A Wolf – how dreadful – cross'd my Way,*
> *Yet fled – he fled from his defenceless Prey:*

38   See, concerning this boundary, the remark on Epistle [10 of Book 1].

> Cervius haec inter vicinus garrit anilis
> Ex re fabellas —   (*Sat.* 2.6.77–78)

> *While thus we spend the social Night,*
> *Still mixing Profit with Delight,*
> *My Neighbour Cervius never fails*
> *To club his Part in pithy Tales*

In another of his epistles he likewise mentions his neighbours:

> Rident *vicini* glebas & saxa moventem.   (*Epist.* 1.14.39)

> *My Neighbours laugh to see with how much Toil*
> *I carry Stones or break the stubborn Soil*

but we are left much in the dark concerning their particular place of abode. Upon a little hill called Colle Franco on the east side of the Digentia, and from whence there is the most pleasant prospect of the valley, there were dug up some years ago a marble chariot,[40] and two Ionic columns of marble. The shafts of the pillars and the chariot were broken to pieces by the country people from the absurd hopes of finding money in them. But the capitals still exist at a blacksmith's door at the farther end of the town of Licenza. They are of elegant workmanship and shew the diameter of the pillars at the top to have been of [ ][41] inches. On the flat ground at the bottom of this hill near the rivulet – and directly opposite to that spot to be mentioned in my remarks on Epistle 14 as the portone of Horace's ground – was likewise found an altar to Jupiter, which had stood some years at the door of a peasant in Licenza to hold water for his chickens. The undermost or perhaps two undermost lines have been broken off, or disfigured. But the letters which have suffered no violence are very distinct and elegantly formed:[42]

I O M
T·COCCEIUS·FELIX·HORR
SEVIR·AUG·UXOR·AEMILIA
AMERCISI....·/

Having copied this inscription the best way I could, I left ten pauls with the   39
Arciprete of Licenza to purchase it of the proprietor,[43] and desired him to find
a place for it in Count Orsini's villa, where it might be safe for the inspection
of the learned. Perhaps these ten pauls may be the means of preserving other
inscriptions which the country people would neglect or employ in some
wretched building, turning the letters inward not to deform their wall. The
name of Cocceius[44] was very illustrious amongst the Romans, and it is to be
found in many inscriptions.*

Epistle 10 [Book 1]:

> Vivere naturae si convenienter oportet,
> Ponendaeque domo quaerenda est area primum;
> Novistine locum potiorem rure beato?
> Est, ubi plus tepeant hiemes? ubi gratior aura   15
> Leniat & rabiem Canis, & momenta Leonis,
> Cum semel accepit solem furibundus acutum?

> *Would you to Nature's Law's Obedience yield;*
> *Would you a House for Health or Pleasure build,*
> *Where there is such a situation found,*
> *As where the Country spreads its Blessings round?*
> *Where is the temperate Winter less severe?*
> *Or, when the Sun ascending fires the Year,*
> *Where breathes a milder Zephyr to assuage*
> *The Dog-Star's Fury, or the Lion's Rage?*

The whole of this epistle, though it sounds like a panegyric upon the country
in general, has a particular reference to the Sabine valley from whence it is
dated, and would not be strictly true if otherwise applied./ What he says   40
here with regard to its being warm in winter and cool in summer is
confirmed by the present inhabitants and probably arises from the manner in
which it is sheltered on all hands from winds, which in Italy sometimes blow
from the north very cold and from the south and southeast so as to be both
hot and unwholesome. It is at least certain that he was sincere in the praises
he here bestows upon this valley by his making it his place of residence,
though a valetudinarian, in all seasons of the year; as may be gathered from
various parts of his writings. In Satire 3 [Book 2] Damasippus says to him:

> Atqui voltus erat multa & praeclara minantis,
> Si vacuum tepido cepisset villula tecto.   10

> *And yet you threatened something wondrous great,*
> *When you should warm you in your Country-seat.*

---

*In summer 1783, a sepulchre was discovered on the right side of the road leading from S. Maria
Maggiore to S. Croce in Gerusalemme, very near the ancient aqueduct, containing inscriptions of the
family of Cocceius to the number of 40 or 50, all which, being of marble, were taken out and transported
into the neighbouring vineyard. This sepulchre is *in extremis Esquiliis;* and those of Maecenas and Horace
are probably not far distant.

and a little higher:

> — at ipsis
> Saturnalibus huc fugisti sobrius. ergo   5
>
> *When Saturn's jovial Feast,*
> *Seem'd too luxuriant to your sober Taste,*
> *Hither you fled.*

that is to say, about the middle of December, and we find him (Book 3, Ode 18) promising a sacrifice to Faunus and a feast to all his country vassals, upon the Faunalia, the fifth of that month:

> Cum tibi Nonae redeunt Decembres: 10
> Festus in pratis vacat otioso
>   Cum bove pagus:
>
> *When through the Winter's Gloom thy Day*
> *Festal shines, the Peasants play*
> *On the grassy-matted Soil,*
> *Round their Oxen, free from Toil.*

Here likewise we find him in the greatest summer heat inviting Tyndaris to partake of his refreshment, Book 1, Ode 17:

> Hic in reducta valle caniculae
> Vitabis aestus —   18
>
> Here in a secluded valley you will avoid
> the Dog-Star's heat

and in Ode 29 of Book 3, inviting Maecenas he says:/

41
> Jam clarus occultum Andromedae pater
> Ostendit ignem; jam Procyon furit,
>   Et stella vesani Leonis,
>   Sole dies referente siccos   20
>
> *Andromeda's conspicious Sire*
> *Now darts his hidden Beams from far;*
> *The Lion shews his madning Fire,*
> *And barks fierce Procyon's raging Star,*
> *While Phoebus, with revolving Ray,*
> *Brings back the Burnings of thirsty Day.*

We find him, Book 3, Odes 8, making a sacrifice on the first of March, in commemoration of his having narrowly escaped being killed by the fall of one of his own trees on the same day of a former year:

> Martiis caelebs quid agam Calendis   1
>
> What should I, a bachelor, do on the first of March

and in Book 4, Ode 11, he invites Phyllis to partake of a feast which he makes at his villa the 13th of April, the birthday of his patron Maecenas:

> Idus tibi sunt agendae,
> Qui dies mensem Veneris marinae
>   Findit Aprilem   15

This Day the smiling Month divides,
O'er which the sea-born Queen presides

He begins Epistle 7 [Book 1] to Maecenas with:

Quinque dies tibi pollicitus me rure futurum   1
Sextilem totum mendax desideror —

I promis'd at my Country Farm to stay
But a few days; yet August roll'd away,
And left your Loiterer here

and in his Epistle to Quintius, Book 1, Epist. 16, he says:

Hae latebrae dulces, & (jam si credis) amoenae,   15
Incolumem tibi me praestant Septembribus horis.

This pleasing, this delicious soft Retreat
In Safety guards me from September's Heat.

In short it appears that his whole delight was in this retreat, and that he never
went to Rome except when drawn thither, as he says, in his epistle to his
vilicus, by *odious business./*

post fanum putre Vacunae   (*Epist.* 1.10.49)   42

behind the crumbling shrine of Vacuna.

Porphyrion, the ancient commentator of Horace, says in his note upon this
passage:

Vacuna apud Sabinos plurimum colitur. Quidam Minervam alii Dianam, nonnulli
Cererem, et Bellonam, esse dixerunt. Sed M. Varro in 1 Res Divin. Victoriam ait, et ea
maxime hi gaudent, qui sapientia vincunt.[45]

The precise situation of this temple may not at this day be easily ascertained,
but it appears to have been on, or near, Rocca Giovine by the following
inscription still preserved there over the door of a house:[46]

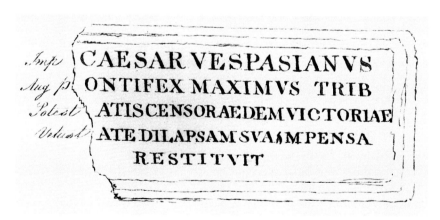

6.1. Drawing of the Rocca
Giovine inscription [*CIL*
xiv.3479], ucla Bound Mss.,
Coll. 170/376, p.42

Vespasian might perhaps be induced to make the rebuilding of this little
temple his own private concern, from a sort of provincial devotion, being

himself a Sabine, but without some other relation to it, it is difficult to guess
how a ruined chapel in an obscure and impervious part of the Sabine country
above 30 miles distant from Rieti, the place where he was born, could ever
come within his knowledge and become an object of his attention. To solve
this, we must call to mind that Horace had left his whole estate by will to
Augustus, and that it had continued to his successors in the Empire, as a part

43   of their private domain. This might/ naturally lead Vespasian to visit this
valley or, at least, to inform himself of every thing it contained, especially
after it had become illustrious by being the residence of two such
distinguished men as Horace and Burrus. There is a very pleasant spot of
ground on the declivity of Mount Lucretilis, between Rocca Giovine and
what I apprehend to be Horace's boundary, where there are foundations and
vaults supposed by the Abbé Chaupy remains of the Fanum Vacunae. The
place is called by the country people *Formicella* probably from a small clear
stream of water that runs close by it. Here Horace may have written this
epistle to Fuscus Aristius, and the little rill might naturally have suggested
the lines:

> Purior in vicis aqua tendit rumpere plumbum,
> Quam quae per pronum trepidat cum murmure rivum
> > (*Epist.* 1.10.20–21)

> *Is Water purer from the bursting Lead,*
> *Than gently murmuring down its native Bed?*

It is likewise possible that the Fanum Vacunae might have stood where is
now the chapel of La Madonna delle Case, as it was a common practice of the
first Christians to dispossess the heathen divinities of their dwellings, by
putting their own in their places: substituting a he saint for a god, and a
Madonna, or she saint, for a goddess. This chapel is upon what I believe was
the south boundary of Horace's estate and, by its title of 'Delle case' was
probably within it. A little digging about the foundations of these buildings,
might perhaps give farther lights.[47] The last time I was at Rocca Giovane June
15, 1777, the man over whose door the inscription of Vespasian is placed took
me into his house and shewed me, as a part of the pavement a bit of marble/

44   containing the greatest part of what was wanting of the inscription:

> IMP
> AUG P
> POTE

None of the other enquirers into Horace's affairs had ever seen this
fragment;[48] and I was sorry to see it, having been in hopes that the
underground discovery of it might have ascertained the original situation of
the old temple. Perhaps according to the first idea of Holstenius, the Fanum
Vacunae stood upon Rocca Giovane, where the inscription is now preserved.
It is a very particular situation, the ground all round it is uncommonly
pleasant, with plenty of trees and springs, and not above a mile from
Horace's house: but I thought it right to bring forth all I knew or could

conjecture concerning the situation of the old temple, for the sake of promoting farther and more critical enquiry./

Epistle 14 [Book 1]:   45

> Villice silvarum & mihi me reddentis agelli   1
>
> *Thou steward of the woods and Country-Seat,*
> *That give me to myself*

Whenever Horace mentions his favourite farm it is constantly in diminutive terms. Here it is *agellum*, at another time *modus agri non ita magnus* [*Sat.* 2.6.1]; at another, *mihi parva rura* [*Odes* 2.16.37], and so forth. In like manner speaking of his wood, it is *paullum silvae* [*Sat.* 2.6.3], or *Silva iugerum paucorum* [*Odes* 3.16.29-30]. But all these methods of speaking are only relative, and serve little to give us a just idea of the real extent of the subjects. The whole of the Valley of Licenza would not make the possessor a very rich man, and yet it is certain that it did not all belong to him; for he had neighbours who were near enough to observe and to laugh at his own manual operations in husbandry as he tells us in this epistle:

> Rident vicini glebas & saxa moventem.   39
>
> *My Neighbours laugh to see with how much Toil*
> *I carry stones or break the stubborn Soil*

and to come at night to sup with him as he says in Sat. 6 [Book 2]:

> Cervius haec inter vicinus garrit anilis
> Ex re fabellas   78
>
> *My neighbour Cervius never fails*
> *To club his Part in pithy Tales*

In the uncertainty in which his writings leave us, I have endeavoured to find out from the inspection of the ground some natural boundaries which might probably limit his property, and believe that it was bounded to the east by the Digentia; on the west by the top of the Mount Lucretilis; on the north by the stream of Fonte Bello; before and after its junction with the Maricella; and on the south by a deep ravine,/ called Fossa Sainese, which now divides the lands of Licenza from those of Rocca Giovane [cf. Fig.ii]. At the upper, or western, end of this ravine stands the little chapel called 'La madonna delle case', which now makes a part of the Rocca Giovane territory, but from the nature of the ground, which is there flat, might have anciently belonged to either. Within the boundary I have described, and at the south east corner of it, is a hill, part of the foot of Mount Lucretilis, called Colle Franchisi. Near the highway from Vicovaro where, in turning the east corner of this hill, we first get sight of the open valley and Horace's Villa, Bernardo Pomfili, the proprietor, told me he had some years ago dug up the stone sides of a *portone* or gate which pointed from that part of the highway, slanting towards Horace's house; and that there was a neat pavement went from that gate, part

                                                     46

of which he had likewise dug up. I had not an opportunity of digging when I was last at Licenza in June 1777, but was shown upon the spot some dozens of these stones said to have composed this pavement and which were scattered about in the land.[49] They are a sort of wedges of about 7 inches deep, the heads of them which formed the outside of the pavements being a square of about 3 inches and a half of the common white rock of these hills, which is a coarse marble. The fact, as related by Bernardo, would have been of consequence for shewing that Horace's ground extended at least so far south and the more conclusive that at the remains of the villa itself, which is about three quarters of a mile off, there are thousands of stones to be gathered exactly formed like this pretended pavement. But as these stones – though very proper for causewaying – are formed precisely like those made use of in the *opus/ reticulatum* to be found in the Mausoleum of Augustus and almost all the buildings of the first emperors as far down as Caracalla, thus:

47

6.2. Illustration of the building technique of *opus reticulatum*, UCLA Bound Mss., Coll. 170/376, p.47

We must suspend belief concerning the alleged pavement until it is actually uncovered and seen in its unbroken state.

Following the Colle Franchisi, or Francolisi, westward, up the Lucretilis, and along the north side of the Fossa Sainese, the ground has the name 'Il Sainese', that is the *Sabinenses*, as I learned from several of the country people. Abbé Chaupy had received some information of the same sort, but being naturally quick in applying what he heard to his preconceived system, he has extended this description to all the ground on the west side of the Digentia, as distinguishing it from the east side, which he says was the country of the Marsi. His distinction may be of itself very just; but as I am engaged in writing an *enquiry*, I should act very inconsistently if I were to take upon me to ask others what I had not learned by going farther than my evidence leads me; thinking it better to leave to future/ enquirers, upon more compleat information, to extend, explain, or reject what I have provided for them. In the meantime it seems to follow from the above intelligence that Horace's farm, including the Chapel of the Madonna delle Case, probably the *Fanum Vacunae*, were in the Sabine territory; and that the lands of Rocca Giovane were belonging to some other district. And upon this occasion I cannot refrain from observing that upon the Rocca Giovane side of the Fossa Sainese there is a house, now employed for keeping cows, called 'La Romina', and where the country people say there are ancient walls without being able to assign any reason for the name it bears.

48

— habitatum quinque focis, &
Quinque bonos solitum Variam dimittere Patres;

(*Epist.* 1.14.2–3)

five worthy Fathers sent,
One from each House, to Varia's Parliament

Here Horace means to show his *vilicus* that his farm could not be very contemptible, as it had been sufficient for the maintenance of five families of distinction. In the common editions, the above mentioned town is called *Baria* by a change very usual in the lower times of the Roman Empire, the inscriptions of which often present us with BIXIT and SEBIBO instead of *vixit* and *sevivo*. But Dr. Bentley gives us *Variam* upon the authority of the most ancient manuscripts. It is now called Vicovaro, standing upon the Valerian Way eight miles from Tivoli. In the later times of the Romans it seems to have been confounded with the highway near it and to have itself obtained the name of Valeria. This probably misled the transcribers of Strabo at that time, who in his account of the towns upon the Valerian way, which/ began at Tivoli, gives us, first Valeria and next Carseoli, and then Alba Fusiensis: εἰσὶ δ'ἐν αὐτῇ, that is in the Valerian way, Οὐαλέρια καὶ Καρσέολοι καὶ Ἄλβα; and it is certainly this town which is, under the name of Valeria, mentioned by Anastasius, the Bibliothecarian, as the birthplace of Pope Boniface the Fourth, although he speaks of it as being in the country of the Marsi – a country in more ancient times confined to the east of the Digentia, which is above a mile beyond Vicovaro. In Peutinger's tables, which are supposed to be more ancient than Anastasius, it is named *Varia*,[50] and is said to be eight miles beyond Tivoli, which is precisely the distance of Vicovaro. It had been a *municipium* or corporation town, as appears by the following inscription still extant in the staircase of the Villa Bolognetti in Vicovaro, where it was dug up:

M·HELVIVS·M·F·CAM·RVFVS
CIVICA·PRIM·PIL
BALNEVM
MVNICIPIBVS·ET·INCOLIS
DEDIT[51]

It farther appears by this inscription that there were *incolae* ['inhabitants'] in this town who were not *municipes* ['citizens'] and it is probable that there were *municipes* in the adjacent country who were not *incolae*, and of this last class we must suppose the *quinque boni patres*, or senators, to have been – for the common notion of their being peasants or farmers who cultivated Horace's land agrees very ill with that of their being members of/ a town council.[52] Nor do his words imply it. The houses might be still *habitati* ['inhabited'] by his working servants of which we know he had eight, but the *solitum demittere* ['accustomed to send'] is a separate circumstance, and certainly alludes to a time past. We know, however, that some of his slaves lived under his own roof by what he says in Sat. 6 [Book 2] concerning his giving supper to their children:

49

50

O noctes, cenaeque Deûm! quibus ipse meique   65
Ante Larem proprium vescor, vernasque procacis
Pasco libatis dapibus: cum, ut cuique libido est

'O nights, that furnish such a Feast
As even Gods themselves might taste!'
Thus fare my Friends, thus feed my Slaves,
Alert, on what their Master leaves.
Each Person there may drink, and fill
As much, or little, as he will

Which *vernae* are no doubt the same mentioned in Book 4, Ode 11 where speaking of the preparations for celebrating Maecenas's birthday he says:

Cuncta festinat manus: huc & illuc
Cursitant mixtae pueris puellae: 10

All Hands employ'd; my Girls and Boys,
With busy Haste, prepare our Joys

Whether it had its origin from motives of health or safety from invaders, I know not, but the country people in the middle regions of Italy live now altogether in villages very inconveniently perched upon the top of very steep hills. And there is not now in all the Valley of Licenza one fireside or any bed to sleep upon – the miller near Horace's Villa every night locking up his mill, and retiring with his family to Licenza, which is about a mile from it.[53] /

51

— & quod
Angulus iste feret piper et tus ocius uva
(*Epist.* 1.14.22–23)

While my small Farm yields rather Herbs than vines

By the turn of this expression it appears to allude to some peevish reflection of the *vilicus*, and if by *angulus* is meant some particular corner of Horace's ground, such as the ravine of Fonte Bello, where there are now scattered vines, it might be just; but if applied to the whole, not at all so. Horace mentions this wine as tolerable when, in Epistle 15, Book 1:

— (nam vina nihil moror illius orae:
Rure meo possum quidvis perferre patique:
Ad mare cum veni, generosum & lene requiro,
Quod curas abigat etc.   19

Their Country-Vintage is not worth my Care,
For though at home, whatever Wine, I bear,
At Sea-port towns I shall expect to find
My wines of generous and of smoother kind
To drive away my Cares

and in Book 1, Ode 20, he finds it sufficiently good for the entertainment of Maecenas:

Vile potabis modicis Sabinum   1
Cantharis, Graeca quod ego ipse testa
Conditum levi —

A Poet's Beverage, humbly cheap
(Should great Maecenas be my Guest)
The Vintage of the Sabine Grape,
But yet in sober cups, shall crown the Feast:
'Twas racked into a Grecian Cask,
Its rougher Juice to melt away,
I sealed it too – a pleasing Task!

I once had some wine sent me by the Arciprete of Licenza made of grapes, which grew upon and near the ruins of Horace's house and which in colour and taste resembled Burgundy of the middling sort. The common wine of the valley is white and is tolerably good, notwithstanding that the poverty of the people deprives them of the proper vessels, instruments, and other conveniences for making and keeping it to advantage./ All sort of fruit grows here in perfection, but is at least three weeks later than in the Campagna di Roma.

52

> Addit opus pigro rivus, si decidit imber,
> Multa mole docendus aprico parcere prato.
>
> (*Epist.* 1.14.29–30)

Then feels your Laziness an added Pain
If e'er the Rivulet be swollen with Rain;
What mighty Mounds against its Force you rear
To teach its Rage the sunny Mead to spare!

These two lines very well agree with the present state of the Valley of Licenza, and particularly with that part of it which I have assigned to Horace. The valley has at its bottom a certain quantity – not very extensive – of very rich meadow ground, through which the Digentia and its associating streams have their course and are some times so impetuous after great rains collected in the neighbouring hills as to cut up new channels for themselves, and at some distance from where they ran the day before. As this occasions great loss and confusion to the proprietors of the several bits of this valuable ground, the more industrious among them defend themselves against it by piles of dry white stone, not built up, but laid sloping in the nature of a bank, to defend those parts of the natural bank which appear likely to give way. In June 1777 I saw parts of that meadow, which had been the northmost part of Horace's possession, sheathed in this manner. The meadow ground of most consideration in this valley is that which lies to the northwest end of it and through which run the streams of Fonte Bello and the Maricella. They are used only for the pasture of cattle, which with the addition of some good trees, here and there, and the women washing their clothes makes altogether a most delightful pastoral scene. Horace had, no doubt this spot in his eye when he says Book 3, Ode 18:/

53

> Festus in pratis vacat otioso   11
> Cum bove pagus

the Peasants play
On the grassy-matted Soil,
Round their Oxen, free from Toil.

Epistle 16 [Book 1]:

Continui montes nisi dissocientur opaca   5
Valle

There is a chain of hills, unbroken were it not divided by a
shady valley —

This is a pretty good general description of the present Valley of Licenza, which, to those who stand in the middle of it seems to be shut up by high hills, at all quarters. For the entrance to it from San Cosimato by the foot of Rocca Giovane, the only entrance to it by even ground, is too narrow to be there observable, being little broader than what is necessary for the passage of the rivulet Digentia. After passing this strait the valley opens considerably, and continues for about two miles till it is entirely shut up at the north end by the hills of Licenza and Civitella.

— sed ut veniens dextrum latus aspiciat Sol,
Laevum decedens curru fugiente vaporet.   7

The right wide spreading to the rising Day,
The left is warm'd beneath his setting Ray.

From its receiving so readily the rising and setting sun, those who formerly read this passage have been led by it to believe that Horace's valley extended itself from east to west and with this idea have hunted for it in several places in the Sabine country. But upon sight of the ground itself – concerning the identity of which we are not permitted/ from the concurrence of circumstances any longer to doubt – we find that it is not so. The valley is of an oval figure, and longest from south to north; at the northern part indeed a little bending to the northwest. In this southward direction, with a great many small serpentines, runs the rivulet Digentia, and the Convent of San Cosimato and the village of Licenza are according to the compass nearly in the same meridian, as I have often had occasion to observe with sufficient accuracy in my several visits to this spot. Thus, likewise they are marked in Padre Boscovich's map of the Ecclesiastical State, and in other maps of that country.[54] But in that of the Valley of Licenza drawn by Abbé de Chaupy [see Fig.5.4], for the illustration of his book upon Horace's country house, the good Abbé has suffered his pencil to be guided rather by his prepossessions than his eyesight and has moved heaven and earth in order to make the actual situation of things correspond with what he believed to be Horace's description of them. For in his map, the village of Licenza is placed almost west of San Cosimato, instead of being, as it is in reality, exactly north of it.[55] He judged, indeed, very right in supposing that Horace could not be mistaken with regard to the four points of the compass in a place where he had spent all the hours of the day, and all the months of the year. But after seeing that the situation of the ground did not agree with the description, he ought to have suspected that he had mistaken Horace's meaning. Upon a reconsideration of the passage, I find it will admit of another construction, much less exceptionable than that which is generally given to it, by making *sed ut* relate not to *dissocientur* but to *opaca,*

54

and interpret it thus: A cluster of hills, except in this place where they are/ separated by a *deep* Valley; *yet not so deep* as to be deprived of the rays of the sun when rising or where he is going to set. Here some small allowance must be given to the exaggerating poet and the fond proprietor; for the description cannot be strictly true of any small valley surrounded with hills, and to my own knowledge is not true of the Valley of Licenza. The distinction, however, which he makes between the rising and the setting sun is full of that propriety which never fails to attend those who write from the life. The elevated spot which, in my remarks upon Satire 6 [Book 2], I have assigned for the situation of Horace's house, lies at a considerable distance from the hills to the east; and which, besides, are not the highest that surround the Valley: But on its west, it has the Lucretilis [Fig.ii], the highest mountain in the neighbourhood, to which it is so near that it may be properly said to be only an excrescence; so that, although he might have had the benefit of the sun soon after his rise, he must have been at certain seasons of the year deprived of it long before he sunk beneath the general horizon. It is only about the summer solstice, when the sun sets to the north of the *Campanile*, or forked top of Lucretilis, that his description approaches to truth. By a peculiarity in the little elevation upon which Horace's house stood, it enjoys the rays of the sun half an hour after it has ceased to shine on the rest of the valley; but I observed at the same time that an hour after the sun was set to Horace also, he continued to shine on the hills of Saracinesco on the other side of the Anio [Fig.i].*

> dextrum latus ... laevum (*Epist.* 1.16.6–7)
>
> the right side ... the left

It is difficult to say what can ever be meant by the *right* and *left* side of a valley, and it is therefore probable that the description here alludes to something that is not expressed in it. To me, who have some knowledge of this particular valley and its circumstances the words furnish two conjectures very differently derived, but both terminating in the same point. The first is that Horace forms this description of the valley from the course of the rivulet, which, running through the middle of it from north to south, makes the west the right side, and the east the left side of it.

The other conjecture is that knowing his house to have its front and principal prospect to the north, he means by *right* and *left* the right and left sides of his house – a description which by inverting the position of the describer coincides with the first in respect of the sun, as the first relates to the inside of the valley, the other to the outside of the house.

---

* To make all this description perfectly intelligible I am sensible that a map becomes necessary: and, in Spring 1783 I was actually in search of a land-surveyor for/ that purpose, when, happily, I was relieved from that task by a person much more capable than myself to see it duly performed. This was Mr Philip Hackert the landscip painter at Rome, who had then undertaken to publish by subscription ten views from the neighbourhood of Horace's Villa; and who, upon conversing with me upon the subject, conceived that, besides the pleasure arising from the sight of picturesque views of nature, the work would become more acceptable to men of erudition if he could point out with precision the relation which these views bore to their favourite poet. The map was accordingly drawn with all that accuracy and elegance which was to be expected from the superintendency and assistance of so eminent an artist.³⁶

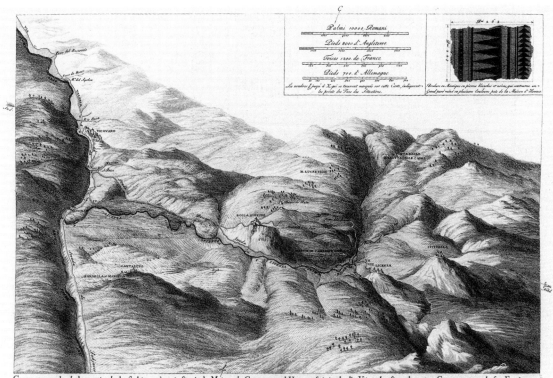

Carte generale de la partie de la Sabine où etoit situèe la Maison de Campagne d'Horace, suivie de dix Vûes des sites de cette Campagne et de ses Environs, nommès dans les Oeuvres d'Horace, et relatives aux dissertations que M.^r l'Abbé de Santis, M.^r l'Abbé Capmartin de Chaupy et Mr de Ramsay ont publiè à ce sujet

Dediées à Sa Majesté
Roi de Suede des Goths

Gustave III
et des Vandales &c.&c.&c.

A Rome chez Georg: Hackert Graveur Place d'Espagne

Par son très humble très obeissant
et très Soumis Serviteur Ja: Ph: Hackert

6.3. Relief map of the Licenza valley by Jakob Philipp Hackert, National Gallery of Scotland

57

That Horace's house must have had its principal prospect towards the north becomes very manifest upon the first sight of/ the ground where it stood. For he was deprived of prospect to the southeast by a hillock of his own. His west windows had the Lucretilis too near them, and his south, though the hills are at a mile's distance, afforded nothing that was particularly beautiful; whereas those on the north side, looking down the declivity gave a very pleasant view of all the rivulets which form the Digentia with their meadows, and behind them the picturesque hills where now stand the villages of Licenza, Civitella, etc. The last time I was upon this spot, June 27, 1777, I desired the master of the vineyard to take his spade and lay open a piece of the mosaic pavement, by the lines of which I found that the building had been exactly set by the four points of the compass. I had, at other times been shown parts of this mosaic composed of flowering foliages. What I saw, upon this occasion was a border of black and white marble, of the following figure.*

---

*I went with my son on the 27th of September 1783 to take another sight of this pavement, but as it is of considerable extent, and its plan unknown, the country people laid open a piece of border different from any I had before seen, and nearly as follows:

6.4. Detail of the mosaic in room G1 Lugli [cf. Fig.5.8], UCLA Bound Mss., Coll. 170/376, p.57

6.5. Detail of the mosaic in room G1 Lugli [cf. Fig.5.8], UCLA Bound Mss., Coll. 170/376, p.57

Temperiem laudes. quid, si rubicunda benigni
Corna vepres & pruna ferunt? si quercus et ilex
Multa fruge pecus, multa dominum juvat umbra?   10
Dicas adductum propius frondere Tarentum.

58

(*Epist.* 1.16.8–11)

How mild the Clime, where Sloes luxurious grow,
And blushing Cornels on the Hawthorn glow!
With plenteous Acorns are my Cattle fed,
Whose various Oaks around their Master spread;
For you might say, that here Tarentum waves
Its dusky Shade, and pours forth all its Leaves.

For this wood so often mentioned by Horace, see remarks upon Satire 6 [Book 2]. In the place there pointed out, a wood is still to be seen producing all the trees and plants here mentioned, with abundance of other wild fruits, such as the *sorbe*, or wild pear.

Fons etiam rivo dare nomen idoneus, ut nec
Frigidior Thracam nec purior ambiat Hebrus,
Infirmo capiti fluit utilis, utilis alvo.

(Epist. 1.16.12–14)

A fountain to a rivulet gives its Name,
Cooler and purer than a Thracian Stream,
Useful to ease an aching Head it flows,
Or when with burning Pain the Stomach glows.

This is the Fonte Ratini, or rather Fonte de' Ratini, for the country people give the name of Ratini to the whole ground under it, and which to the eye and taste very well answers the description given [Fig.ii]. The country people of the neighbourhood esteem this very wholesome water and say it is often sent to sick people at a distance. For its wholesomeness we may very safely trust Horace, who appears to have had very weak health and to have been particularly attentive to the preservation of it. The virtues he ascribes to this water may, indeed, be only the result of its lightness and purity which comparatively with the less clear water of Rome might have entitled it to all the praises he bestows upon it, at least as far as regarded his own 59 constitution. His nicety with regard to wholesome/ water appears very strongly in Epistle 15 [Book 1], written at a time when his health seems to have been in a declining state, and when he was making diligent enquiry for the properest place on the sea coast for passing the winter, whether Velia or Salernum; and where, amongst other things he desires his friend Vala to inform him:

Collectosne bibant imbris, puteosne perennis
Jugis aquae —   (Epist. 1.15.15–16)

Would they drink rainwater collected in tanks, or do they have wells with ever-
flowing spring water?

Upon a general review of this Epistle, I suspect that it has come down to us mutilated and confused, and very different from what it was when sent by Horace to his friend, if ever it was sent. He begins it with a number of questions concerning the produce of his farm, all which he promises to answer *loquaciter* or in a very particular manner. But we look in vain for those answers, and after sixteen lines of general and desultory hints, fall all at once into a string of moral precepts, very good in themselves, and very much in the spirit of Horace, but as little connected with one another, as with the proposed subject of the epistle. The whole is probably made up of memorandums left unfinished at the author's death, or of fragments of his finished works picked up afterwards by his admirers, and stuck together in the best way they could. It may some time or other please heaven to inspire the King of Naples or some of his ministers with a curiosity to know what may be contained in the 800 manuscript volumes found at Herculaneum and now piled up, like lumps of charcoal, in a cupboard at Portici. Perhaps 60 amongst them might be found the works of Horace in his own/ handwriting, which would clear up this and many other difficulties, in which all the genius and learning of Bentley have not been able to assist us.[57]

Epistle 18 [Book 1]:

> Me quotiens reficit gelidus Digentia rivus,
>
> (*Epist.* 1.18.104)

How often does the cold Digentia refresh me,

This rivulet is now called the Licenza, being the old name a very little changed by a carelessness in the pronunciation. It rises in three principal sources, one crossing from Percile called La Risecca, the other from Civitella, called the Maricella, and the third called Fonte Bello, which with the Fonte Ratini joining together at the north end of the valley run southward through the middle of it, and at about half a mile to the east of the Convent of San Cosimato falls into the Anio and makes part of that body of water which forms the several Cascades at Tivoli. This circumstance is what Horace probably alludes to in his ode to Melpomene, Book 4, Ode 3:

> Sed quae Tibur aquae fertile praefluunt,   10
> Et spissae nemorum comae,
>   Fingent Aeolio carmine nobilem.

> *But Him, the Streams which warbling flow*
> *Rich Tibur's fertile Vales along,*
> *And shady Groves, his Haunts, shall know*
> *The Master of th'Aeolian Song.*

The Digentia anciently divided the Sabine from the country of the Marsi, and the country people to this day call part of the ground on the west side of it the *Sainese*, that is the *Sabinensis*. It is never without a tolerable stream of water, as the hills which/ surround this valley are well provided with perpetual springs, but not in proportion to its channel, which though both wide and deep is sometimes after great rains, not only filled but overflowed to a degree that is terrible and destructive.

61

> Quem Mandela bibit, rugosus frigore pagus
>
> (*Epist.* 1.18.105)

> *which Mandela drinks, a district wrinkled with the cold*

Mandela was a *pagus*, that is a *paese* or tract of ground on the east side of the Digentia. The name corrupted into Bardela is still used by the modern inhabitants and is one of the titles of the family of Nuñez, proprietors of Cantalupo. In the maps of Revillas and Ameti we find a village at the south end of Cantalupo marked *Bardela, olim Mandela*: but upon questioning the people upon the spot, I found there was no town there of that name, but that their phrase was *Cantalupo di Bardela*, which much better agrees with the appellation of *pagus* given to it by Horace [Fig.i]. But what puts it out of all doubt that this ground is the true Mandela is an inscription which was dug up there about the 1766,[58] the adventures of which – its being buried a second time as a common stone in repairing an altar in the church of San Cosimato, its being delivered from thence and finally fixed for preservation in the staircase of the Villa Bolognetti at Vicovaro – are very circumstantially related by the Abbé de Chaupy, whose zeal and activity upon the occasion merit the grateful acknowledgments of all true lovers of antiquity. The inscription is as follows:/

62

VAL·MAXIMA MATER
DOMNIPREDIA VAL
DVLCISSIMA FILIA
QVE VIXIT ANNIS XXX
VIMENIIDXII IN PRE
DIIS SVIS MASSE MAN
DELANE SEPRETORVM
HERCVLES QVESQN PACE[59]

This inscription being probably of the second or third century, the composition of country people little instructed in Latin grammar or orthography, and whose bad spelling might become still worse by the execution of a bungling mason, it may not be easy to explain with certainty in all its parts. But it is exceedingly clear and conclusive in that part of it which relates to my subject: to wit, in fixing the situation of the *Massa Mandelana* or as Horace would have called it, the *Pagus Mandelanus*.[60] But as an explanation of the whole may be desirable, I will attempt it as well as I can, availing myself of some conjectures of the Abbé Chaupy's, which are ingenious and possibly true.

The many palpable inaccuracies of this inscription both in grammar and orthography – such as putting all the names of persons, those who erected the monument and those for whom it was erected, equally in the nominative case; the ending words with a single E which ought to have been ended with an Æ diphthong – gave the Abbé a right to suppose that there might be the like inaccuracies in other words less/ understood. And that where the word was totally unintelligible, like SEPRETORVM, he might try to divide it into such initials and abbreviations as would produce a consistent meaning, without expecting the authors of the inscription to have been acquainted with the rules or practice of abbreviating (they having given a sufficient proof of the contrary in their manner of marking the three last words, Q[V]ESQNPACE). After these preliminary considerations the Abbé finds that this sepulchral monument had been set up by Valerius Maximus Hercules upon his own estate to the memory of his mother and his daughter, whose monument had been either defaced by accident, or had been set up in some place less to his mind. The only thing in which I differ from the Abbé is in the meaning of the words DOMNI PREDIA to which he has given several turns, none of which connect with the other words of the inscription, or conduce to establish his own hypothesis, such as *doti omni*, or *dotibus omnibus praedita*, or *domini prebia* or *praevia*. My conjecture is that these words ought to have been carved *domini predii*,[61] that they connect with the word *mater*, which immediately precedes them and that they were inserted to shew that the first Valeria was not the mother but the grandmother of the second, the mother being probably alive at the time of restoring the monument. With this supposition, the whole may be read thus:

63

Valeriae Maximae, matri domini praedii,
Valeriae, dulcissimae filiae, quae vixit annis 36,
Mensibus 2, diebus 12. In praediis suis
Massae Mandelanae sepulchrum restituit/
et ornavit Valerius Maximus Hercules
   Quiescant in pace.

64

Quem Mandela bibit, rugosus frigore pagus,

(*Epist.* 1.18.105)

which Mandel drinks, a district wrinkled with the cold

From a long and attentive consideration of the works of Horace, I am so impressed with an opinion of his *curiosa felicitas*, that when any of his descriptions or epithets exhibit only a flat or dubious meaning, I immediately conclude that either the words have been vitiated by the transcribers, or that I do not understand them. Of these difficulties I find no less than two in the above line. *Quem Mandela bibit*, is certainly a description of an extraordinary kind. Rivers are, fixed and permanent objects in Nature and are often very properly employed by poets to ascertain the geographical situation of people. Thus Virgil says, *Qui Tyberim Fabrimque bibunt*[62] by which we have the exact situation, above the confluence of those two rivers, of the nation he means to describe. And thus Horace says *Rhodanique portor*[63] to describe an inhabitant of the middle of Gaul. But here the Digentia, which is of itself first and immortal, has its situation ascertained by its neighbourhood to a village of which the very name would have long ago perished if it had not been for this single line of Horace. I am, therefore, led to suspect that the idea here meant to be conveyed was of a very confined sort, and, in searching for it, it occurs to my memory that in all my wanderings about the Digentia, I never met with any rivulet or spring of water on the east, which I have always supposed to be the Mandela side of it, while I can now/ distinctly recollect no less than seven on the Sabine side of excellent water and of which there are three singly which are able to furnish drink for a capital city. Perhaps Horace, who was vain of his little possession, means here to set forth its superior value to those of his neighbours by insinuating their total want of spring water in which he so happily abounded. A more accurate examination of the ground itself would increase or diminish the weight of this conjecture: for I only give it as such.

65

The other difficulty lies in the *rugosus frigore pagus* [*Epist.* 1.18.105]; for it does not appear why any part of that neighbourhood, which is not higher, should be colder than the rest. The Abbé Chaupy, indeed, says (vol.3, page 279) that he was sensible of the propriety of this description upon feeling a piercing cold wind while he was employed in drawing his map between Cantalupo and San Cosimato, near the place where the sepulchral inscription of the Valerian family had been found. This wind, attended with a *brouillard*, or fog, he had, he says, the curiosity to investigate as quickly as he could for four miles and found that it came from the quarter of La Scarpa, Rio Freddo, and Valle in Freddo [Fig.i], precipitating itself in a column through a valley where it met with no resistance between the hills of Anticoli and Saracinesco on the left, and the *continui montes* which enclose Horace's valley, on the right. I have never had an opportunity of confirming this observation of the Abbé's, so I must leave it as I found it and shall conclude these remarks by observing that though they contain all the lights I have been able to acquire, I am far from thinking that the subject has received all the light/ that may be possibly thrown upon it. Something more certain and precise may still be learned concerning the particular situation of Mandela and the extent of the Massa Mandelana by an examination of the title deeds of the family of Orsini, anciently Lords of all this territory; or of those of Nuñez and Borghese, who derive from them; and still more from the Archives of the Vatican, and of the Church of St. John Lateran, if they happen to be accessible. Much, likewise, may be still learned concerning the true situation of the Fanum Vacunae, and other particulars of this interesting valley, if any man of classical curiosity with 20 or 30 spare sequins in his pocket would employ the country people to dig upon Colle Franco, and other places already mentioned by me in these remarks. But I must caution such a virtuoso either to begin his digging early in the spring, or to defer it till after harvest. For the country people, who know nothing about odes or epistles, believe that all who dig do it from the expectation of finding hidden treasure; and that the demon who watches over the treasure would raise a wind which might destroy their little crop of corn, wine, and oil.

Having mentioned the country people, I should not do them justice if I did not take notice of them amongst the antiquities of the place; for, excepting their religion (which it is hardly necessary to except) they seem to be of the same stamp with those who, according to the poets and historians, inhabited that country in the days of Numa Pompilius, with the same laborious manner of living, the same contented poverty, and the same innocence; so that when my wife, my daughter Amelia, and I took our leave/ of them upon the 28th of June, 1777, we did it with much regret.

Notes

1. Ramsay refers here to the death of his second wife, Margaret Lindsay, who died on 4 March 1782; to his daughter, Amelia, whose marriage took her to Bermuda; and to his son, John (*b* 1768), whose diary of the trip to Italy survives (NLS, MSS 1833–4).

2. The Latin text of Horace cited throughout is the one that Ramsay says he generally used: R. Bentley's *Q. Horatius Flaccus*. All translations in plain text are those of the editor; those in italics are from P. Francis, *Poetical Translation of the Works of Horace*, 1756. 'Francis ranks as the Horatian translator-general of the second half of the eighteenth century and the first half of the nineteenth with new editions constantly called for. Though now hardly more than a name even to connoisseurs of English poetry, he has good claims to be considered the best translator of Horace, certainly of the Odes, to date, and Johnson's praise is just: "Francis has done it best; I'll take his, five out of six, against them all"'; D. S. Carne-Ross, 'Introduction', 1996, p.23.

3. cf. F. Biondo, *De Roma*, 1527, fols 78–9. A Papal secretary and noted humanist, Flavio Biondo wrote *Italia Illustrata*, a treatise on the geography of Italy, from 1446 to 1453; see *Dizionario Biografico degli Italiani*, vol.10, 1968, pp.536–59; N. T. de Grummond, *Encyclopedia*, 1996, vol.1, pp.160–61. Judging from the fact that his description of Italy jumps from Vicovaro to Rio Freddo, he appears not to have known the Licenza Valley. Throughout his work, Biondo shows an interest in locating ancient villas, including Hadrian's Villa (fol.68r); the Villa of Cicero at Puteoli (fol.148v); and the Villa of Lucullus near Naples (fol.148v).

4. cf. P. Cluverius, *Italia Antiqua*, 1624. Cluverius (Philipp Clüver), who taught at Leyden and who

66

67

travelled in Italy in 1617–18 gathering notes for his book, treats Horace's villa at vol.1, pp.671–2. Like Biondo, he shows no awareness of the existence of the Licenza Valley (nor even of nearby Vicovaro). For Cluverius's map, see D. Cremonini, *L'Italia nelle vedute*, 1991, no.16 (pp.22–3); A. P. Frutaz, *Le carte del Lazio* 1972, vol.1, pp.45–6 (no.XXIV). On Cluverius see de Grummond, *Encyclopedia*, 1996, vol. 1, p.294.

5. G. R. Volpi, *Vetus Latium profanum*, 1704–45. Volpi discusses Horace's villa at vol.10, pp.275–325.

6. The modern Anio River.

7. See L. Holstenius, *Annotationes*, 1666, p.106. (On Holstenius see R. Almagià, *L'opera geografica*, 1942, and on Holstenius and Cluverius see pp.3, 67–72.) Holstenius was born in Hamburg and educated at Leyden. From 1641 until his death he was Librarian of the Vatican Library. Holstenius had been Cluverius's student at Leyden and had accompanied his teacher on the expedition to Italy in 1617–18. He criticized his teacher for travelling too fast to do a thorough job (pp.68–9), and as his correspondence with Peiresc makes clear, he planned to issue a corrected edition of Cluverius's *Italia Antiqua* (cf. Almagià, pp.71–2). He was prevented by other duties from doing so, and in the event only his marginal notes on Cluverius (often written in a disagreeable tone) were published after his death.

8. Holstenius, ibid., p.106: 'Cluverius, p.672, line 38, "behind the shrine of ruined Vacuna" (Horace, *Epist.* 1.10.49). [The place is now called Rocca Giovine. The Emperor Vespasian restored here a temple of Victory ruined by age, as is attested by an inscription found there ... Line 43] The village of Digentia, which is now Licenza, next follows nearby.'

9. cf. D. G. De Revillas, *Dioecesis et agri Tiburtini*, 1739 and 1767; A.P. Frutaz, *Le carte del Lazio*, vol.1, pp.82–5 (no.XXXVII). On Revillas see M. Pedley, 'The Manuscript Papers', 1991.

10. cf. G. F. Ameti and D. de Rossi, *Il Lazio*, 1693; see P. Arrigoni and A. Bertarelli, *Le carte geografiche*, 1930, no.2158; A. P. Frutaz, ibid., vol.1, pp.75–7 (no.XXXIII). Ameti says of Rocca Giovine that it was 'olim Fanum Vacunae' and Licenza (the town and stream) 'olim Digentia'.

11. Whereas it is true that Holstenius was the first to equate Licenza with Digentia and Rocca Giovine with Fanum Vacunae, it is not correct to say that he was the first to notice in print the Licenza valley; cf., for example, Magini's map of the Roman Campagna of 1620, which has the town and river of Licenza and the towns of Rocca Giovine and Civitella: A. Magini, *Campagna di Roma*, 1620 = D. Cremonini, *L'Italia nelle vedute*, 1991, no.15; Frutaz, ibid., vol. 1, pp.35–6 (no.XVIII). Oddly, Magini situates the town of Vicovaro to the north of Civitella, several miles from its true positon near the Anio. Vicovaro and the river and town of Licenza also appear in N. Sanson, *Estats de l'Eglise*, 1648.

12. cf. D. de Sanctis, *Dissertazione*, 1761 and later.

13. C. De Chaupy, *Découverte de la maison*, 1767–9. On the Abbé Capmartin De Chaupy see *Biographie universelle*, 1854, vol.8, pp.45–6; E. Galletier, 'L'Abbé Capmartin de Chaupy', 1935; N. Mathieu, 'Capmartin du Chaupy', 1987.

14. Anastasius the Librarian, *Vitae Romanorum Pontificum: XXXIV. Sanctus Silvester*, 44 (J.-P. Migne, *Patrologiae*, vol.127, pp.1523–4). Anastasius had a colorful career as a churchman and writer in ninth-century Rome, suffering excommunication in 850 and even serving as Anti-Pope for a few days in 855. He held the post of Librarian of the Holy Roman Church from 867 until his death in around 878. St Silvester was Pope under Constantine.

15. Anastasius, ibid., p.34: 'The Valerian property in the Sabina, which is worth 40 solidi; the Statian property in the Sabina, which is worth 55 solidi; the property "Two Houses" in the Sabina, which is worth 40 solidi; the Percilian property in the Sabina, which is worth 20 solidi.'

16. D. De Francesco, 'Le donazione costantiniane', 1990, p.48, and Z. Mari, 'La valle dell'Aniene', 1995, p.38, also hold that the Constantinian donation to the Church of Saints Peter and Marcellinus concerned land located in the area of Horace's Villa in the Licenza Valley.

17. *CIL* XIV.3479.

18. On Abate Giuseppe Petrocchi, notary of Vicovaro and antiquarian, see G. Petrocchi, *Orazio*, 1958, p.36, note 6. De Francesco, ibid., places the *fundus Statianus* in the zone of Stazzano, about 3 km southeast of Moricone and far from the Licenza Valley.

19. Ramsay refers here to Bosius 1632.

20. Ramsay is inaccurate here. The extant property records for Licenza, dating to 1782 and preserved in the Archivio di Stato, Rome, show that although much of the land around the site of Horace's Villa (a parcel known then and now as 'Le vigne di San Pietro') was owned by the parish church of Licenza, a certain amount was also owned by the Prince Borghese.

21. cf. below, at p.39.

22. Not translated by Philip Francis (see note 2 above). A literal translation would be: 'whenever, Tyndaris, the sloping valleys of Ustica and the smooth rocks have resounded with the sweet pipe'.

23. 'Ustica is the name of a mountain and valley in the Sabina. He calls it delightfully "reclining", directing his attention to the area that slopes. So, too, in the *Epistles* [he writes about] "the hills,

unbroken except for one shady valley [*Epist.* 1.16.5–6]. "Reclining" means "low", as, for example, in the following [Virgil, *Aen.* 3.689]: "the Megarian harbor and the low-lying Thapsus".'

24. The words 'to a degree … from Civitella' are not in NLS. Ramsay added them after visiting Civitella for the first time on 13 September 1783.

25. The word is omitted from Francis's translation of line 14 above. A more literal translation would read: 'lying beneath either the high plane tree or this pine tree'.

26. 'Ode 16' is the reading of the mss. Ramsay means *Odes* 2.17, where mention is again made of the tree that almost killed the poet. The infamous tree is also mentioned in *Odes* 3.4 and 3.8. 'Horace's escape from a falling tree is a familiar but puzzling episode. The historicity of the experience should not be doubted: it is associated in time with Maecenas's recovery from illness (*Odes* 2.17.25ff.), compared with the battle of Philippi as one of the crises of the poet's life (*Odes* 3.4.26ff.), and assigned with circumstantial particularity to the first of March (3.8.1). The year is much more problematical.' R. G. M. Nisbet and M. Hubbard, *Commentary on Horace*, 1978, p.201.

27. Ramsay's etymology is correct; see C. Battisti and G. Alessio, *Dizionario*, 1954, vol.4, p.2719.

28. In a personal communication, Prof. Brent Vine, a classical linguist at UCLA, writes that Ramsay's etymology of Cotiso is unlikely.

29. The reference is to a passage in Juvenal's third satire, in which the poet laments the sadly ostentatious appearance of the spring of Egeria as it appeared in his day, *Sat.* 3.18–20: 'quanto praesentius esset / numen aquis, viridi si margine lauderet undas / herba' ('how much more near to us would be the spirit of the fountain, if its waters were fringed by a green border of grass').

30. Bentley's reading has been generally accepted. It was anticipated by J. Cruquius, *Q. Horatius Flaccus*, 1579.

31. 'He promises a sacrifice for the Fons Blandusia in the Sabine territory, where he owned a villa.'

32. cf. C. De Chaupy, *Découverte de la maison*, 1767–9, vol.3, p.364, citing vol. 2, p.123 of a *bullarium*, or collection of Papal bulls and documents. Of the several *bullaria* in print by the mid-eighteenth century, only that of C. Cocquelines, *Bullarum privilegiorum*, 1739–62, has the document on the page De Chaupy cites.

33. cf. P. F. Kehr, *Regesta pontificum*, 1962, p.464 (no.9) for the text and confirmation of De Chaupy's reading and identification of the Fons Bandusius.

34. C. Cocquelines, *Bullarum privilegiorum*, 1739–62, vol.2, p.123. The editor gratefully acknowledges the help of Dr Ann Scott in the translation of the text.

35. Virgil, *Eclogues* 2.33: 'Pan cares for the sheep and the shepherds.'

36. After 'it', NLS has: 'Over the spring is the rugged remains of an ancient building, part of which now lies in the water, having been undermined by the peasants, from their usual hope of finding treasure under it. Running aslant down the hill …'. No traces of this building survive today, so Ramsay's report is of great interest to contemporary archaeologists studying the Licenza Valley.

37. cf. C. De Chaupy, *Découverte de la maison*, 1767–9, vol. 3, p.11.

38. That the priest of Licenza should have used the pipe to make birdshot is not surprising in view of the following report (D. de Sanctis, *Dissertazione*, p.xi) about his lack of culture: 'non si piccò mai ne di erudizione, ne di Antichità' ('he never claimed any erudition or interest in antiquity'). Pope Benedict XIV founded the Pontificia Accademia Romana di Archeologia in 1740, but it ceased activity in 1756 and was refounded by Pius VII in 1810; see R. E. A. Palmer in N. T. de Grummond, *Encyclopedia*, 1996, pp.915–16. The Society of Antiquaries, London (of which Ramsay had been a Fellow since 1743) published inscriptions of various kinds in its journal *Archaeologia*, which started appearing in 1770.

39. cf. *CIL* xv.7897 and *CIL* xiv.3487. Ramsay has confused Sextus Afranius Burrus, the Prefect of the Praetorian Guard under Claudius and Nero (cf. *PIR* I², 74, no.441), and the T(i). Claudius Burrus whose name was inscribed on a lead pipe at Horace's Villa. The latter was possibly (Ti. Claudius) Burrus, the son of Domitian's chamberlain (Ti. Claudius) Parthenius, discussed in *Paulys Real-Encyclopaedie*, vol. 3 (1899), col. 2681 (Claudius 89). On father and son, cf. also *PIR* I B 154, 176, *PIR* II C 951a, recently confirmed by W. Eck, 'Ti. Claudius Parthenius', 1997, coll.19–20. Martial mentions Parthenius in a number of his epigrams (4.78, 5.6, 8.28 etc.) and wrote a birthday poem for Burrus (4.45). See J. P. Sullivan, *Martial*, 1991, p.33. Ramsay is correct in assuming that a name in the genitive (possessive) case on a Roman lead water pipe probably indicates the owner of the conduit; see C. Brunn, *Water Supply*, 1991, especially pp.59–62.

40. Ramsay here has probably misunderstood his informer's Italian, taking 'un carro di marmo' (i.e. 'a cartload of marble') to mean 'a marble chariot'.

41. Left blank in EUL, NLS and UCLA.

42. This inscription is not to be found in *CIL* xiv among the inscriptions from the Licenza Valley; it is also not mentioned by G. Lugli, 'La villa sabina', 1926, and Z. Mari, 'La valle del Licenza', 1994. Mari, in a personal communication, would emend I O M in the first line to D M.

43. See *OED* s.v. Paul 2. [tr. It. Paolo, Paul] 'The Paolo, an obsolete Italian silver coin, worth about fivepence sterling. 1767 STERNE, Tr. Shandy, IX.xxiv, "I paid five Pauls for two hard eggs."' So ten pauls was not very much money.

44. cf. *CIL* VI.15882–943 for Cocceius inscriptions from the city of Rome. It is not clear whether Ramsay refers to any of these in his note (*) that follows.

45. 'Vacuna is frequently worshipped among the Sabines. Certain scholars said she was [equivalent to the Roman goddess] Minerva, others to Diana, some to Ceres and Bellona. But M. Varro in Book I of his *Res Divin.* said [she was equivalent to] Victory, and they take greatest joy at this who are persuaded by wisdom.'
    The standard text of this passage in [Ps.] Acro today (see A. Holder and O. Keller, *Scholia antiqua*, 1894) has a different reading: 'Vacunam apud Sabinos plurimum cultam quidam Minervam, alii Dianam putaverunt; nonnulli etiam Venerem esse dixerunt; sed Varro primo rerum divinarum [fr. 1 Cardanus=127 Funaioli] Victoriam ait, quod ea maxime hi gaudent, qui sapentiae vacent' ('Some thought that Vacuna, who was frequently worshipped among the Sabines, was Minerva, others Diana; some even said that she was Venus. But Varro in Book I of the *Res Divinae* says [she was equivalent to] Victory, which greatly pleased those who lack wisdom').
    On the various problems arising from Vacuna's appearance in *Epistles* 1.10.49 see A. Traina, 'Vacuna', 1997.

46. *CIL* XIV.3485: 'The Emperor Vespasian, Pontifex Maximus, holder of Tribunician Power, Censor, at his own expense restored the temple of Victory ruined by age'.

47. Z. Mari, 'La valle del Licenza', 1994, pp.28–31, notes that the problem of the identification of the Fanum Vacunae in the area of Rocca Giovine is still unsolved, largely because we do not know the provenance of the Victoria inscription (*CIL* XIV.3485). He points out that the nineteenth-century travellers Sebastiani and Gori reported that the inscription was found near St Maria delle Case but traces this back to unreliable local tradition. Nevertheless, Mari (like Ramsay) is attracted by the idea that the church was built on the foundations of a pagan shrine, which may well have been dedicated to Vacuna/Victoria.

48. The fragment has in the meantime been rejoined with the rest of the inscription on the wall of the Orsini Castle at Rocca Giovine.

49. The name of Bernardo Pomfili does not appear in the books of property records for Licenza and Rocca Giovine dated 1783, preserved in the Archivio di Stato, Rome. Thus it is not possible to determine exactly where Ramsay saw the 'dozens of stones' in June 1777. Field survey in 1998 of the eastern slope of the Colle Franchisi, near the modern road from Vicovaro to Licenza, has found stones of uncertain date that may have been used for terraces, retaining walls and road pavement.

50. Ramsay's identification of Strabo's Valeria with Varia was conjectured by Cluverius, who emended Strabo's text accordingly. The emendation is now generally accepted in modern editions. The first scholar to identify Varia with Vicovaro was L. Torrentius, *Q. Horatius Flaccus*, 1608, p.679.

51. *CIL* XIV.3472. H. Dessau (the editor of the inscription in *CIL*) and Z. Mari, 'La valle del Licenza', 1994, p.23, note that since we do not in fact know where this inscription was found, it is risky to use it (as Ramsay does here) as evidence that Varia was a *municipium*.

52. Modern commentators on Horace's *Epistles* (e.g. A. Kiessling and R. Heinze, *Q. Horatius Flaccus*, 1957, and R. Mayer, *Horace Epistles*, 1994) disagree with Ramsay, interpreting 'boni patres' to be 'patresfamilias,' or simply the heads of households. Ramsay's interpretation derives from the ancient scholiasts on the passage.

53. The process of resettlement on fortified hilltops ('incastellamento') in the Anio and neighbouring valleys dates to the tenth century AD; see Z. Mari, 'La valle dell' Aniene', 1995, pp.39–40. Settlement in the fields and on the hillsides outside the hilltop town of Licenza began in earnest only after World War II.

54. Ramsay's point is correct, but he is wrong about Boscovich's map, which does not include San Cosimato; see C. Maire and R. Boscovich, *Carta geografica*, 1769; A. P. Frutaz, *Le carte del Lazio*, 1972, vol.1, pp.90–92 (no.XL). On Boscovich, see J. B. J. Delambre, *Grandeur et figure*, 1912; D. Nikolic, 'R. Boskovich', 1962; L. Cubranic, 'Il contributo de Ruggero Boskovic', 1963; on Boscovich and Maire, see M. Pedley, 'I due valentuomini', 1993.

55. Ramsay is correct in noting the mistaken orientation of Licenza with respect to San Cosimato.

56. cf. J. P. Hackert, *Carte generale*, c.1780.

57. Ramsay's wish was granted, when later in the century Father Antonio Piaggio invented a machine for unrolling the delicate Herculanean papyri that had been discovered in the Villa of the Papyri by Karl Weber. The papyri rolls contained no manuscript of Horace, consisting mainly of a library of Epicurean philosophical texts (the bulk by the mid first-century BC philosopher Philodemus). No more than a few scraps of Latin poetry have been found among them; see, in general, M. Gigante, *Philodemus in Italy*, 1995. Ramsay followed the excavations at Herculaneum since his first trip to Rome in the 1730s. Upon his return to London he helped his reputation by publishing

translations of letters he received in 1739 and 1740 from Camillo Paderni about the work in progress at Herculaneum; see p. 11 above and A. Smart, *Allan Ramsay*, 1992, p.30. Not surprisingly, the Herculanean papyri were never far from his mind. A few years before writing his treatise on Horace's Villa, Ramsay had expressed the wish that the Herculanean rolls include 'one Single Ode of Alcaeus, or one of Sappho'; see Ramsay's manuscript 'An Enquiry into the Principles of English Versification', fol. 37v.

Ramsay's sarcastic remark about the King of Naples and his ministers recalls William Stukeley's famous outburst against the 'supine indolence' of the British government in preserving Hadrian's Wall; see S. Piggott, *William Stukeley*, 1985, p.146. William Hamilton, in 'Account of the Discoveries at Pompeii', 1777, p.167, speaking of the inscription now known as *CIL* x.846, expressed annoyance with the Neapolitan authorities for the way they removed monuments from their context and put them into the museum at Portici. Other eighteenth-century scholars were impressed by the scale of the effort made by the King of Naples in recovering the antiquities of Herculaneum and Pompeii; see for example the Chevalier de Jaucourt, 'Herculaneum', 1777: 'voilà l'avantage des potentats: un particulier … aurait encore trouvé quelques fragments d'antiquités; mais le roi de Naples faisant creuser dans le grand et en ayant les moyens, a deterré une ville entière'.

What Ramsay writes about Horace, *Epistles* 1.16 ('[it] is probably made up of memorandums left unfinished at the author's death, or of fragments of his finished works picked up afterwards by his admirers, and stuck together in the best way they could') is less eccentric than one might think. R. Kilpatrick, *The Poetry of Friendship*, 1986, p.97, writes that 'the structure of this epistle has often been criticised. Morris ['The Form of the Epistle', 1931] regarded it as a *sermo* with epistolary machinery added, and generally not well constructed. The transition between vv. 1–16 and 17–end has bothered critics too.'

58.   The inscription was found at the monastery of San Cosimato in 1757 by Abate Giuseppe Petrocchi of Vicovaro; see D. de Sanctis, *Dissertazione*.

59.   *CIL* xiv.3482; see Fig.5.5

60.   A *massa* was a collection of properties belonging to one owner. In central Italy, they began to appear in the fourth century AD and persisted into the Middle Ages; see D. De Francesco, 'Le donazione costantiniane', 1990, p.67; Z. Mari, 'La valle dell'Aniene', 1995, p.38.

61.   H. Dessau, the editor of the inscription in *CIL* xiv, notes that the word 'domnipraedius' is known from other inscriptions. He also finds the language of the text to be problematic in parts and is as stymied by SEPRETORUM as were De Chaupy and Ramsay.

62.   Virgil, *Aen.* 7.715 ('the people who drink the Tiber and Fabaris'). The context is the catalogue of Italian peoples who make war on Aeneas and the Trojans after Juno opens the gates of war at *Aen.* 7.620.

63.   Horace, *Odes* 2.20.20 ('they who drink the waters of the Rhone').

Catalogue:
**Illustrative Works
Relating to Allan Ramsay's Search
for Horace's Villa**

Patricia R. Andrew

Allan Ramsay

Ramsay 1

Sketchbook 1755
NGS D4878
20.5 x 14.2 cm (8.0 x 5.5 in)
Includes sketches and map of Licenza
area. See Figure 5.3.

Ramsay 2

View of Horace's Farm, 1777
NGS RSA 509
44.7 x 61.0 cm (17.5 x 24.0 in). Black chalk
on paper.
Inscribed: 'View of Horace's farm from
the window of Count Orsini Villa at
Licenza, drawn exactly by me A.R. by
the help of pack thread squares, June 21
1777 / a. The field in which is the mosaic
pavements – / b. the place where stands
amongst the bushes the remains of some
old walls – c. The Cypress a litle below
the source of Fonte Ratini – d. the
Mill / e. Rocca Giovane – f. The spot
where the stones of a portone were dug
up a few years ago – g. Colle Franchisi –
h. The Convent of San Cosimato,
bearing due South'.
Fig.8.1

Ramsay 3

Group of sketches, probably 1783
(otherwise 1777), bound with the
'Enquiry' MS in the National Library of
Scotland, MS 730. Slightly irregular
paper sizes.

Ramsay 3.1

f.36
13.8 x 20.8 cm (5.50 x 8.25 in) on paper
18.0 x 23.8 cm (7.00 x 9.25 in). Squared
pencil drawing.
Inscribed beneath image: 'Taken from
Licenza looking towards Mons
Lucretilis / Horace's villa a little above
the house that is in this drawing'.
See Introduction, Fig.iv.

Ramsay 3.2

f.37
18.1 x 23.7 cm (7.25 x 9.50 in) on paper
14.0 x 20.5 cm (5.5 x 8.0 in). Pencil
drawing with lightly coloured washes in
grey, brown, green and pink.
Inscribed beneath image: 'View of Rocca
Giovane'. Washes probably added by
Jacob More.

Ramsay 3.3

f.38
13.8 x 20.5 cm (5.5 x 8.0 in) on paper 18.2
x 23.7 cm (7.25 x 9.25 in). Squared pencil
drawing.
Inscribed beneath image: 'from the road
[?] Licenza, looking toward Horace's
villa / Rocca Giovane and St Cosimato'.

Ramsay 3.4

f.39
16.4 x 21.8 cm (6.5 x 8.5 in) on paper 18.8
x 22.9 cm (7.5 x 9.5 in), small hole in
paper. Pencil drawing.
Inscribed beneath image: 'view near the
mill looking toward Licenza. Horace's
villa / on the Left'.
Fig.8.2

Ramsay 3.5

f.40
18.0 x 20.5 cm (7 x 8 in) on paper 18.4 x
23.1 cm (7.5 x 9.0 in). Pencil drawing,
whole sheet squared up.
Inscribed above image: 'View of Licenza
on the east side looking towards
Lucretilis'.

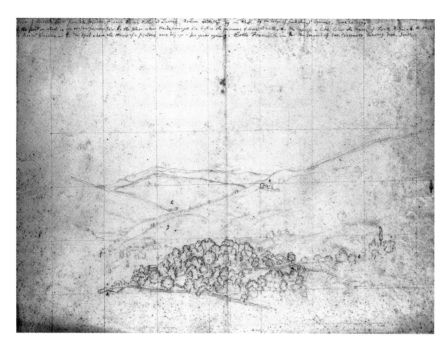

8.1

8.2

8.3

8.4

Jacob More

For further details of each painting see
P.R. Andrew, 'Jacob More: Biography
and a Checklist of Works', [1993],
updating 1990; and J. Holloway, 'Two
Projects to Illustrate Allan Ramsay's
Treatise on Horace's Sabine Villa', 1976.

[Group of 3]

More 1

View near Licenza, 1777
NGS RSA 505
33.4 x 44.6 cm (13.25 x 17.50 in). Pen and
ink with green and brown wash over
black chalk. A panel of approx. 8 cm
(3.25 in) down the right-hand side of
paper remains uncoloured except for a
brown wash.
Inscribed: 'L23'. View down valley with
meandering river, hill slopes on either
side.
Fig.8.3

More 2

View near Horace's Villa
NGS D1417
34.5 x 53.8 cm (13.50 x 21.25 in).
Watercolour over pencil, faintly
coloured. Laid down on old mount.
Inscribed verso: 'View of the Valley of
Digentia, the Situation of Horace's
house Rocca Giovane, Colle Franchise,
Colle Franco and San Cosimato',
probably in Allan Ramsay's hand.
Composition as More 5. Formerly
attributed to Sir William Gell.

More 3

Valley of Ingentia, 1777
NGS D1415
45.1 x 60.4 cm (17.75 x 24.25 in)
Watercolour over ink and pencil;
squared up.
Inscribed verso: 'View from Count
Orsini. Window of the Valley of Ingentia
– not drawn in proportion', probably in
Ramsay's hand. Formerly attributed to
Sir William Gell.
Fig.8.4

[Group of 4]

More 4
View of Licenza, 1777
NGS RSA 506
33.4 × 44.5 cm (13.25 × 17.50 in). Pen and ink and wash over black chalk.
Inscribed: 'L22'.

More 5
A View of Licenza, 1777
NGS RSA 374
33.3 × 44.4 cm (13.25 × 17.50 in). Yellow-green and brown washes over pencil or black chalk. Executed on same original sheet of paper as More 6.
Transferred from NGS 'English unidentified'.
Fig.8.5

More 6
View near Licenza, 1777
NGS RSA 504
34.0 × 51.5 cm (13.50 × 20.25 in). Green and brown wash over black chalk. Executed on same original sheet of paper as More 5.
Inscribed: 'L21'.
Fig.8.6

More 7
A View near Horace's Villa, 1777
NGS D1416
34.2 × 53.4 cm (13.5 × 21.0 in). Watercolour over pencil. Pale washes, mainly yellows and greens, laid down. A worked-up version of More 2.
Inscribed on mount: 'View of the Hillock to the east of Horace's house, Mons Lucretilis, and the Mill of Licenza. The source of Fonte Rabini just above the two little Cypresses Taken from a little rising a little to the north of Colle'.
Formerly attributed to Sir William Gell.
Pl.V

8.5

8.6

8.7

[Group of 3]

More 8
View of Horace's Villa, 1778
Coll. James Holloway
36.1 x 50.3 cm (14.25 x 19.75 in).
Watercolour.
Signed and dated 'Jacob More Rome
1778' on the mount, and inscribed 'A
VIEU OF HORAC'S VILLA taken near the
MILL OF LICENZA'.
Fig.8.7

More 9
View of Horace's Villa
NGS D5028
51.0 x 72.0 cm (20.00 x 28.25 in).
Watercolour and bodycolour over pencil.
Finished for presentation.
Signed and inscribed on backing paper.
Pl.VI

More 10
View of Licenza
NGS RSA 538
37.1 x 54.4 cm (14.50 x 21.25 in).
Watercolour and bodycolour. Highly
coloured. Very damaged, with creasing
and tears.
A town, not Licenza (possibly Subiaco)
in distance centre, with buildings
delineated in detail. Finished for
presentation.

[Group of 6]

More 11
View near Licenza
Yale Center for British Art, Paul Mellon
Collection, B.1977.14.5766.
28 x 40 cm (12.50 x 15.75 in). Pen and
black ink and watercolour over pencil
on laid paper.
Inscribed: 'View near the Mill, looking
towards Licenza. Horace's Villa on the
left' and 'No 1'.
Fig.8.8

More 12
View of Licenza
NGS D4938
27.6 x 39.6 cm (11.0 x 15.5 in). Pen and
ink and wash in light grey and pink
over pencil.
Inscribed on old mount (now detached):
'A view of Licenza on the East side,
looking towards Mons Lucretilis' and
'No 4'. Worked up from a sketch by
Ramsay (Ramsay 3.5).
Fig.8.9

More 13
A View from Licenza, looking to the West
Location unknown (Christie's, London,
17 November 1992 (82))
27.7 x 40.2 cm (11.00 x 15.75 in).
Watercolour.
Inscribed verso: 'View from Licenza,
looking to the west, towards Mons
Lucretilis. Horace's villa lies a little
above the house in this drawing' and
'No 5'. Worked up from a sketch by
Ramsay.

More 14
Rocca Giovane
NGS RSA 355
27.5 x 40.3 cm (10.75 x 16.00 in). Pencil
and wash, mainly greys and pinks, laid
down.
Inscribed on old mount: 'View of Rocca
Giovane/No 6'. Worked up from a
squared study by Ramsay.
Pl.VII

8.8

8.9

8.10

More 15
Horace's Villa
BM, 1870-12-10-237
35.4 x 49.4 cm (14.0 x 19.5 in).
Watercolour over pencil.
Worked up from a sketch by Ramsay
Fig.8.10

More 16
Rocca Giovane
Location unknown (Spink's, London,
1978).
35.0 x 49.5 cm (13.0 x 19.5 in). Pencil and
wash.
Composition almost identical to
More 14.

(?)Carlo Labruzzi

*View of the Bridge and Ruined Aqueduct
near San Cosimato*
NGS D5014
34.4 × 48.3 cm (13.5 × 19.0 in). Pen and
watercolour.
Inscribed verso: 'Vicovaro in the Valley
of the Aniene above Tivoli – Italy'.
Previously attributed to Jacob More.
Pl.VIII

Jakob Philipp Hackert

Hackert 1
Set of gouaches, 1780, all 33 × 44 cm
(13.00 × 17.25 in). All Düsseldorf,
Goethe-Museum, Anton-und-Katharina-
Kippenberg-Siftung (on permanent loan
from the Federal Republic of Germany),
Inv. No. NW 1796–1805/1982.

Hackert 1.1
View of Vicovaro
Inscribed: 'à Vicovaro. Ph. Hackert pinx.
1780'.
Pl.IX

Hackert 1.2
*Via Valeria and View of the Convent of
San Cosimato*
Inscribed: 'Voi Valérienne avec le
Couvent St. Cosimato. Ph. Hackert.
f.1780'.
Fig.8.11

Hackert 1.3
*View of the Bridge and Ruined Aqueduct
near San Cosimato*
Inscribed: 'Rest des Aqueduc de Claude
à S.Cosimato près de Vicovaro Ph.
Hackert 1780'.
Fig.8.12

Hackert 1.4
View of Cantalupo and Bardella
Inscribed: 'Cantalupo. Ph. Hackert.
f.1780'.
Pl.X

Hackert 1.5
View of Rocca Giovane
Inscribed: 'Rocca jovene Ph. Hackert
f.1780'.
Fig. 8.13

Hackert 1.6
View of Licenza
Inscribed: 'Licenza Ph. Hackert f.1780'.
Pl.XI

Hackert 1.7
View of the Site of Horace's Villa
Inscribed: 'Endroit ou la Maison de
Campagne d'Horace ete situe. Rocca
Giovine'.
Fig.8.14

Hackert 1.8
View of Mons Lucretilis
Inscribed: 'Monte Lucretilus Ph. Hackert
1780'.
Fig.8.15

Hackert 1.9
View of Fonte Bello on Mons Lucretilis
Inscribed: 'La Sorce du ruisseau Digenza
sur le Mont Lucretilus près de la
Campagne d'Horace Ph. Hackert 1780'.
Pl.XII

Hackert 1.10
View of the Grotto of Goats near Fonte Bello
Inscribed: 'Ph. Hackert 1780. La Grotte
de Chèvres sur le Mont Lucretilus Ph.
Hackert f.1780'.
Fig.8.16

Hackert 2
Prints after Jakob Philipp Hackert's
gouaches, dated 1780 and published 1784.
The series of etching/engravings
discussed and reproduced in this
publication was produced entirely in
Rome. A second series was later produced
in Naples, with the last line of the
inscription amended to read: 'à Naples
chez George Hackert graveur de S. M./le
Roi de Deux Siciles. Avec Privilége'.
Illustrations 8.17–8.20 are from the
collection of Bernard Frischer.

Hackert 2.1
View of Vicovaro
Plate: 37.5 × 46.1 cm (14.75 × 18.25 in);
image: 32.5 × 44.3 cm (12.75 × 17.50 in).
Inscribed: 'N° I Peint à Gouache par J.
Ph. Hackert 1780./Gravé à l'eau forte
par B. A. Dunker/et terminé par George
Hackert/VÜE DE VICOVARO anc. VARIA./
En venant de Tivoli par la Voie
Valérienne/Quinque bonos, Solitum
Variam dimittere Patres/Hor: Ep: XIV.

8.11

8.12

8.13

8.14

8.15

8.16

Lib. I/ A Rome chez George Hackert Place d'Espagne'.

Hackert 2.2
View of the Convent of San Cosimato
Plate: 37.4 x 46.1 cm (14.75 x 18.25 in); image: 33.1 x 43.7 cm (13.00 x 17.25 in). Inscribed: 'N° II/Peint à Gouache par J. Ph. Hackert 1780./Gravé à l'eau forte par B. A. Dunker /et terminé par G. Eichler/VÜE DU COUVENT DE ST COSIMATO/En venant de Vicovaro sur la Voie Valérienne anc: Via Valeria/ Valeria via a Tibure incipit ducitque in Marsos/Strabo'.
Fig.8.17

Hackert 2.3
View of the Bridge and Ruined Aqueduct near San Cosimato
Plate: 37.4 x 46.1 cm (14.75 x 18.25 in); image: 32.8 x 43.4 cm (13 x 17 in). Inscribed: 'N° III/Peint à Gouache par J. Ph. Hackert 1780./Gravé à l'eau forte par B. A. Dunker/et terminé par George Hackert/VÜE D'UNE PARTIE DU COUVENT DE ST COSIMATO/Avec le pont moderne sur l'Anio et une partie de l'aqueduc de Claude'.
Fig.8.18

Hackert 2.4
View of Cantalupo and Bardella
Plate: 37.4 x 45.7 cm (14.75 x 18.00 in); image: 33.2 x 43.8 cm (13.00 x 17.25 in). Inscribed: 'N° IV/Peint à Gouache par J. Ph. Hackert 1780/Gravé à l'eau forte part B. A. Dunker/et terminé par G. Eichler/VÜE DE CANTALUPO ET BARDELLA anc: MANDELA/Prise du Côté de St Cosimato/Me quoties reficit gelidus Digentia rivus. – Quem Mandela bibit rugosus frigore pagus/Hor: Ep: XVIII Lib I'.
Fig.8.19

Hackert 2.5
View of Rocca Giovane
Plate: 37.4 x 46.5 cm (14.75 x 18.25 in); image: 33.2 x 44.0 cm (13.00 x 17.25 in). Inscribed: 'N° V/Peint à Gouache par J. Ph. Hackert 1780/Gravé à l'eau forte par B. A. Dunker/et terminé par G. Eichler/ROCCA GIOVINE/Généralement Supposé l'ancien Fanum Vacunæ/Haec tibi dictabam post Fanum putre Vacunæ/Hor: Ep: X. Lib. I'.

Hackert 2.6
View of Licenza
Plate: 37.0 x 45.3 cm (14.50 x 17.75 in); image: 32.6 x 43.3 cm (12.75 x 17.00 in). Inscribed: 'N° VI/Peint à Gouache par J. Ph. Hackert 1780/Gravé à l'eau forte par B. A. Dunker/et terminé par Lorieux/ VÜE DU VILLAGE DE LICENZA/Et du petit bourg de Civitella prise sur la route avant d'arriver à la Maison de Campagne d'Horace'.

Hackert 2.7
View of the Site of Horace's Villa
Plate: 37.5 x 47.0 cm (14.75 x 18.50 in); image: 32.8 x 44.0 cm (13.00 x 17.25 in). Inscribed: 'N° VII/Peint à Gouache par J. Ph. Hackert 1780/Gravé à l'eau forte par B. A. Dunker/et terminé par Lorieux/ VÜE DE LA SITUATION DE LA MAISON DE CAMPAGNE D'HORACE/Avec Rocca giovine prise du Village de Licenza/Hoc erat in votis: modus agri non ita magnus; – Hortus ubi, et tecto vicinus jugis aquae fons, – Et paulum sylvæ super his foret/Hor: Sat: VI. Lib: II./ Endroit où etoit la Maison d'Horace/ Rocca giovine'. Birds engraved bottom left of plate outside image.
Fig.8.20

Hackert 2.8
View of Mons Lucretilis
Plate: 37.5 x 46.0 cm (14.75 x 18.00 in); image: 33.2 x 43.7 cm (13.00 x 17.25 in). Inscribed: 'N° VIII/Peint à Gouache par J. Ph. Hackert 1780/Gravé à l'eau forte par B.A. Dunker/terminé par G. Eichler/ LE CAMPANILE anc MONS LUCRETILIS/Avec la Ravine par ou passe Fonte Bello une des Sources de la Digentia/Velox amænum sæpe lucretilem – – – Hic in reducta Valle caniculæ viatabis æstus – – – Hor: Od: XVII. Lib: I / Ibid:'.

Hackert 2.9
View of Fonte Bello on Mons Lucretilis
Plate: 37.2 x 46.0 cm (14.5 x 18.0 in); image: 33.0 x 44.2 cm (13.0 x 17.5 in). Inscribed: 'N° IX/Peint à Gouache par J. Ph. Hackert 1780./Gravé à l'eau forte par B. A. Dunker/et terminé par G. Eichler/VÜE DE FONTE BELLO/Ou une des Sources du Ruisseau Digentia sur le Mont Lucretilis/Fons etiam rivo dare nomen idoneus/Hor: Ep: XVI: Lib.I'.

8.17

8.18

8.19

8.20

Hackert 2.10
View of the Grotto of Goats near Fonte Bello
Plate: 37.8 × 46.5 cm (15.00 × 18.25 in);
image: 28.7 × 46.8 cm (11.25 × 18.50 in).
Inscribed: 'N° X./Peint à Gouache par J.
Ph. Hackert 1780./Gravé à l'eau forte
par B.A. Dunker/et terminé par G.
Eichler/VÜE DE LA GROTTE DES
CHEVRES/Près de Fonte Bello/Impune
tutum per nemus arbutos – Querunt
latentes et thyma deviae – Olentis
Uxores Mariti / Hor: Od: XVII: Lib: I'.

Hackert map
Plate: 37.0 × 47.2 cm (14.5 × 18.5 in);
image: 29.0 × 44.0 cm (11.50 × 17.25 in).
Inscribed: 'Carte generale de la partie de
la Sabine où etoit située la Maison de

Campagne d'Horace, suivie de dix Vües
des sites de cette Campagne et de ses
Environs, nommés dans les Oeuvres
d'Horace, et relatives aux dissertations
que M.^{r} l'Abbé de Santis, M.^{r} L'Abbé
Capmartin de Chaupy et Mr de Ramsay
ont publié à ce sujet/Dedieés à la
Majesté Gustave III Roi de Suede des
Goths et des Vandales &c. &c. &c./A
Rome chez George Hackert/Graveur
Place d'Espagne/Par son très
humble/très obeissant e très/Soumis
Serviteur/Ja: Ph: Hackert'. Inset top
right includes measurements of
distances and the engraving of the piece
of mosaic found at the Villa site.
See Fig.6.3.

8.21

Luigi Sabatelli

Second set of engravings after Hackert's goauches, undated (?1790) by Luigi Sabatelli. Inscription on title page transcribed in full; abbreviated transcription of all other engravings. All are inscribed in both French and English. Sabatelli 1.1–1.10 are inscribed: 'Paint par J. Ph. Hackert/Gravé par Franc Morel'. Illustrations 8.21–8.25 are from the collection of Bernard Frischer.

Sabatelli title page
Plate: 17.2 x 23.0 cm (6.75 x 9.00 in). Inscribed: 'RACCOLTA/di N° 10 Vedute rappresentanti/LA VILLA D'ORAZIO/O LA SUA ABITAZIONE DI CAMPAGNA/Ed i siti circonvicini/CON UNA CARTA TOPOGRAFICA DELLA STESSA GRANDEZZA/Che indica con N^i Romani I punti,/dai quali il Pittore Filippo Hackert le ha espresse,/con le figure allegoriche al poeta sud^o, d'invenzione e disegno di Luigi Sabatelli/Incise a bulino da Francesco Morel – /IN ROMA /presso Agapito Franzetti/Calcografo e Marcante di Stampe a Torsanguigna/Con Privilegio Pontificio'.
Fig.8.21

Sabatelli map
Plate: 17.0 x 20.3 cm (6.75 x 8.00 in); image: 14.0 x 18.9 cm (5.5 x 7.5 in).

Sabatelli 1.1
View of Vicovaro
Plate: 17.1 x 20.2 cm (6.75 x 8.00 in); image: 13.8 x 18.4 cm (5.50 x 7.25 in). Titled: VUE DE VICOVARO anc. VARIA.

Sabatelli 1.2
View of the Convent of San Cosimato
Plate: 17.2 x 20.3 cm (6.75 x 8.00 in); image: 14.0 x 18.7 cm (5.5 x 7.5 in). Titled: VUE DU COUVENT DE ST COSIMATO.

Sabatelli 1.3
View of the Bridge and Ruined Aqueduct near San Cosimato
Plate: 17.2 x 20.3 cm (6.75 x 8.00 in); image: 14.1 x 18.7 cm (5.50 x 7.25 in). Titled: VUE D'UNE PARTIE DU COUVENT DE S. COSIMATO.
Fig.8.22

Sabatelli 1.4
View of Cantalupo and Bardella
Plate: 17.3 x 20.4 cm (6.75 x 8.00 in); image: 14.0 x 18.7 cm (5.50 x 7.25 in). Titled: VUE DE CANTALUPO ET BARDELLA anc MANDELA.
Fig.8.23

Sabatelli 1.5
View of Rocca Giovane
Plate: 17.1 x 20.2 cm (6.75 x 8.00 in); image: 14.0 x 18.8 cm (5.50 x 7.25 in). Titled: VUE DE ROCCA GIOVINE.

Sabatelli 1.6
View of Licenza
Plate: 17.2 x 20.3 cm (6.75 x 8.00 in); image: 14.3 x 19.1 cm (5.5 x 7.5 in). Titled: VUE DU VILLAGE DE LICENZA.

Sabatelli 1.7
View of the Site of Horace's Villa
Plate: 17.1 x 20.2 cm (6.75 x 8.00 in); image: 14.0 x 19.1 cm (5.5 x 7.0 in). Titled: VUE OU ETOIT LA MAISON DE CAMPAGNE D'HORACE.
Fig.8.24

Sabatelli 1.8
View of Mons Lucretilis
Plate: 17.2 x 20.3 cm (6.75 x 8.00 in); image: 14.0 x 18.9 cm (5.5 x 7.5 in). Titled: LE CAMPANILE anc MONS LUCRETILIS.

VUE D'UNE PARTIE DU COUVENT DE S. COSIMATO | V.^a D'UNA PARTE DEL CONVENTO DI S. COSIMATO

8.22

VUE DE CANTALUPO ET BARDELLA sur MANDELA | V.^a DI CANTALUPO E BARDELLA sull MANDELA

8.23

VUE OU ETOIT LA MAISON DE CAMPAGNE D'HORACE | V.^a OVE ERA LA CASA DI CAMPAGNA D'ORAZIO.

8.24

VUE DE FONTE BELLO | VEDUTA DI FONTE BELLO

8.25

Sabatelli 1.9
View of Fonte Bello on Mons Lucretilis
Plate: 17.1 × 20.2 cm (6.75 × 8.00 in);
image: 14.0 × 18.6 cm (5.5 × 7.5 in).
Titled: VUE DE FONTE BELLO.
Fig.8.25

Sabatelli 1.10
View of the Grotto of Goats near Fonte Bello
Plate: 17.1 × 20.2 cm (6.75 × 8.00 in);
image: 14.2 × 19.0 cm (5.5 × 7.5 in).
Titled: VUE DE LA GROTTE DES CHEVRES.

Bibliography

Ackerman, J., *The Villa: Form and Ideology of Country Houses*, London: 1990.

Adam, R., *Ruins of the Palace of the Emperor Diocletian at Spalatro in Dalmatia*, London: 1764.

Alberti, J.B., *De re aedificatoria*, Florence: 1485; trans. J. Rykwert, N. Leach and R. Tavernor as *On the Art of Building in Ten Books*, Cambridge, MA, and London: 1988.

Almagià, R., *L'opera geographica di Luca Holstenio*, Vatican City: 1942.

Aluffi, H.M., *Balthasar Anton Dunker: 1746–1807*, exhibition catalogue, Kunstmuseum, Berne: 1990.

Ameti, G.F., and de Rossi, D., *Il Lazio, con le sue più cospicue strade antiche e moderne e principali casali, e tenute*, Rome: 1693.

Andrew, P.R., 'Jacob More, 1740–1793', unpublished Ph.D. thesis, University of Edinburgh: 1981.

—'An English Garden in Rome', *Country Life*, vol.169, 23 April 1981, pp.1136–8.

—'Jacob More's Falls of Clyde Paintings', *Burlington Magazine*, vol. 129, 1987, pp.84–8.

—'Jacob More and the Earl-Bishop of Derry', *Apollo*, vol.124, 1986, pp.88–94.

—'Rival Portraiture: Jacob More, the Roman Academician', *Apollo*, vol.130, 1989, pp.304–307.

—'Jacob More: Biography and a Checklist of Works', *The Walpole Society*, vol.56, 1990 [1993], pp.105–96.

Armstrong, D., *Horace*, New Haven and London: 1989.

Arrigoni, P., and Bertarelli, A., *Le carte geografiche dell' Italia*, Milan: 1930.

Ayres, P., *Classical Culture and the Idea of Rome in Eighteenth-Century England*, Cambridge: 1997.

Barrington, D., 'Observations on Caesar's Invasion of Britain, and more particularly his Passage across the Thames', *Archaeologia*, vol.2, 1772, pp.134–40.

Battisti, C., and Alessio, G., *Dizionario etimologico italiano*, Florence: 1954.

Bentley, R., *Q. Horatius Flaccus, ex recensione et cum notis atque emendationibus Richardi Bentleii*, Cambridge: 1711.

Bergmann, B., 'Painted Perspectives of a Villa Visit', in Gazda, E.K., ed., *Roman Art in the Private Sphere*, Ann Arbor, MI: 1991, pp.49–70.

Bignamini, I., and Jenkins, I., 'The Antique', in Wilton, A., and Bignamini, I., eds, *Grand Tour: The Lure of Italy in the Eighteenth Century*, exhibition catalogue, Tate Gallery, London, London: 1996, pp.203–205.

Biographie universelle, Paris: 1854.

Biondo, F., *De Roma instaurata libri tres … Blondii Flauij Florliuiensis de Italia illustrata*, Turin: 1527.

Boissier, G., *The Country of Horace and Virgil*, London: 1896.

Bosius, A., *Roma sotterranea*, Rome: 1632.

Boswell, J., *Life of Johnson*, ed. G. Birkbeck Hill, revised L.F. Powell, 6 vols, Oxford: 1934.

—*Boswell in Extremes*, ed. C.M. Weis and F.A. Pottle, London: 1971

Bradstreet, R., *The Sabine Farm, A Poem: into which is interwoven a series of translations, chiefly descriptive of the Villa and Life of Horace, occasioned by an excursion from Rome to Licenza*, London: 1810.

Brower, R.A., *Alexander Pope: The Poetry of Allusion*, Oxford: 1959.

Brown, I.G., 'Critick in Antiquity: Sir John Clerk of Penicuik', *Antiquity*, vol.51, 1977, pp.201–10.

—'Sir John Clerk of Penicuik (1676–1755): Aspects of a Virtuoso Life', unpublished Ph.D. thesis, University of Cambridge: 1980.

—*The Hobby-Horsical Antiquary*, Edinburgh: 1980.

—*Poet and Painter: Allan Ramsay, Father and Son, 1684–1784*, Edinburgh: 1984.

—'Allan Ramsay's Rise and Reputation', *The Walpole Society*, vol.50, 1984, pp.209–47.

—'Young Ramsay in Edinburgh', *Burlington Magazine*, vol. 126, 1984, pp.778–81.

—*Poet and Painter: Allan Ramsay, Father and Son, 1684–1784*, exhibition catalogue, NLS, Edinburgh: 1985.

—*The Clerks of Penicuik: Portraits of Taste and Talent*, Edinburgh: 1987.

—'The Pamphlets of Allan Ramsay the Younger', *The Book Collector*, vol.37, 1988, pp.55–85.

—*Monumental Reputation: Robert Adam and the Emperor's Palace*, Edinburgh: 1992.

—'"Emulous of Greek and Roman fame": a lost profile portrait of his father by Allan Ramsay', *Apollo*, vol. 141, no.397, 1995, pp.36–42.

—'A Painter in Search of a Poet: Allan Ramsay and Horace's Villa', in Bignamini, I., ed., *Archives and Excavations. Essays on the History of Excavations in Rome and Southern Italy from the Renaissance to the Early Twentieth Century: Antiquarianism, Archaeology, Art Market and Collections*, London: forthcoming.

Brunn, C., *The Water Supply of Ancient Rome*, Helsinki: 1991.

Budgen, F., *James Joyce and the Making of Ulysses*, Oxford: 1972.

Burgevin, L.G., 'A Little Farm: The Horatian Concept of Rural Felicity in English Literature', in *Horace: Three Phases of his Influence*, Chicago: 1936.

Butt, J., *Alexander Pope: Imitations of Horace*, London: 1966.

Carne-Ross, D.S., 'Introduction', in Carne-Ross, D. S., and Haynes, K., eds, *Horace in English*, London: 1996.

Carré, J., *Lord Burlington (1694–1753): le connoiseur, le mécène, l'architecte*, 2 vols, Clermont-Ferrand: 1993.

Castell, R., *The Villas of the Ancients Illustrated*, London: 1728.

Chambers, D., 'The Translation of Antiquity: Virgil, Pliny and the Landscape Garden', *University of Toronto Quarterly*, vol.60, 1991, pp.354–73.

Chiarini, P., *Il Paesaggio Secondo Natura: Jacob Philipp Hackert e la sua cerchia*, exhibition catalogue, Palazzo delle Esposizioni, Rome: 1994.

Cluverius, P., *Italia antiqua: Opus post omnium curas elaboratissimum; tabulis geographicis aere expressis illustratum*, 2 vols, Leyden: 1624.

Coarelli, F., *Lazio: Guide archaeologiche Laterza*, Rome and Bari: 1984.

Cocquelines, C., *Bullarum privilegiorum ac diplomatum Romanorum Pontificum amplissima collectio cui accessere Pontificum omnium vitae, notae & indices opportuni*, 6 vols, Rome: 1739–62.

Le Corbusier [C. E. Jeanneret], *Précisions sur un présent de l'architecture et de l'urbanisme*, Paris: [1930]; trans. E. S. Aujame as *Precisions: On the Present State of Architecture and Urbanism*, Cambridge, MA, and London: 1991.

Le Corbusier [C. E. Jeanneret] and Jeanneret, P., *The Complete Architectural Works*, Zurich: 1964.

Cremonini, D., *L'Italia nelle vedute e carte geografiche dal 1493 al 1894: Libri dei viaggi e atlanti*, Modena: 1991.

Cruquius, J., *Q. Horatius Flaccus cum commentariis & ennarationibus commentatoris veteris*, Antwerp: 1579.

Cubranic, N., 'Il contributo di Ruggero Boskovic allo sviluppo della geodesia', in *Atti del convegno internazionale celebrativo del 250° anniversario della nascita di R.G. Boscovich e del 200° anniversario della fondazione dell' Osservatorio di Brera*, Milan: 1963, pp.103–13.

Curtis, W.J.R., *Modern Architecture since 1900*, 3rd edn, London: 1996.

—'Principle v Pastiche', *Architectural Review*, vol.186, August 1984, pp.11–21.

Dacier, A., *Oeuvres d'Horace en latin et en françois, avec des remarques critiques et historiques*, Paris: 1733.

D'Anna, G., 'É veramente esistita una villa di Orazio a Tivoli?', *Cultura e scuola*, vol. 130, 1994, pp.34–42.

De Angelis, G., *Le 'Dieci vedute della casa di campagna di Orazio' (1780) di Jacob Philipp Hackert*, Monti Lucretili: Parco Regionale Naturale, exhibition catalogue, Rome: [1994].

De Chaupy, C., *Découverte de la maison de champagne d'Horace: ouvrage utile pour l'intelligence de cet auteur, & qui donne occasion de traiter d'une suite considérable de lieux antiques*, 3 vols, Rome: 1767–9.

De Francesco, D., 'Le donazione costantiniane nell' Agro Romano', *Vetera Christiana*, vol. 27, 1990, pp.47–75.

de Grummond, N.T., ed., *An Encyclopedia of the History of Classical Archaeology*, 2 vols, Chicago and London: 1996.

de Jaucourt, Chevalier, 'Herculaneum', in Diderot, D., *Encyclopédie*, suppl. III, 1777, pp.349–58.

Delambre, J.B.J., *Grandeur et figure de la terre*, Paris: 1912.

Del'Isle, G., *Tabula Italiae Antiquae in regiones XI ab Augusto divisae et tum ad mensuras itinerarias tum a observationes astronomicas exactae*, Paris and Amsterdam: 1711, reprinted 1745.

Del Re, A., *Dell' antichità tiburtine capitolo V: Diviso in due parti*, Rome: 1611.

De Revillas, D.G., *Dioecesis et agri tiburtini topographia nunc primum trigonometrice delineata et veteribus viis villis ceterisque antiquis monumentis adornata*, Rome: 1739, 2nd edn 1767.

de Sanctis, D., *Dissertazione sopra la villa de Orazio Flacco*, Rome and Ravenna: 1761, 2nd edn 1768, 3rd edn 1784.

de Seta, C., *Philipp Hackert: Vedute del Regno di Napoli*, Milan: 1992.

di Gastaldi, G., *I nomi antichi e moderni della Italia*, Venice: 1564.

Dizionario biografico degli Italiani, Rome: 1968.

[Ducros, L.], *Images of the Grand Tour: Louis Ducros, 1748–1810*, exhibition catalogue, Kenwood House, London; Whitworth Art Gallery, Manchester; and Musée Cantonal des Beaux-Arts, Lausanne, Geneva: 1985.

Eck, W., 'Ti. Claudius Parthenius', in *Der Neue Pauly*, Stuttgart and Weimar: 1997, coll. 19–20.

Eliot, T.S., 'Ulysses, Order and Myth', *Dial*, November 1923.

Ellman, R., *James Joyce*, 2nd edn, Oxford: 1982.

Emiliani, A., *Leggi, bandi e provvedimenti per la tutela dei beni artistici e culturali negli antichi stati italiani 1571–1860*, Bologna: 1996.

Evans, J., *A History of the Society of Antiquaries*, Oxford: 1956.

Everett, N., *The Tory View of Landscape*, New Haven and London: 1994.

Fabretti, R., *De aquis et aquaeductibus veteris Romae*, Rome: 1680.

Folkes, M., 'On the Trajan and Antonine Pillars at Rome', *Archaeologia*, vol.1, 1770, pp.130–34.

Ford, B., 'James Byres: Principal Antiquarian for the English Visitors to Rome', *Apollo*, vol.99, 1974, pp.446–61.

Forty, A., *Words and Buildings: A Vocabulary of Modern Architecture*, London: 2000.

Francis, P., *Poetical Translation of the Works of Horace: with the Original Text. Critical Notes collected from his best Latin and French Commentators*, 4 vols, 6th edn, London: 1756.

Frischer, B., *Shifting Paradigms: New Approaches to Horace's Ars Poetica*, Atlanta, GA: 1991.

—'Fu la villa Ercolanese dei Papiri un modello per la villa Sabina di Orazio?', *Cronache Ercolanesi*, vol. 25, 1995, pp.211–29.

—'Notes on the First Excavation of Horace's Villa near Licenza (Roma) by the Baron de Saint'Odile and the Abbé Capmartin de Chaupy', in Hamesse, J., ed., *Roma, Magistra Mundi: Itineraria culturae medievalis. Mélanges offerts au Père L. E. Boyle à l'occasion de son 75ᵉ anniversaire*, Louvain La-Neuve: 1998: pp.265–89.

Frutaz, A.P., *Le carte del Lazio*, 3 vols, Rome: 1972.

Fuchs, J., *Reading Pope's Imitations of Horace*, London and Toronto: 1989.

Fuller, T., *Gnomologia: Adages and Proverbs, Wise Sentences and Witty Sayings, Ancient and Modern, Foreign and British*, London: 1732.

Galletier, E., 'L'Abbé Capmartin de Chaupy et la découverte de la ville d'Horace', *Les Etudes classiques*, vol. 4, 1935, pp.74–92.

Gigante, M., *Philodemus in Italy: The Books from Herculaneum*, trans. D. Obbink, Ann Arbor, MI: 1995.

Gilbert, S., *James Joyce's Ulysses*, London: 1931.

Giornale dell belle arti e della incisione antiquaria, musica e poesia, vols 47–51, 1784, pp.313–15.

Givens, S., ed., *James Joyce: Two Decades of Criticism*, New York: 1948.

Glover, T.R., *Horace: A Return to Allegiance*, Cambridge: 1932.

Goad, C., *Horace in the English Literature of the Eighteenth Century*, New Haven: 1918.

Goethe, J.W. von, *Jakob Philipp Hackert: Biographische Skizze, meist nach dessen eigenen Aufsätzen entworfen von Goethe*, Tübingen: 1811.

—*Italienische Reise, 1786–1788*, Munich: 1961.

—*Winckelmann und sein Jahrhundert: In Briefen und Aufsätzen*, Tübingen: 1805, reprinted Leipzig, ed. H. Holtshauer: 1969.

Gow, I., 'The Edinburgh Villa', *The Book of the Old Edinburgh Club*, new series, vol. 1, 1991, pp.34–46.

Griffiths, A., and Carey, F., *German Printmaking in the Age of Goethe*, exhibition catalogue, BM, London: 1994.

Grimal, P., *Les Jardins Romains*, Paris: 1943.

Guillemin, A.M., *Pline et la littérature de sons temps*, Paris: 1929.

Hackert, J.P., *Brieven van Jacob Philipp Hackert aan Johann Meerman uit de jaren 1779–1804, met enkele brieven van Johann Friedrich Reiffenstein*, ed. J. van Heel and M. van Oudheusden, exhibition catalogue, Rijksmuseum Meermanno-Westreenianum, The Hague: 1988.

Hallam, G.H., *Horace at Tibur and the Sabine Farm*, 2nd edn, Harrow: 1927.

Hamilton, W., 'Account of the Discoveries at Pompeii', *Archaeologia*, vol. 4, 1777, pp.160–75.

Harris, J., *The Palladian Revival: Lord Burlington, his Villa and Garden at Chiswick*, New Haven and London: 1994.

Highet, G., *Poets in a Landscape*, London: 1957.

Holder, A., and Keller, O., eds, *Scholia antiqua in Q. Horatium Flaccum*, Innsbruck: 1894.

Holloway, J., 'Two Projects to Illustrate Allan Ramsay's Treatise on Horace's Sabine Villa', *Master Drawings*, vol. 14, 1976, pp.280–86.

Holstensius, L., *Annotationes in geographiam sacram Caroli a S. Paulo, Italiam antiquam Cluuerii, et Thesaurum geographicum Ortelii*, Roma: 1666.

Horsfall, N., *A Companion to the Study of Virgil*, Leiden: 1995.

Hume, D., *The Letters of David Hume*, ed. J. Y. T. Greig, 2 vols, Oxford: 1932.

—*An Enquiry Concerning Human Understanding*, ed. L.A. Selby-Bigge, 3rd edn revised P. H. Nidditch, Oxford: 1975.

Hunt, J.D., 'Pope's Twickenham Revisited', *Eighteenth-Century Life*, new series, vol.8, 1983, pp.26–35.

—*Garden and Grove: The Italian Renaissance Garden in the English Imagination, 1600–1750*, London: 1986, 2nd edn, Philadelphia: 1996.

—'Pope, Kent and "Paladian" Gardening', in Rogers, P., and Rousseau, G.S., eds, *The Enduring Legacy: Alexander Pope Tercentenary Essays*, Cambridge: 1988.

—'Gard'ning Can Speak Proper English', in Leslie, M., and Raylor, T., eds, *Culture and Cultivation in Early Modern England: Writing and the Land*, Leicester: 1992.

—'Making Virgil Look English', in Heusser, M., et al., eds, *Word and Image Interactions*, Basel: 1993.

Hunt, J.D., and Willis, P., eds, *The Genius of the Place: The English Landscape Garden, 1620–1820*, Cambridge, MA: 1988.

Jones, T., 'Memoirs of Thomas Jones', *The Walpole Society*, vol.32, 1946–8 [1951], pp.1–142.

Kehr, P.F., *Regesta pontificum romanorum*, vol. 9, Berlin: 1962.

Kennett, B., *Romae Antiquitae Notitia*, 2nd edn, London: 1699.

Kiessling, A., and Heinze, R., eds, *Q. Horatius Flaccus: Briefe*, Berlin: 1957.

Kilpatrick, R., *The Poetry of Friendship: Horace, Epistles I*, Edmonton, Alberta: 1986.

Kircher, A., *Latium. Id est, Nova et parallela Latii tum veteris tum novi descriptio qua quaecunque vel natura, vel veterum romanorum ingenium admiranda efficit, geographico-historico-physico ratiocinio, juxta rerum gestarum, temporumque seriem exponitur & enucleatur*, Amsterdam: 1669.

Knight, R.P., *Expedition into Sicily, 1777*, ed. C. Stumpf, London: 1986.

Krönig, W., *Hackerts Zehn Aussichten, 1780*, Cologne: 1983.

Krönig, W., and Wegner, R., with Kreiger, V., *Jakob Philipp Hackert, der Landschaftmaler der Goethezeit*, Cologne: 1994.

La Lande, J.J., *Voyage d'un François en Italie, fait dans les années 1765 et 1766*, Venice and Paris: 1769.

La Laurentine et l'invention de la Villa Romaine, Paris: 1982.

Landucci, J., *Voyage de Rome à Tivoli … au quel on a joint la description de la Villa Adrienne et de celle d'Horace situées dans la Sabine aux environs de Tivoli*, Rome: 1792.

Lavagne, H., 'Piranèse archéologue à la Villa Hadrien', in *Piranesi e la cultura antiquaria: Gli antecedenti e il contesto. Atti del Convegno, 14–17 Novembre 1979*, Rome: 1985, pp.259–71.

Lees-Milne, J., *Earls of Creation*, London: 1962.

Lethieullier, S., 'Part of a Letter from Smart Lethieullier, Esq., to Mr. Gale, concerning the old Roman Roads', *Archaeologia*, vol.1, 1770, pp.62–5.

Levi, P., *Horace: A Life*, London: 1997.

Litchfield, R.B., *Emergence of a Bureaucracy: The Florentine Patricians, 1530–1790*, Princeton: 1986.

Lucan, J., ed., *Le Corbusier, une encyclopédie*, Paris: 1987.

Lugli, G., 'La villa sabina di Orazio', *Monumenti Antichi*, vol.31, 1926, coll. 457–598.

Lumisden, A., 'Letter to John MacGouan, Esq., Rome, December 1, 1765', in *Remarks on the Antiquities of Rome and its Environs: Being a Classical and Topographical Survey of the Ruins of that Celebrated City*, London: 1797.

Lyne, R.O.A.M., *Horace: Beyond Public Poetry*, New Haven and London: 1995.

MacDonald, W.J., and Pinto, J.A., *Hadrian's Villa and its Legacy*, New Haven and London: 1995.

Mack, M., *The Garden and the City: Retirement and Politics in the Later Poetry of Pope, 1731–1743*, Toronto and London: 1969.

Macmillan, D., 'The Scottishness of Scottish Art: A Historical View', Talbot Rice Memorial Lecture, University of Edinburgh: 1984.

—*Scottish Art, 1460–1990*, Edinburgh: 1990.

Magini, A., 'Campagna di Roma olim Latium', map 41 in *Italia di Gio. Ant. Magini*, Bologna: 1620.

Mai, E., and Götz, C., *Heroismus und Idylle: Formen der Landschaft um 1800, bei Jackob Philipp Hackert, Joseph Anton Koch und Johann Christian Reinhart*, exhibition catalogue, Wallraf-Richartz-Museum, Cologne: 1984.

Maire, C., and Boskovich, R., *Carta geographica dello stato della Chiesa, Granducato di Toscana, e de' stati adjacenti*, Paris: 1769.

McKay, A.G., *Houses, Villas and Palaces in the Roman World*, Ithaca, NY: 1975.

Mari, Z., 'La valle del Licenza in età romana', in *Comitato nazionale per le celebrazioni del bimillenario della morte di Q. Orazio Flacco. Atti del convegno di Licenza, 19–23 Aprile 1993*, Venosa: 1994, pp.17–76.

—'La valle dell' Aniene nell' antichità, *Atti e Memorie della Società Tiburtina di Storia e d'Arte*, vol.68, 1995, pp.25–52.

Martindale, C., and Hopkins, D., eds, *Horace Made New*, Cambridge: 1993.

Masson, J., *Q. Horatii Flacci Vita ordine chronologico sic delineata, ut vice sit commentarii historico-critici in plurima & praecipua poetae carmina; quae veris redduntur annis, nova donantur luce, a prava vindicantur interpretatione celeberrimorum commentatorum*, Leyden: 1708.

Mathieu, N., 'Capmartin du Chaupy, découvreur de la maison de campagne d'Horace, ou petit promenade archéologique au sujet du domaine d'Horace en Sabine, au XVIIIe siècle', *Caesarodunum*, vol.23 bis, 1987, pp.177–98.

Maugeri, M., 'Il trasferimento a Firenze della collezione d'antichità di Villa Medici in epoca leopoldina', forthcoming in *Mitteilungen des Kunsthistorischen Instituts in Florenz*.

Mayer, R., *Horace Epistles, Book I*, Cambridge: 1994.

Mazzoleni, A., 'La villa di Quinto Orazio Flacco', *Rivista di filologia e d'istruzione classica*, vol. 19, 1891, pp.175–241.

Mielsch, H., *Die römische Villa: Architektur und Lebensform*, Munich: 1987, 2nd edn 1997.

Milman, H.H., *The Works of Quintus Horatius Flaccus … with a Life*, London: 1849.

Migne, J.-P., *Patrologiae cursus completus, series secunda, in qua prodeunt patres, doctores, scriptoresque ecclesiae latinae a Gregorio Magno ad Innocentium III*, Paris: 1852.

Monferini, A., 'Piranesi e Bottari', in *Piranesi e la cultura antiquaria: Gli antecedenti e il contesto. Atti del Convegno, 14–17 Novembre 1979*, Rome: 1985.

Moore, J., *A View of Society and Manners in Italy*, 2 vols, London: 1781, 4th edn 1787.

von Moos, S., 'Charles Edouard Jeanneret and the Visual Arts', in *Le Corbusier, Maler og Arkitekt/Le Corbusier, Painter and Architect*, exhibition catalogue, Nordjyllands Kunstmuseum, Aalborg: 1995.

Moroni, G.C., *Dizionario di erudizione storico-ecclesiastica*, Venice: 1846.

Morricone Matini, M.L., *Mosaici antichi in Italia. Regione prima. Rome: Reg. X Palatium*, Rome: 1967.

Morris, E. P., 'The Form of the Epistle in Horace', *Yale Classical Studies*, vol. 2, 1931, pp.18–114.

Nikolic, D., 'R. Boscovich et la géodesie moderne', *Archives internationales d'histoire des sciences*, vol. 15, 1962, pp.31–42.

Nisbet, R.G.M., and Hubbard, M., *A Commentary on Horace: Odes Book II*, Oxford: 1978.

Nordhoff, C., and Reimer, H., *Jakob Philipp Hackert, 1737–1807: Verzeichnis seiner Werke*, Berlin: 1994.

Noyes, A., *Portrait of Horace*, London: 1947.

Olin, L., *Across the Open Field: Essays Drawn from English Landscapes*, Philadelphia: 1999.

O'Malley, T., and Wolschke-Bulmahn, J., eds, *John Evelyn, the 'Elysium Britannicum' and European Gardening*, Washington, DC: 1998.

Pace, C., 'Pietro Santi Bartoli: Drawings in Glasgow University Library after Roman Paintings and Mosaics', *Papers of the British School at Rome*, vol.47, 1979, pp.117–55.

Palladio, A., *I quattro libri dell'architettura*, Venice: 1570; trans. I. Ware, London: 1738, reprinted New York: 1965; also trans. R. Tavernor and R. Schofield, Cambridge, MA, and London: 1997.

Passmore, J.A., *Hume's Intentions*, Cambridge: 1952.

Paulys Real-Encyclopaedie der classischen Altertumswissenschaft, 33 vols and 15 supplement vols, Stuttgart: 1893–1978.

Pedley, M., 'The Manuscript Papers of Diego De Revillas', *Papers of the British School at Rome*, vol. 59, 1991, pp.319–24.

—' "I due valentuomini in defessi": Christopher Maire and Roger Boscovich and the Mapping of the Papal States (1750–55)', *Imago mundi*, vol. 45, 1993, pp.59–76.

Petrocchi, G., *Orazio, Tivoli, e la società di Augusto*, Rome: 1958.

Phillipson, N., 'The English Garden in Enlightened Scotland: Some Preliminary Reflection', in *Park und Garten im 18. Jahrhundert: Colloquium der Arbeitsstelle 18. Jahrhundert, Wuppertal, 1977*: 1978.

Pietrangeli, C., *Scavi e scoperti di antichità sotto il pontificato di Pio VI*, Rome: 1943, 2nd edn 1958.

—'The Discovery of Classical Art in Eighteenth-Century Rome', *Apollo*, vol. 117, 1983, pp.380–91.

Piggott, S., *Ruins in a Landscape: Essays in Antiquarianism*, Edinburgh: 1976.

—*Antiquity Depicted: Aspects of Archaeological Illustration*, London: 1978.

—*William Stukeley: An Eighteenth-Century Antiquary*, 2nd edn, London: 1985.

Pine, J., ed., *Quinti Horatii Flacci Opera*, 2 vols, London: 1733–7.

Pinto, J., 'Piranesi at Hadrian's Villa', in Scott, R.T., and Scott, A.R., eds, *Eius Virtutis Studiosi: Classical and Postclassical Studies in Memory of Frank Edward Brown (1908–1988)*, Washington, DC: 1993.

Piranesi, G.B., *Le antichità romane*, Rome: 1756.

—*Della magnificenza ed architettura de' Romani*, Rome: 1761.

—*Diverse maniere d'adornare i cammini*, Rome: 1769.

Pope, A., *The Poems*, ed. J. Butt, Twickenham edn, 7 vols, New Haven and London: 1951 [vol.III/iii contains the 'Epistle to Burlington', vol.IV the 'Imitations of Horace' and other quasi-Horatian epistles].

—*The Correspondence*, ed. G. Sherburn, 5 vols, Oxford: 1956.

Pottle, F.A., *James Boswell: The Earlier Years, 1740–1769*, London: 1966.

Pottle, M.S., Abbot, C.C., and Pottle, F.A., *Catalogue of the Papers of James Boswell at Yale University*, 3 vols, Edinburgh, New Haven and London: 1993.

du Prey, P. de la Ruffinière, *The Villas of Pliny: From Antiquity to Posterity*, Chicago and London: 1994.

Price, T.D., 'A Restoration of Horace's Sabine Villa', *Memoirs of the American Academy at Rome*, vol.10, 1932, pp.135–55.

Ramsay, A. [the elder], *The Poems of Allan Ramsay. A New Edition, corrected and enlarged; with a Glossary*, 2 vols, London: 1800.

—*The Works of Allan Ramsay*, Scottish Text Society edn, vol.4, ed. A.M. Kinghorn and A. Law, Edinburgh: 1970.

Ramsay, A., [the younger], 'An Enquiry into the Principles of English Versification. With some analogical remarks upon the versification of the ancients', BL, MS. Add. 39999.

—'Extracts of Two Letters from Camillo Paderni at Rome to Mr Allan Ramsay, Painter, in Covent-Garden, concerning some antient Statues, Pictures, and other Curiosities, found in a subterraneous Town, lately discovered near Naples. Translated from the Italian by Mr Ramsay, and sent by him to Mr Ward, F.R.S.', *Philosophical Transactions*, vol. 41, part 2, 1740, pp.484–9.

—*The Investigator. Containing the following Tracts: I. On Ridicule. II. On Elizabeth Canning. III. On Naturalization. IV. On Taste*, London: 1762.

Rand, E.K., *A Walk to Horace's Farm*, Boston and Oxford: 1930.

Rieu, E. V., *Virgil: The Pastoral Poems*, Harmondsworth: 1949.

Rosa, P., 'Notizie intorno alla Villa di Orazio', *Bullettino dell' Istituto di Corrispondenza Archeologica*, vol. 7, 1857, pp.105–10.

Rowe, C., 'The Mathematics of the Ideal Villa', *Architectural Review*, vol.101, March 1947, pp.101–104.

—*The Mathematics of the Ideal Villa and Other Essays*, Cambridge, MA, and London: 1976.

Sabatelli, L., *Pensieri diversi di Luigi Sabatelli incisi da Damaniano Permiati*, Rome: 1795.

—*(1772–1850): Designi e Incisioni*, exhibition catalogue, Gabinetto Designi e Stampe degli Uffizi, Florence: 1978.

Sandner, O., ed., *Angelika Kauffmann e Roma*, Rome: 1998.

Sanson, N., *Estats de l'Eglise et de Toscane*, n.p.: 1648.

Scamozzi, V., *Idea dell' architettura universale*, Venice: 1615.

Schmidt, E.A., *Sabinum: Horaz und sein Landgut im Licenztal*, Heidelberg: 1997.

Scott, W., *The Journal of Sir Walter Scott*, ed. W. E. K. Anderson, Oxford: 1972.

Seidl, J., 'Das Lothringische Hausarchiv', in Bittner, L., ed., *Gesamtinventar des Wiener Haus-, Hof- und Staatsarchivs*, Vienna: 1937.

Sherwin-White, A.N., *The Letters of Pliny: A Historical and Social Commentary*, Oxford: 1966.

Showerman, G., *Horace and his Influence*, London: 1922.

Skinner, B.C., *Scots in Italy in the 18th Century*, Edinburgh: 1966.

Smart, A., *Allan Ramsay: Painter: Essayist and Man of the Enlightenment*, New Haven and London: 1992.

—'Allan Ramsay', in Turner, J., ed., *The Dictionary of Art*, London: 1996, vol.25, pp.881–4.

—*Allan Ramsay: A Complete Catalogue of his Paintings*, ed. J. Ingamells, New Haven and London: 1999.

Spence, J., *Observations, Anecdotes and Characters of Books and Men, Collected from Conversation*, ed. J.M. Osborn, 2 vols, Oxford: 1966.

Stack, F., *Pope and Horace: Studies in Imitation*, Cambridge: 1985.

Stolberg, F.L., *Travels through Germany, Switzerland, Italy and Sicily. Translated from the German of Frederic Leopold Count Stolberg, by Thomas Holcroft*, 4 vols, 2nd edn, London: 1797.

Stukeley, W., 'The Sanctuary at Westminster', *Archaeologia*, vol. 1, 1770, pp. 43–8.

Sullivan, J.P., *Martial: The Unexpected Classic*, Cambridge: 1991.

Summerson, J., *The Unromantic Castle and Other Essays*, London: 1990.

Switzer, S., *Ichnographia rustica*, 3 vols, London: 1718.

Tanzer, H., *The Villas of Pliny*, New York: 1924.

Torrentius, L., *Q. Horatius Flaccus cum erudito Laevini Torrentii commentario*, Antwerp: 1608.

Traina, A., 'Vacuna', in *Enciclopedia oraziana*, vol.2, Rome: 1996, pp.506–507.

Vertue, G., 'Vertue Notebooks, III', *The Walpole Society*, vol.22, London: 1934.

Vichi, G., *Gli Arcadi, 1690–1800: Onomasticon*, Rome: 1977.

Virgil, *Georgics*, trans. C. Day Lewis, London: 1940.

Volpi, G.R., *Vetus Latium profanum. Auctore Josepho Rocco Volpio*, 10 vols, Rome: 1704–45.

Walpole, H., *Horace Walpole's Correspondence with Sir Horace Mann*, ed. W. H. Smith, W. S. Lewis and G. L. Lam, 48 vols, New Haven: 1937–83.

Watkin, D., *Sir John Soane: Enlightenment Thought and the Royal Academy Lectures*, London: 1996.

Wilkinson, L.P., *Horace and his Lyric Poetry*, 2nd edn, Cambridge: 1968.

Williams, R., *The Country and the City*, London: 1973.

Wilton, A., and Bignamini, I., eds, *Grand Tour: The Lure of Italy in the Eighteenth Century*, exhibition catalogue, Tate Gallery, London: 1996.

Wilton-Ely, J., *Piranesi as Architect and Designer*, New York, New Haven and London: 1993.

— *Giovanni Battista Piranesi: The Complete Etchings*, 2 vols, San Francisco: 1994.

Winckelmann, J.J., *Dokumente zu Lebensgeschichte*, vol.4 of *Briefe*, ed. W. Rehm, Berlin: 1957.

—*Lettere italiane*, ed. G. Zampa, Milan: 1961.

Wittkower, R., *Architectural Principles in the Age of Humanism*, London: 1949, 3rd edn 1962.

Worsley, G., *Classical Architecture in Britain: The Heroic Age*, New Haven and London: 1995.

Zutter, J., ed., *Abraham-Louis Ducros: un peintre suisse en Italie*, exhibition catalogue, Musée Cantonal des Beaux-Arts, Lausanne, and Musée du Quebec, Milan: 1989.

Index